DAYS *of* VICTORY

CANADIANS REMEMBER: 1939-1945

TED BARRIS · ALEX BARRIS

Macmillan Canada
Toronto

Canadian Cataloguing in Publication Data
Barris, Ted
        Days of Victory

Includes index.
ISBN 0-7715-7301-4

1. World War, 1939-1945 - Personal narratives, Canadian. 2. World War, 1939-1945 - Canada. 3. Canada - History - 1939-1945.* I. Barris, Alex, 1922- . II. Title.

FC582.B37 1995   940.54'8171   C94-932677-1
F1034.B37 1995

Macmillan Canada wishes to thank the Canada Council, the Ontario Ministry of Culture and Communications and the Ontario Arts Council for supporting its publishing program.

Endpaper art: Fran Dowie

Macmillan Canada
A Division of Canada Publishing Corporation
Toronto, Canada

1 2 3 4 5 FP 99 98 97 96 95

Printed in Canada

To all the Canadians
who survived the Second World War...
And especially to those who didn't...
This book is respectfully dedicated.

Acknowledgements

As with most books, this one is the result of much collaboration. The first collaboration was between the authors and hundreds of veterans (and their families); their gift of memories on paper, in photographs and in face-to-face interviews is the heart of this manuscript. Those who helped put us in touch with those reminiscences include Vicki Gabereau, Bob Burt, Fred Davis and Judy Webb; as well as such organizations as the Canadian Association of Retired People, Canadian Legion Magazine, CBC Radio and Real Radio.

In particular, the authors thank those who took this project as much to heart as we did, giving time and energy above and beyond the call; among them J.D. MacFarlane, Art Cole, Dr. Carl Christie, Don Warner, Alan Skaife, Toyo Takata, Fran Dowie, Sam Levine, W. Ray Stephens, Harry Rasky, Eric Koch, Leslie Wyle and Gordon and Eva MacLeod.

We acknowledge the contribution of family and friends who collaborated with their enthusiasm and support. But perhaps the most important collaboration and cherished one was a blood collaboration—between a father who experienced the Second World War first-hand as a medic in the armed forces, and his son, born after the war but eager to know more about that experience.

In this the fiftieth anniversary year of those *Days of Victory*, we look forward to the final collaboration between authors and you, our readers.

Contents

Introduction

Canada came of age during the Second World War.

We stumbled out of the soul-searing Dirty Thirties into the most momentous experience that has ever befallen this country. On the war front, Canadians strode courageously across the battlefields of Hong Kong, Dieppe, Sicily, and Normandy, and on the home front, hard working Canadians fashioned an economic miracle. By mid-1945, as Ted and Alex Barris note in their poignant, human portrait of the war, "The boys were coming home, but they were not the same boys who had gone off to fight Hitler. They had grown up, matured, become wiser..."

Nor were the people at home the same. They, too, had grown up. We all had been transformed by the crucible of war. We had gone from Depression, to war, and to the brink of one of the greatest booms in history. From 1939 to 1945 Canada had turned itself inside out from being an essentially backwater, rural nation into an economically vibrant, urban society and one of the world's industrial giants. That transformation was brought about by twelve million Canadians striving to change their world into a strong, caring society. They did it by millions of individual acts of heroism on the war front and on the home front.

In the summer of 1939, the Prairies were one giant dust bowl, and the cities empty shells with closed factories, open soup kitchens, and hobo jungles on the outskirts. For those who could get a job, the starting pay for Toronto school teachers was $28 a week, a three-piece men's suit cost $9.98 at Eaton's, a broadcloth shirt cost 84 cents. The laughter of "The Happy Gang" on CBC and Jack Benny on NBC deflected some of the Depression agony as did the movies where, for a dime, you could see a double feature, a Flash Gordon serial, a cartoon, a newsreel, and the coming attractions. As war clouds gathered, downtown movie theatres were showing for 25 cents such blockbusters as *The Wizard of Oz*.

But then, towards the end of that glorious summer of 1939, we marched out of the Depression and off to war, although it was not with the same exuberance that heralded our entry into the First World War. Even the announcement of war was treated unceremoniously when, on a Sunday at noon, the CBC broke into an NBC program to deliver the news. Announcer Austin Willis interrupted the orchestra playing "Smoke Gets in Your Eyes," read a brief news bulletin, and then immediately returned the listeners to the orchestra playing "Inka Dinka Doo."

But the CBC was aboard the troopship *Aquitania* when the first Canadian soldiers sailed from Halifax three months later, and with Lorne Green and Earl Cameron anchoring the news, the CBC vividly brought to Canadians on the home front the spine-tingling battlefield reportage of the galaxy of daredevil war correspondents, including the best of them all, Matthew Halton.

Burned into our memories were the radio and newspaper reports of the Blitz, Dunkirk, El Alamein, Pearl Harbor, Stalingrad, and Hiroshima. Spitfires, Hurricanes, and Lancaster Bombers carried the war to Germany while Canadian destroyers and corvettes waged war in the North Atlantic on the German U-boats, including those which prowled into the Gulf of St. Lawrence to sink merchant ships. Aside from the million men in uniform, there were the women: CWACS, Wrens, and WDs, as well as a quarter of a million Canadian women in war plants.

On everyone's lips were Canada's military leaders such as General Andrew McNaughton and General Guy Simonds, political leaders such as Mackenzie King and C.D. Howe, and military heros such as glamorous air ace Buzz Beurling and Victoria Cross recipient Padre John Foote.

But it was the unsung foot soldiers who seized our hearts as we read the seemingly endless list of casualties, or whose pencilled letters home brought joyous relief to wives and sweethearts. They were the ones slogging through the mud and cold, often scared to death but knowing they had to go on. "We were told, you have fifteen minutes to live. Kill or be killed," one Queen's Own Rifles corporal recalled as he hit the Normandy beach on D-Day. It is their story which Ted and Alex Barris have captured so evocatively in *Days of Victory* and their story which propelled Canada into adulthood. But this also is the story of the wartime home front with its worries about spies and fifth columnists, about rationing of food, clothes, and gas, with "Meatless Fridays," Victory Bonds, youngsters collecting tin cans and aluminum foil for the war effort while their older sisters and mothers knitted socks and sweaters for the boys overseas. Through it all we heard the voices of Vera Lynn, Gracie Fields and the Andrews Sisters, as well as the music of Mart Kenney and Art Hallman.

For those on the home front and those on the war front, the end of the fighting in 1945 let loose a whooshing sense of joy, hope, and anticipation, and the VE and VJ Day dancing in the streets soon gave way to the transformation of Canada's industrial war machine into a peacetime economic powerhouse. The nation had come of age. So had we all.

Knowlton Nash

1

Back to Business

During the first week of May 1945, peace was in the air. Anticipation mounted inexorably. But nobody knew which day the surrender would be signed.

Major Doug MacFarlane, managing editor of *The Maple Leaf,* the Canadian Army's daily newspaper in Europe, waited in Brussels. He had made arrangements to cover the surrender of Germany to the Allies as one of twenty war correspondents who would be allowed to witness the signing ceremonies at Rheims, France.

But the army being the army, MacFarlane was not notified in time to make the journey to Paris, from where General Dwight D. Eisenhower was to take his party—including the twenty war correspondents—in a Dakota aircraft to Rheims. Annoyed at the poor communications, MacFarlane telephoned Sergeant Ross Parry, *The Maple Leaf*'s man in Paris, to take his place.

"I told him there was a seat reserved for *The Maple Leaf* on the plane," MacFarlane remembers, "and he was to tell them he was going in my place. I said I'd get to Paris and back him up. Parry did a magnificent job."

"Great lights flooded the room," Parry wrote, "as cameramen prepared to record this greatest moment in recallable history. The light was dazzling as it reflected from the cellophane-covered battle maps of Europe that covered all the walls. Still there were the pins and cardboard signs and arrows which had followed Allied progress to this victory and showed present conditions of Allied and German land, sea, and air forces."

When MacFarlane got to Paris on May 7, Parry had already returned. MacFarlane went to the U.S. Signal Corps office, where official photographs of the signing were being processed for later release. He knew the public relations man on duty—their paths had crossed in Italy—and he got a set of the photos.

Next, he went to the censor's office. "And darned if I didn't know somebody there, too. Also from Italy." He got his friend in the censor's office to put a stamp of approval on the pictures—clearly in advance of the intended release time—and got out of there before the man might have second thoughts.

"I shoved them underneath my battledress and went back to the Scribe Hotel... A guy came up to me that I'd never seen before, an American, and he said, 'I understand that some Canadian by the name of MacFarlane has got a collection of photos of the signing of the surrender that he's not supposed to have.' I said, 'Oh?' He said, 'If I were him I'd get in a goddam jeep and get back to Brussels just as fast as I bloody well could.' I took the hint and took off in a jeep headed for Brussels."

And that was how *The Maple Leaf* scooped the rest of the journalistic world, being first to publish the historic pictures—twelve of them over two newspaper pages—before any other paper in the world.

Predictably, MacFarlane couldn't resist writing a story himself, from SHAEF (Supreme Headquarters Allied Expeditionary Force) in Paris, giving an overview of the day's events. His byline read: "Maj. J. D. MacFarlane, Staff Writer, *The Maple Leaf*."

For the beefy, twenty-nine-year-old J. Douglas MacFarlane— referred to by his staff as "JDM"—it was just another feather in a well-festooned cap. One of four children of a Methodist minister, Doug had had to adjust to periodic moves, which were customary at the time for Methodist clergymen—from Ottawa to Cornwall, to Montreal, to Chatham. At seventeen, he joined the Chatham bureau of *The Windsor Star*, then moved to the main Windsor office. He covered the Ontario Legislature for several years, then moved to *The Toronto Star*.

In Windsor, he had joined the reserve battalion of the Essex Scottish Regiment. When he became a full-time soldier in 1942, MacFarlane trained as an infantry officer in Victoria, did well, and was invited to stay on as an instructor. "I got completely fed up [with training] so I appealed to some of my contacts in Ottawa. Next thing you know, I was an adviser to General McNaughton at Canadian Army Corps Headquarters in England."

Later he was attached to General Crerar's headquarters in Sicily, which made him the right man in the right place when the Canadian Army decided to start a newspaper. MacFarlane was chosen to become its managing editor.

He had learned the game of fencing with officialdom for the release of information. Even though *The Maple Leaf* was an army paper, he never lost the newsman's zeal for getting The Story.

This wasn't always as easy as the Rheims incident might suggest. Throughout the war (indeed, most wars) governments and the military prefer to control the press, choosing what to release and when to release it.

When the disastrous raid on Dieppe took place, the military purposely added an extra layer of censorship to delay the release of the news. Similarly, when the minesweeper *Esquimalt* was torpedoed and sunk off the coast of Nova Scotia on April 16, 1945, the government withheld release of the news until VE Day, three weeks later, when the bad news could be swept under the carpet of good news.

The government rationale for holding back news was to "protect security." But it wasn't so much the public's security as the government's that it wanted to protect. During the war years, Canada's government had become experienced at manipulating public opinion.

Before the war, Canadians had paid scant attention to the rest of the world. There were numerous signs pointing towards the coming world conflict, but somehow these went unnoticed. Mussolini's invasion of Ethiopia, Franco's rebellion in Spain, Japan's aggression against China, Hitler's incessant expansionism—all these looming clouds were ignored. Canadians were preoccupied by the Depression—and by occasional signs that it might be ending.

So when Hitler invaded Poland and the Allies, including Canada, declared war, the reaction was shock and dismay—as if war had suddenly erupted like a volcano.

Nadia Boshuck remembers hearing the news late at night in Saskatoon when she was eleven. "When war was declared, that was a time when the news boys came out running up and down the streets, yelling, 'Extra! Extra! War Declared! War Declared!'

"I kept bothering my aunt and saying, 'What is this war declared?' She was very impatient with me. She just turned away quickly and said, 'Oh, it just means that your brother is going to have to go to the war as a soldier and be killed.'

"That was what hit me... My brother was nine years older. He did go away to the war. He had finished high school and was about to start university, and instead he joined the army... But this was an explanation that hit home. It was rather cruel. She didn't think of it that way, she was just impatient because they were all concerned with the imminence of war and I was just like a mosquito bothering them, 'What's this war, what's war?' But imagine not to have any concept of war..."

For many young men, war meant signing up, the possibility of adventure or of a new career. For eighteen-year-old Wallace Bambrough, the news represented an opportunity to quit his job at a bakery in Toronto. "I'd grown tired of cleaning dirty pans, so I enlisted with my brother, at the same time. This was in 1940, and we joined the Royal Canadian Engineers. My mother said, 'You'll be home for Christmas.' We'd only been in the army for a month. And Christmas we were in England...building camps and living in tents. We worked at that right up until six months before D-Day.

"I'd do it again. I mean, there was a lot of bad times, homesickness and all, but when you balance it up, I don't think I'd be able to live it down if I was able to go and didn't go."

Joe Oggy was born in Montreal of Ukrainian parents, but during his childhood he lived in Winnipeg, then Port Colborne, Ontario, before settling in Toronto with his widowed mother and three brothers and one sister. He was twenty-one when the war started and soon began worrying that he had been "too young for the first war and might be too old for this one." He had joined the militia, then transferred to the army when he was twenty-two.

"I felt it was something you were supposed to do," Joe says. "There was a little twinge of adventure, I guess, but not much. It was more that I felt it was my duty."

The Carty family of Saint John, N.B., felt much the same way. Albert Carty had served during the First World War in No. 2

Construction Battalion, which consisted of black Canadians. But despite that experience of racial segregation, Carty raised his family to be proud Canadians. Seven of his ten sons served in Canadian armed forces in the Second World War.

The oldest, Donald Carty, spent three years in the RCAF, and relied on his wit to combat occasional racist attitudes. He remembers being welcomed to one station by an RAF type who addressed him as "Darky."

"He walked on a few paces," Carty recalls, "and I said, 'One moment, please.' He turned around. I said, 'It's quite obvious that you don't know me, and thanks for the welcome, but I assure you that my name is not Darky, it is Donald Carty. And if you do not feel up to addressing me as such, I would appreciate it if you would call me Airman.' And I turned around and went upstairs in a very military fashion and left him with his mouth wide open."

Signing up was sometimes something of a test of one's loyalty or mettle. Scott Young and Ben Malkin were working newspapermen in Winnipeg. When war broke out, Malkin promptly joined up and Young jokingly said: "Shouldn't you wait and see who's likely to win?" According to Scott, Ben replied: "Listen, there's going to be people around saying that the Jewish guys are not joining up and it's their battle." In time, both men became war correspondents overseas.

When he heard that war had been declared, amateur photographer Ken Smith went to the recruiting office on York Street in Toronto. He was transferred to No. 110 RCAF Auxiliary Squadron for medical testing, which he failed because he had a varicocele (a varicose vein). "I was classified B, which meant I was unfit, unless it was removed.

"Some time before, while working at Simpson's, I had had a slight injury and got an outpatient card for the Toronto General Hospital. So I immediately went up there, told them this must be done immediately for the air force... The next day I was operated on, was discharged... and returned to the air force medical officers and was passed A-1.

"For almost six years I did photography for the air force...from the Battle of Britain to VE and VJ Day."

Sometimes signing up was a badge of maturity. At seventeen, Alan Skaife was too young to enlist in 1940. But that didn't stop him. His father had been a bugler with the 42nd Black Watch. Skaife tried to join both the Royal Montreal Regiment and the 42nd Black Watch. He was kicked out of both because he needed his parents' permission to join.

"When I got down to the artillery at Military District 4, the major knew my father, and he said, 'Do your parents know you're here?' I said, 'Nope, and I don't want them to know until I go home.' I joined up on May 28, 1940...was attested by Major Lane and in June 1940... proceeded to Petawawa, Ontario, for training.

"I had a cousin, Boyd Kettison. He and I were good friends. Boyd and I went to the Royal Military Regiment and to the 42nd Black Watch and we also went down to the artillery. We both got sworn in. His parents said no, and they were able to get him out. How, I don't know... He went to the air force in 1943 or '44... On the first flight Boyd was killed. When I came home after the war, [his parents] wouldn't speak to me."

For others, signing up required some ingenuity. Stephen Bell left Govan, Saskatchewan, in the spring of 1940. He was seventeen and flat broke. He went to Toronto in search of work and "spent the last ten cents I had on toast and coffee in a White Spot Grill at the corner of Queen and Bay." A soldier sat down next to him and they talked. The soldier suggested that Steve join up. "So I went to the University Armouries, and they asked me how old I was. I was seventeen. 'Oh, no,' they said, 'you're too young, come back in a couple of years.'"

There were a number of different line-ups in the Armouries. Bell switched lines several times, each time upping his age. Eventually he said he was twenty. The officer didn't believe him, but agreed to let him join up. He trained in the infantry with the 48th Highlanders, and transferred to the Calgary Tank Corps in June 1941 because it meant a chance to get overseas. He was in plenty of time for the Dieppe raid.

Some who were anxious to join went to even greater lengths. Bob Jarvis, born into an old and well-to-do Toronto family, was at a private school in St. Catharines during most of the war. His two older brothers, Bill and John, served in the war, and his father, who had been commissioned in the First World War, was stationed in Manitoba, training other officers.

"Bill was, in fact, my half-brother. His mother had died leaving him several million dollars. Bill heard that any Canadian male, if he owned his own airplane, could in fact be commissioned into the RCAF. So he bought a Tiger Moth, learned to fly, and was overseas in England by 1940. From there he was assigned to fly in Burma...

"Bill flew photo-reconnaissance in Burma. The only armament they carried was the speed of their Spitfires, because with all the photographic equipment they carried, they could not carry armaments as well. They relied on out-manoeuvring and out-running. However, somewhere in Rangoon, Bill picked up a 10-gauge shotgun which he carried with him in the Spitfire. He swore he shot down two Zeros. Those kills were not verified."

Roy Harbin hoped that the opportunity to travel would let him explore his roots. Harbin's parents were from Twillingate, Newfoundland, but they married in Toronto, where Roy was born, one of three brothers. A strapping kid who looked older than his fifteen years, he joined the Sea Cadets when he was still a student at Northern Vocational High School. In 1943, when he was sixteen, he joined the Royal Canadian Navy, but he needed his parents' permission.

He and three of his classmates went to the navy recruiting office, but he was the only one under seventeen. "I wasn't even sure they were going to take me, but anyway we got called. Went down one morning, they gave me all my equipment, a whole bunch of needles, and I was sent home before noon. They told me to be back in time to catch the train for Edmonton that night and have the uniform pressed. So I went home and told my folks, said that I would probably be in basic training for six months, around Toronto. My (older) brother had just gone down to Debert (Nova Scotia) where they go overseas.

"So there's my mother ironing my uniform. I didn't realize how much she hated ironing uniforms, because I never saw her crying when she was ironing anything else."

Having studied at Northern Vocational to be an electrician, he took further training in Edmonton, Windsor, and Halifax, before being assigned to a frigate, HMCS *Montreal*, which escorted convoys. When he got to Newfoundland to begin the first of several St. John's-to-Londonderry runs, he hoped to visit his grandmother and aunts, none of whom he had ever met.

"I put my little nickel in the phone and I tried to call. They told me there's no phone connection to Twillingate. And Twillingate is like from Toronto to Bracebridge. So I went down to the railroad station and I says, 'Is there any way I can get to Twillingate?' and the guy says, 'If you have five days.' He says you'd have to take a train and a schooner and a bus or something like that... So I never got to see them. Never, ever met my grandmother."

For many people, signing up was a taste of freedom. Broadcaster Cy Strange was working at CJKL in Kirkland Lake, Ontario, early in the war and remembers an announcer whose idea of a weather report was to tell his listeners, "Jeez, it's cold." Or he would announce: "The time now is the same time you have."

Just before the CBC national news, the local stations used to air a thirty-second commercial. At CJKL, Seymour's Men's Wear in Kirkland Lake sponsored that spot and his advertisement always ended with, "If Seymour's clothes don't fit, Seymour won't let you wear them."

"Well, one night," Strange recalled, "this chap had had it up to here with Seymour, and he said, 'Remember, if Seymour's clothes don't fit, Seymour doesn't give a shit. And neither do I.'

"He had joined the army. He walked out of the station, went to Toronto with the Queen's Own Rifles, and eventually wound up as a prisoner of war. Jack Kent Cooke (the owner of the station) said at the time, 'I hope the Germans shoot him, because if they don't, I will.'"

Even if signing up was exciting, the military life was usually unglamorous. On the day Canada declared war on Germany, September 10, 1939, John MacCormack joined the 1st Anti-Aircraft Battery in Halifax. The unit was training with First World War guns. "And not only that," he remembers. "Our ammunition was, of course, First World War ammunition. On the boxes it had printed: 'Not to be fired later than July 1926.'"

Bill Gibson had several hurdles to clear before he saw action. By rights, Gibson should have joined any service but the air force. His father had retired as a regimental sergeant major, so family tradition might have steered him into the army. He'd grown up within walking distance of the HMCS *Stadacona* (the Royal Canadian Navy barracks) in Halifax, so the navy might have attracted him. But Gibson was determined to join the RCAF. In 1939 he was seventeen and in Grade 9;

the air force minimum entry requirement was eighteen years of age with a matriculation. Nevertheless, he got as far as a medical inspection at the RCAF recruiting office.

"The doctor found something wrong with my ears and couldn't pass me for air crew... At some point I had had an abscess in my ear; it had broken and skin was now covering my eardrum, so my ears wouldn't pop"—a normal and necessary function when flying.

No matter. The doctor simply used a darning needle to pull the scarred skin away from his eardrum and instructed Gibson "to hold my nose and close my mouth and blow every half hour or so... Sure enough within a week my ear popped and I tore down to the recruiting centre again to be re-examined."

Bill Gibson's war began on May 12, 1943, when he became an AC2—Aircraftman Second Class. His choice to pursue air gunnery soon put him into action. Gibson was sent to Toronto, where he lived on his air force pay of $1.30 a day and studied math, English, navigation, meteorology, and wireless operation. By October 1943, when he was eighteen, he had become an RCAF sergeant air gunner and was sent home to Halifax on embarkation leave to await an overseas posting.

"One morning as I was leaving the house, I told my mother I'd better take my shaving kit with me. I don't know why, but I took it... When I got to the station, they called out thirty names. Mine was among them... They made us get all our equipment—full kit bag of flying clothing, plus rifle and bayonet—loaded us on a truck, took us down to Pier 21, and loaded us on the SS *Mauritania*. I was put in charge of anti-aircraft guns (on board the ship) changing crews every four hours."

Eleven days later, after alternately freezing at the anti-aircraft gun positions and freezing in his bunk "in the bowels of the ship," Gibson landed at Southampton. At the air force reception centre in Bournemouth, on the south coast of England, he was assigned to a .303 machine gun position on the rooftops to defend the city from low-flying German bombers and fighters coming in off the English Channel.

Frank Pellerin, of French-Acadian descent, joined the Halifax Rifles reserve when he was seventeen, but later switched to the artillery. "I didn't realize what war was all about," he says, "but we had a Sergeant Major Cook... He was like a father to me. He would do anything for the troops. I think discipline was the thing which we had, and it worked out, it helped you grow up." Pellerin fought in Normandy and was wounded just outside Caen.

Thousands of Canadians joined up in thousands of ways. Late in December 1939, *The Halifax Herald* printed a dispatch datelined "Somewhere in the United Kingdom." It began: "Britons tonight received the most welcome and heartening news since the outbreak of war—news that the first contingent of the Canadian Active Service Force had landed safely in the United Kingdom... Behind a veil of secrecy, troop-laden transports glided ghostlike into this port as devout citizens were returning from church service on a cold, bleak Sunday."

But the war was not fought by the armed forces alone. Civilians in essential services also helped to win the war. The day that Hitler invaded Poland, September 1, 1939, Dick Dee and Marie Philp got married in Vancouver. "It was rather an odd wedding, just two friends of ours, in fact, my boss and his wife. They stood up for us, and when we came out we thought we must have some pictures. We got the milkman, who was just coming up the drive, and he took pictures of us." Winnipeg-born Dee was new to Vancouver, having been transferred there from the offices of Canadian Comptometer in Toronto. The next day, he received a telegram from his former Toronto co-workers: "You just made it." Canadian Comptometer provided equipment to Boeing Aircraft and Dee's work was considered an essential service, so he did not enter the armed services.

Peggy Tucker was just finishing high school in Toronto when the war started. "We set up a Red Cross unit at Jarvis Collegiate and would do knitting and fund-raising for the Red Cross," she remembers.

She began training to become a nurse in February 1941, at the Hospital for Sick Children. "Of course, you didn't get any time off or anything. I had been working at the Active Service Canteen on quite a heavy volunteer basis... I would work a twelve-hour shift and then change my shoes and go down and dance at the canteen until ten."

There were two dances a week, and the volunteers couldn't dance more than two dances with any one man. "You had to go back and be doled out again."

Peggy Tucker's father was general manager of Consumers Gas, a company that converted part of its premises in downtown Toronto into a hostel for servicemen. "The guys (in uniform) could get a bed and shower and breakfast for, oh, I think it was twenty-five cents a night."

In cities or towns across Canada, people got involved, somehow, to help the war effort, to show their support of the boys in uniform, not knowing how long the war would last. The weeks dragged into months which stretched into years. War work, rationing, Victory Bonds, sacrifices, making do, casualty lists, shortages—somehow, all of it was endured with a sigh of resignation and a glimmer of hope that, one distant day, it would all be over.

And then, finally, peace rushed in.

Six days before the end of the war, the *Calgary Herald* captured a touching moment in a story about some veterans arriving home:

> World shaking news—reports of Hitler's death, rumors of peace, and announcements of the steady defeat of the enemy—meant little to almost 100 veterans of five or more years' service overseas as a special train brought them to their homes on rotation leave. Tuesday evening, they had but one interest—to rush from the train and embrace smiling wives and mothers and, in many cases, children who for the past several years have been familiar to them only in snapshots.
>
> Happiness at being home after 5 1/2 years' service gave almost superhuman strength to one young Calgary soldier. As his train pulled slowly into the CPR depot, Pte. L. A. Denman decided he just couldn't wait another minute to see his wife and seven-year-old daughter.
>
> To the three men who obstructed his route to Calgary ground, each craning for a glimpse of a relative or friend, Denman shouted: 'If you're not going to get off, get out of my way.'
>
> None of the men moved, so the athletic young soldier hurdled them, hit the pavement in a flat run, leaped a picket fence, raced through the back entrance to the Red Cross reception centre and took his wife and daughter from the rear by surprise as they looked through the centre's windows

at the train which was just beginning to disgorge its throng of grinning soldiers.

After five and a half strife-ridden years, the war finally came to an end, and Canada, along with the rest of the western world, gave thanks and celebrated. Bells in large cathedrals and small churches pealed the happy news. Clergymen led solemn prayers of thanksgiving. Politicians of every stripe paid lavish tribute to valiant young men, especially the living ones, who might soon become voters. Journalists struggled to catch the mood of VE Day.

> A thin young woman, without a hat, her hair whipped by a bitter prairie wind, read the newspaper bulletin board.
>
> The chubby little boy held her hand and gazed at the bulletin without understanding.
>
> She smiled and then tears ran down her face. She snatched up the boy, kissed him. Then she put him down, and they went down the street, hand in hand, dancing, and the little boy's laughter was lost in the wind.
>
> This was VE Day in Regina. (Regina *Leader-Post*)

> It was not a large attractive wreath of orchids, chrysanthemums or carnations. It was simply a little cluster of two bright red roses with long green stems.
>
> But in its position on the large ledge at the base of the Cenotaph in Dominion Square yesterday it illustrated impressively the simple, real idea of memorium and thanksgiving behind the large demonstration of citizens undaunted by the rain on VE Day to gather and offer prayers for the men who gave their lives for their country, and for an enduring peace that would last without another tragic world conflict. (Montreal *Gazette*)

> Calm relief in this old port city [Saint John] was the first reaction to today's surrender news.
>
> Later, flags, bunting and other decorations broke out in greater abundance than at any time since the Royal visit of 1939.

Crowds gathered uptown this afternoon and confetti covered the sidewalks. Noise-making started after the official Ottawa announcement of victory over Germany. Then factory and ship whistles blew, sirens sounded and church bells pealed. Throngs at the head of King Street became so packed that traffic was unable to move. (Canadian Press)

Victory was a laughing jade whose hair was entwined with ticker tape and office toilet paper.

Victory was a silent woman standing on the curb, her eyes filled with tears for the son now dead.

Victory was the thoughtless youths who clambered over the heroic bronze figures in Canada's National War Memorial and offered sacrilege to the Dead of the first Great War.

Victory was as you saw it and as you made it tonight in Canada's capital, where lights blazed from every window of the Parliament Buildings and the Tower was bathed in the glow of flood lamps. (Toronto *Globe and Mail*)

John Maycock was seventeen years old and living in Hamilton, Ontario, when the war ended. As a youngster, he had earned money by selling newspapers, and that instinct came to the surface on May 8, 1945. "I headed for uptown Hamilton when the first hint of victory in Europe was heard. I made a beeline for the newspaper building and converted all my cash into newspapers. Then I started from Catherine Street to James Street. I never made it, because I ran out of *Hamilton Spectators*. Papers that usually sold for two cents went for a nickel or a dime; I returned several times to the newspaper office, each time converting all my cash into papers. Only once did I make it to King and James... Prudence told me to pocket my wealth and return home."

In some places—most notably in Halifax—the celebrations got out of hand, resulting in perhaps the worst rioting Canada had seen since the 1930s. But when it was all over, when the last shreds of confetti were swept from the city streets across the country, when the last mayor's stentorian utterances trailed off, when the last loud drunks were locked up, Canadians, like an audience when a show has ended, stood up, stretched, put on their coats and hats, and went out to face the real world again. It was time to get back to business and face the cost of five and a half years of war.

No one in Canada was unaffected: more than a million Canadian men and women had served full time in the three services, including nearly 50,000 women. The death toll was just under 42,000. The service with the highest percentage of fatalities was the RCAF—more than 17,000 dead out of 232,000.

The newspapers that heralded the arrival of peace still included depressing lists of casualties, some of them "old" news that had not yet been released. Medical authorities knew hundreds of thousands would be coming home—many of them wounded, disabled, or suffering from psychological trauma. Military authorities knew thousands would be bringing war brides or sending for them. Things could not simply return to normal.

The boys were coming home, but they were not the same boys who had gone off to fight Hitler. They had grown up, matured, become wiser, perhaps a bit cynical. Certainly, many expected something more than the life they had left as eighteen- or twenty-year-olds.

And things had changed at home, too. Not all the girls had remained faithful, just as not all the boys had. More important, many women wanted more than the life they had led before the war. As early as 1943, Lotta Dempsey had written: "You can tell your great-granddaughter some day that this was the time and place it really started: the honest-to-goodness equality of Canadian women and men in all the work of this country that is to be done; and the pay, and the kudos and the rights and the problems.

"And you can say that it wasn't done by club women at luncheons; or orators on soap boxes; or legislators in parliaments.

"It began to happen that hour when Canadian girls left desks and kitchens, elevators and switchboards, stepped into overalls and took their places in the lines of workers at lathes and drills, cranes and power machines, tables and benches in the munitions plants of Canada."

Some women were content to leave the war plants and unglamorous office jobs they had taken, others were not. They had sipped from the cup of freedom, and they liked it. This was particularly true of those young women who had donned uniforms in one of the services.

Mothers, sisters, sweethearts, and wives wept tears of joy, gave thanks to the Almighty, then pulled themselves together and started thinking about tomorrow.

But "tomorrow" meant different things to different people. To many, it meant reunion with long-missing loved ones. To others, those whose loved ones would not be returning, tomorrow was but another day of mourning and emptiness.

To men and women in uniform, it meant an end to an ordeal of pain and sacrifice; the happy thought of returning home and starting a new, possibly better life.

To those who had changed their lives by going to work in war plants, it meant a period of unease. What would happen now, when the boys came marching home?

To many, it meant a welcome end to the irritating business of shortages, rationing, doing volunteer work that ranged from packing prisoner-of-war parcels to knitting socks for loved ones far away.

To enterprising businessmen, it meant shifting gears again–back to cars and civilian clothes and home appliances and new houses.

The only thing that people could be sure about was that the Canada of 1945 was not the Canada of 1939. Everyone hoped it would be better. Some feared it might not. Peace had come, but not yet its meaning.

2

More Trials than Triumphs

For the Allies, the road to 1945 was booby-trapped with early defeats, agonizing setbacks, and constant peril.

Britain endured the havoc of prowling U-boats, the Luftwaffe bombings of its cities, the humiliation of Dunkirk, and the dread of imminent invasion. The United States suffered the destruction of Pearl Harbor and the spread of Japanese domination in the Pacific.

Canada's crucible was equally disheartening, but Canadians faced the new demands of the war, in the beginning, by preparing to do their share. The navy escorted convoys across the Atlantic and the air force set up the British Commonwealth Air Training Plan to train pilots and air crew. Canadian Army troops arrived in England before the end of 1939—only to spend more than two years waiting for action.

Ships carrying the first Canadians overseas—*Duchess of Atholl, Empress of Britain, Ile de France, Queen Mary,* and *Queen Elizabeth*—usually docked first in Liverpool, where photographers "ran along roof tops of dock sheds and banged away with their cameras, while authorities figured out where to send us." These were the first images of overseas postings remembered by Canadian servicemen and women. Among them was a young doctor in the Royal Canadian Army Medical Corps.

"As our ship docked at Liverpool, the band on the wharf began to play 'O Canada,'" recalled Dr. Helen Mussallem. "The tears just ran down; it was so emotional. At the finish of 'O Canada,' up from all the decks below came this great barrage of balloons... Then one of the officers standing next to me grabbed me and took me away. He didn't know what to say. They weren't balloons at all, they were inflated condoms."

After all the fuss and fanfare of arrival, the inactivity of the next two years was hard to endure. Even harder was the debacle at Hong Kong that marked the Canadian Army's first engagement in the fighting.

In August 1940, Britain's military brass decided that Hong Kong was an important outpost of the Empire and must be defended at all costs, even though in October the governor of the island, Sir Geoffrey Northcote, advised the withdrawal of the British garrison there, because of the threat of a Japanese attack.

Britain, however, decided that the Canadian Army should send two battalions to beef up the Hong Kong garrison. Since Canada had no intelligence sources in the Far East, the government had little choice but to accept Britain's suggestion.

Colonel J. K. Lawson, director of military training, rated the various battalions on the basis of their readiness for combat duty. There were three categories: Category A were the best trained; the next best were rated B; Category C meant the battalion was insufficiently trained for combat. The Winnipeg Grenadiers and the Royal Rifles of Canada were both rated C. The Grenadiers were just back from garrison duties in the West Indies and the Royal Rifles from similar duties in Newfoundland. Yet those were the two battalions picked to go to Hong Kong. Lawson was then notified that he would command the very troops he had advised against using in Hong Kong.

Winston Churchill opposed the idea when it was first suggested. "This is all wrong," he said. "If Japan goes to war [at that time Japan was not yet involved] there is not the slightest chance of holding Hong Kong or relieving it. It is most unwise to increase the loss we shall suffer there. Instead of increasing the garrison, it ought to be reduced to a symbolic scale." He was right, but he allowed himself to be drawn from his original position, approved this ill-advised operation, and, in effect, delivered Canada's first casualties to their Japanese captors.

The two battalions—1,975 men—left Vancouver aboard a converted passenger liner, the *Awatea*, on October 27, 1941. They sailed without the 212 vehicles (trucks, carriers, and motorcycles) that would be needed in Hong Kong. The vehicles were put aboard an American freighter in Vancouver a week later but never reached Hong Kong.

Somehow they wound up in the possession of U.S. forces defending the Philippines.

If the Canadian troops sent to Hong Kong were under-trained and ill-equipped, they were in for another let-down when they got there: the British garrison was equally unprepared. (An intelligence officer with the Royal Rifles summed up the extent of the British defence: "They had one of everything: one ack-ack gun, one warship, one fighter plane, and so on.") The level of training was not much higher than that of the Canadians. Arms were scarce and obsolete. British Intelligence had assured everyone—especially the British military in Hong Kong—that the Japanese were untrained, under-armed, and cowardly.

Nobody would have suspected that anything was wrong by reading the Canadian newspapers. Their information came from Britain, and had been laundered by censors. On December 8, 1941, the day the Japanese attacked, a small Canadian Press dispatch from Hong Kong mentioned that the Crown Colony had been attacked by air "but ineffectually, according to official announcements." Next day the Toronto *Globe and Mail*, again with a CP dispatch, was headlined: "Searing Barrage Stops Jap Drive on Hong Kong."

On December 12, British United Press reported that large forces of Chinese troops, under Generalissimo Chiang Kai-Shek, were assailing the rear of the Japanese troops attacking Hong Kong and "threatening to cut the Japanese communications lines."

On December 19, *The Globe and Mail* quoted Canada's Defence Minister Ralston as saying that the Japanese had landed on Hong Kong "in considerable force" and that heavy fighting was in progress. He had no information about casualties.

On that day, in a double tragedy, Corporal Henry Kelso and his brother John, both machine gunners with the Winnipeg Grenadiers, were killed in action in Hong Kong.

On that day, Sergeant Major John R. Osborn of the Winnipeg Grenadiers picked up several live grenades that were thrown by the Japanese and tossed them back. When one more grenade was hurled into their position, there was no time to heave it back. Osborn deliberately rolled over on it, saving the lives of his men at the cost of his own. He was awarded a posthumous Victoria Cross.

On that day, Japanese assault troops closed in on Brigadier Lawson's field headquarters. Lawson, only recently promoted, was killed in a shoot-out with the assaulting forces.

By Christmas Day 1941, the bad news could not be withheld any longer. "The defence of Hong Kong," began a Canadian Press story from London, "has broken under relentless assault by land, sea and air and the Crown colony, which for a century has been a British bastion off the southeast China coast, has fallen to the Japanese." By this time almost 300 Canadians were dead and almost 500 wounded.

The accusations and recriminations resulting from this ignoble defeat were to last longer than the ordeal of the more than 1,400 Canadians who were taken prisoners of war at Hong Kong.

The whole nasty business became the centre of a political controversy. In 1942, a few months after the battle for Hong Kong, Ontario's Conservative leader, Colonel George Drew (who held the rank of lieutenant-colonel from his First World War service) attacked the Mackenzie King government for its "mismanagement" of the Hong Kong affair. "Many gallant young Canadians," Drew charged, "went into one of the bitterest battles in all history with little knowledge of the weapons they were called upon to use." He was right, of course. But he undoubtedly would have been just as irate if King had refused the British government's request for Canadian troops to beef up the Hong Kong garrison.

In late January 1942, when the Canadian government gave its first report to the House of Commons about the Hong Kong debacle, Defence Minister J. L. Ralston said, "The defence of Hong Kong is in accordance with the finest traditions of Canadian armies. All ranks fought it out to the last man and more can not be asked of any man."

George Drew later charged that the King government's military brass had agreed to send Canadian troops to Hong Kong without even consulting a map of the island—simply because there wasn't one in the War Room.

The next blow to the Canadian psyche came less than a year later, with the raid on Dieppe.

On August 19, 1942, 6,086 men crossed the English Channel in what should have been an in-and-out assault on the French coastal port of Dieppe and its environs. Most of the men were Canadians: 4,963 members of the Canadian 2nd Division. The raid, politely called "a tactical failure" by its supporters, constituted the bloodiest nine hours in the Second World War. The 2nd Division suffered 3,367 casualties, including 907 dead and 1,946 taken prisoner.

The architect of Dieppe was Lord Louis Mountbatten, cousin to King George VI and a man of boundless ambition and supreme self-confidence. A master of public relations, he had ingratiated himself with Roosevelt, Churchill, Eisenhower, and the Canadian-born press baron Lord Beaverbrook.

In 1941, Mountbatten's ship, HMS *Kelly*, had been sunk and he was awaiting command of another ship. He was assigned command of the aircraft carrier *Illustrious,* but Churchill soon cancelled that job and gave Mountbatten a "more urgent" mission.

In March 1942, Mountbatten was made vice-admiral and given the honorary ranks of air marshal and lieutenant-general. He was, he would later boast, "the youngest vice-admiral since Nelson." More significantly, he was soon named Chief of Combined Operations, meaning he could supervise land, sea, and air operations. He rapidly became an outspoken proponent of massive raids against Hitler's Europe, and he proposed a full-scale invasion of Cherbourg long before the Western Allies were capable of carrying out such a perilous operation. The scheme was rejected.

Undaunted, Mountbatten and his growing staff planned a series of raids against the northwestern coast of France, the most ambitious of which was the raid on Dieppe. It was originally planned for July 4, 1942, with the approval of the Chiefs of Staff—but had to be called off because of bad weather. At that point, General Bernard Law Montgomery, Commander-in-Chief of Southeastern Command and no fan of Mountbatten's, advised that the whole plan be scrapped. One obvious reason for this was the danger that the aborted July 4 raid might have alerted the Germans. Indeed, the day after the planned raid was cancelled, Hitler issued a communiqué to his top commanders warning of the probability of an Allied raid on the French coast. The most likely area, he warned, was the Channel coast, somewhere between Dieppe and Le Havre.

But Mountbatten stubbornly proceeded with plans for the Dieppe raid, despite a notable lack of enthusiasm among the Chiefs of Staff. The disastrous raid on Dieppe was carried out on August 19.

As usual in wartime, all press reports were heavily censored, but never more heavily than in this case. Mountbatten's public relations experts insisted that all press stories had to be cleared by Combined Operations—and then submitted for further censoring to the Ministry of Information. This resulted in a twenty-nine-hour delay in the publication of eyewitness accounts of the raid.

The Allies' first press stories, carefully orchestrated by Mountbatten's minions, were euphoric: "Hand Luftwaffe Crippling Blow in Dieppe Show" ... "Objectives Attained" ... "Canadian Force in Daring Raid Well Rehearsed."

In the United States, newspapers wrote of an American military triumph—evidently unaware that of the 6,000 men involved in the Dieppe raid, only 50 were American.

A *New York Times* correspondent wrote ten lengthy paragraphs about the U.S. Rangers (the fifty Americans involved in the raid) before getting around to such a minor detail as the fact that Canadians made up ninety per cent of the raiding party.

But the ill-advised delay in releasing press coverage succeeded only in allowing the Germans to deploy their own interpretation of events—that this had been not an in-and-out raid, but an attempted full-scale invasion, which had utterly failed.

One correspondent who declined to join in the chorus of hosannas was Ross Munro, of the Canadian Press. "Canadian shock troops had a rough time of it at several points," he wrote, "and losses probably will not be small."

Munro admitted that he had just spent "the grimmest 20 minutes of my life...when a rain of German machine-gun fire wounded half the men in our boat, and only a miracle saved us from annihilation.

"By the time our boat touched the beach the din was at a crescendo. I peered out at the slope lying just in front of us, and it was startling to discover it was dotted with the fallen forms of men in battledress. The Royals [the Royal Regiment of Toronto] ahead of us had been cut down as they stormed the slope. It came home to me only then that every one of those men had gone down under the bullets of the enemy at the top of the incline...

"I saw 60 or 70 bodies, men cut down before they could fire a shot. A dozen Canadians were running along the beach toward the 12-foot-high seawall, 100 yards long. Some fired as they ran. Some had no helmets. Some were wounded, their uniforms torn and bloody. One by one, they were hit and rolled down the slope to the sea."

Among the greatest problems in the Dieppe raid was the natural obstacle of the high cliffs that overlooked the beaches, topped with the German gun emplacements. Soldiers of the Royal Regiment of Canada were cut down as they entered the water.

Ron Beal went in with the Royals and remembered when "the ramp on the assault landing craft was down...you were looking out and you could see the small-arms fire hitting the water just like rain."

Of the seven Canadian medical officers who landed at Dieppe that day, one was killed, two were wounded, and four were captured. One of the latter was Dr. Wes Clare, of Kingston, Ontario.

"The raid, of course, was a disaster. We landed late, after daybreak, and for the last kilometre the long lines of landing craft were visible and under heavy fire. We landed in chest-deep water and had to crawl up a rough beach under heavy fire. There were many early casualties, and for some time my aid men and I had to crawl around the beach, checking the wounded and dead...

"After 11 a.m. some landing craft came in under heavy fire in an evacuation attempt. Even though many were destroyed, some wounded were returned to England. By then there were 80 to 100 men huddled behind our now burning landing craft, and as the tide came in it became obvious that we had to surrender before the wounded drowned. I was senior officer in our group; I tied a triangular bandage to a rifle, and we surrendered."

The Queen's Own Cameron Highlanders of Canada (the Camerons) were given the objective of taking an aerodrome inland from Pourville, west of Dieppe. After the initial assault by the Essex Scottish Regiment, the Calgary Tank Regiment was supposed to help clear the way for the Camerons to reach the aerodrome.

The Camerons landed late and there were no tanks to meet them (they apparently couldn't land). But the foot soldiers fought their way inland until they were turned back at a heavily defended crossing of the Scie River. When they ran short of ammunition, all the units started retreating to the beach, fighting a rearguard action as they went. Some escaped by sea. Some were captured. Many of those wounded on the beaches were drowned by the incoming tide.

Jay D. Murphy says that his uncle, Basil "Red" James, who fought with the Camerons, rarely talked about the Dieppe raid, except "once [when] we were sitting in a Toronto beer parlour with a full view of the street and the three-storey building on the other side. 'That's about what it was like,' he said. 'Just put some Jerries on the roof with machine guns.'"

Murphy remembers hearing news of his uncle: "One hot August morning, the minister and a representative from the town council arrived at the farm (in Manitoba) with official word that Red had been wounded in action. No details were given. His mother accepted the news calmly, almost gratefully. My mother cried with relief. The entire country knew that the Second Division had been to Dieppe, and what the results had been."

In the years before his death, Red relived the horror of those hours in Dieppe. "He would warn those around him to take cover from the Jerries. The memories of the few hours on a French beach stayed with him to the end."

"We had a foreboding before we left England," said Archie Anderson, a member of the Calgary Tank Regiment. "We knew we didn't have a chance... in their hearts most of them knew that." Anderson remembers "a feeling of almost sickening revulsion at the carnage that was on the beach... It's hard to describe the feeling of fear. The smell of burning flesh and the woollen garments was stifling as well."

By all accounts, les Fusiliers Mont-Royal should have had a slight advantage in the operation. Their rigorous training (they were apparently the first Canadian troops to cover eleven miles in ninety minutes) and their fluent French made them among the best prepared for the Dieppe raid. Norman McLean, a volunteer from Duck Lake, Saskatchewan, went in with the Fusiliers. "For twelve hours, I, along with others who were unable to get away, fought the Germans until I was wounded in the wrist by a bayonet and taken prisoner.

"Together with other Canadians I was marched inland for twenty-five miles. We slept in a shed that night. The next day we were loaded into boxcars, forty men to a car. It was stifling hot with little ventilation. We were taken to Vernielles, France. During the seven days we were kept there, we were literally starved. Our rations consisted of a crust of bread and a cup of water each day. We ate grass to supplement our diet." McLean escaped, was captured, and escaped again.

Stephen Bell, from Govan, Saskatchewan, went to Dieppe with the Calgary Tank Regiment on August 19. Bell's tank had barely begun its descent from the landing craft when "we were hit on the turret, just coming down the ramp. This shell hit the top of it, just blew the lid right off. Three of us in the turret were knocked out cold, but it was just concussion."

When the tanks landed, they could not move forward over the stony beach; they simply bogged down in the crushed rocks. Bell's tank stopped fifteen feet up from the water, leaving the crew stranded. "We got hit maybe three or four times in that fifteen feet. The engines would run, but the tank wouldn't move forwards or backwards."

Bell and another man in his tank crew, Johnny Booker, set up a machine gun in what seemed like a sheltered spot and kept firing at Germans. "Five minutes later, a shell hit the back of the tank, about three feet above our heads. Both of us were wounded. I got shrapnel in my legs, my back and my ass. He got hit in the leg... We tore open his pants and blood just spurted out, it must have hit an artery. I didn't bleed much."

Another Calgary tank man, Bill Willard, was hit first in the ankle, the knee, and the shoulder. Then Bell and another man, Earl Snider, saw him "opened up right from his breastbone right down to his crotch." Bell and Snider had "this first-aid kit, so we got a couple of safety pins and stuck everything back in and pinned him up."

At eleven o'clock that morning, some small (thirty-foot or so) boats started coming in to pick up the faltering raiders, and Steve Bell was among those carrying wounded back to the boats.

"Every boat, except for maybe one or two, got blown up in the water. You could ask anybody who was on that beach and they'll tell you, that water was just like red ink with blood. Bodies? You have no idea—just like cord wood, just floating round and round, arms and legs and guts and heads. It was unbelievable. If I hadn't seen it, I wouldn't believe it myself. The water that was coming up was foaming red with blood."

Half an hour later, Bell, like Norman McLean, was a prisoner of war. More Canadians were taken prisoner that day than the army lost in the eleven months of the 1944–45 northwestern Europe campaign.

Another POW taken at Dieppe, the Reverend John Foote, padre of the Royal Hamilton Light Infantry, was credited with saving at least thirty lives. He picked up wounded men one by one, waded through the water to the nearest boat, deposited the casualty, and went back for another. After an hour of this, two men pulled him into a boat, but he plunged back into the water. "It seemed to me," he said later, "the men ashore would need me far more in captivity than any of those going home." Foote was a prisoner of war until May 1945, and was subsequently awarded the Victoria Cross.

The lasting impressions of those who got off the beach alive were summed up by Ron Beal: "The noise, the explosions of grenades, of mortar bombs, of shells, the flying stones, the flying shrapnel; men being hit and screaming, some men calling for their mothers, other men sitting on the beach trying to tuck their innards in... That's the kind of thing that stays with you, when you have your nightmares, you wake up in the night and it's in your nostrils, you can almost smell it in your sleep, you can hear the noise... If it wasn't for the wife beside you to comfort you, you would be an absolute basket case."

Denis Whitaker came ashore at Dieppe as a captain in the Royal Hamilton Light Infantry. His experience with the Hamilton Tigers football club in the 1930s may have helped him, for he led a charge to the verandah of his objective—the town casino—and got there without a scratch. When he barged in, he found himself facing five German soldiers with their hands in the air ready to surrender. But the order "Vanquish 1100" sent Whitaker retreating to the beach and to the safety of landing craft beyond.

"The objectives were far, far too optimistic," Whitaker insists. "Five times the number of troops couldn't accomplish what we were supposed to accomplish."

Whitaker points to a number of flaws in the planning of the raid— the absence of aerial bombing beforehand, the inability of naval vessels to maintain the time schedule, the general inexperience of everyone concerned. Nevertheless, one of the least reported but most successful aspects of the Dieppe raid was the air engagement over the beaches. It was Fighter Command's first opportunity since the Battle of Britain in 1940 to meet the Luftwaffe in strength on their side of the Channel. Fighter pilots of the RAF, the Royal New Zealand Air Force, the United States Army Air Force, and the RCAF shot down ninety-one German aircraft. One group of Allied pilots—two Royal Norwegian Air Force squadrons of the RAF who had trained in Canada—downed sixteen German aircraft.

To this day, the argument persists as to whether the raid on Dieppe was worth the cost it took in (mostly) Canadian lives. The chief argument in favour of the disastrous raid has always been that the Allies "learned lessons" that would prove valuable when D-Day came. Lord Louis Mountbatten insisted that for every life lost at Dieppe ten were saved in Normandy.

Ralph Allen, war correspondent for *The Globe and Mail,* was at Dieppe. In his own recollections, *Ordeal by Fire,* he called the raid "a magnificent fiasco." But he concluded that "according to the impersonal cost accounting of war and in the jargon of the military-college blackboards, the final verdict may be that Dieppe was a tactical failure but a strategic success." Postwar opinion tended to bear out that view, but more recent studies, especially by history professor Brian Loring Villa, are far more harsh in assessing the "strategic success" of Dieppe, and place the onus for the disastrous adventure squarely on the shoulders of Lord Louis Mountbatten.

What still nags at the Canadian conscience is the feeling that almost 5,000 Canadian sacrificial lambs were offered up to serve in a poorly conceived, ineptly executed raid whose primary aims were political rather than military.

Beth Munro, widow of CP correspondent Ross Munro, says that it was the worst experience of his life. "When he had bad dreams or couldn't sleep, it was Dieppe he thought of." To add to his anguish, Munro was called back to Canada soon after the Dieppe raid and sent on a bond-selling tour—to buck up the morale of civilians at a time when his own had so recently been shaken.

Whatever else it was, the Dieppe raid was the last major setback Canada was to endure—but not the last tough fight.

Of Canada's three armed services, it was the Royal Canadian Navy that had the earliest contact with German forces. Throughout the war, the RCN escorted convoys from points in Canada towards Britain.

In the first two years of the war, the RCN's job was a grim one. German U-boats made increasingly bold attacks on Allied convoys. In June 1941 alone, 500,000 tons of shipping were lost to German submarines.

Terry Manuel, whose later trials would include the sinking of the minesweeper HMCS *Esquimalt*, looked back at his RCN duty escorting convoys as his worst experience:

"The Atlantic was the longest and most deadly of all battles of the war and vital to the children and families of our allies and the theatres of war they actively entered into. Suffering was sheer anguish and death long, heartbreaking and hideous as we watched the sea ablaze with oil and burning ships, the screams of blackened men, instantaneous sinkings, no survivors, cries for help, alive and mangled men determined still, in their struggle for life, and yet, we fought on tooth and nail, sleepless aching nights, wet, dirty, and at times saturated in vomit... I turn my head from it all, I can no longer look from within my heart."

Canada helped to counteract the U-boat menace by designing new methods of locating and destroying subs. The best-known new vessel was the corvette, which could be produced cheaply and quickly and had the ability to outmanoeuvre and attack submarines. While most convoys travelled as slowly as six or eight knots, a corvette could travel at sixteen knots, as Sub-Lieutenant Jim Hazlewood said, "with the cook over the stern with an egg-beater."

Hazlewood, a native of southwestern Ontario, joined the RCN late in 1942. After receiving his commission, he was posted to HMCS *Dunvegan*, escorting convoys on the "triangle run" between Halifax, St. John's, Newfoundland, and New York City. The corvette's job was to pick up a convoy in New York, take it out to a western meeting-place to connect with a mid-ocean convoy, then return to St. John's to pick another one in-bound to New York. Hazlewood clocked some 40,000 miles aboard *Dunvegan*.

Hazlewood recalls chasing subs which "had a habit of blowing up human parts to make you think that you had a kill... Once I think we pulled a guy's chest and a leg out... These were (German) servicemen who had died. They saved the bodies and they'd put them in a torpedo-tube and put a blast of air and a slick of oil out too.

"Just before VE Day, we were ordered out to search for a sub... Using our asdic [echo sounder] we made contact with the sub, dropped all kinds of depth-charges, and waited around. Quite often you would drop your depth-charges and if you sat there silently, they would think there were no ships and come up.

"Well, this fellow came up—U-889, a huge German sub. There he was, as plain as could be. And the fellows came out of the conning-tower and raised a big, dirty black flag. I guess it was a blanket on their small yardarm. They wanted to give up. They figured the war was too close to ending.

"I was signals officer at the time and I coded up a signal in German giving them course and speed... We broke radio silence and got instructions to take them to Bay Bulls, Newfoundland, which was about 200 miles away. So we gave them a course and speed and told them if they varied more than two degrees we'd open fire.

"About seven o'clock that night the captain [of the U-boat] came up on the conning-tower and he flashed the message across, 'And so to bed, goodnight.' Turned out he'd graduated from Oxford University and could speak better English than a lot of us."

RCN officer John Carling's memories of corvette duty were dietary. Carling had joined the Sea Cadets in Ottawa in 1938, trained at Cornwallis, got his commission in 1944, and then served aboard a high-tech Castle Class corvette. His territory was the mid-Atlantic run between England and Newfoundland.

"The senior officer with whom I stood bridge watches [had been] a housemaster at Trinity or Ridley College in Ontario. His name was Earl Doane. He was a specialist navigator, but I stood watch with him because there were always two people on the bridge, and we stood what was called the mid-watch—from midnight until four in the morning.

"When the mid-watch was finished, Earl would say, 'Down to the wardroom,' and he would break open a box of cornflakes and we would have sugar on the cornflakes and condensed milk. This went on forever. I haven't eaten cornflakes to this day."

Another invaluable type of vessel during the war was the minesweeper, whose crews worked tirelessly clearing areas of mines and detecting U-boats. Thirteen-year-old Diana Warren, who spent the war years in England, "formed a little group and we adopted a minesweeper named HMS *Willow*. We knitted for the crew. I wrote cheerful letters. The minesweepers were a forgotten group during the war and after. Their job was so hazardous, sweeping away the mines in the North Sea, with horrible freezing cold temperatures and rough seas."

Despite the minesweepers' diligence, between 1942 and 1944 German subs torpedoed twenty-seven ships in or near the St. Lawrence, including four RCN vessels. Alan Easton, commanding officer of the corvette HMCS *Baddeck* in 1941–42, wrote in his book *50 North*: "During the war I saw many empty lifeboats and never did they fail to give an unhappy feeling, a conviction that the shadow of disaster floated close alongside or was hidden beneath, that its mysterious passengers had known fear, tragedy."

Murray Westgate from Regina, Saskatchewan, began his career in the RCN as a telegraphist and had received his sub-lieutenancy by the summer of 1942, when German U-boats were most active in the Gulf of St. Lawrence. His ship, HMCS *Fort Ramsay* operated out of Gaspé, where Westgate heard stories about marauding U-boats, and even rumours of German spies landing in Gaspé. But he never once saw a U-boat there.

Westgate spent six years in the navy, three of them at sea as an officer. He served on about ten different ships, including HMCS *Hotspur*, doing the St. John's-to-Londonderry convoy escort runs, but "never dropped a depth-charge in earnest. Never dropped one...and I was on three ships that were torpedoed and sunk the trip after I left them.

"I was on one [ship] when the acoustic torpedoes came in. The Germans had invented a torpedo that would home in on the noise [made] by the ship's propeller. We were in mid-Atlantic, there were frantic signals. Everybody was dreaming up ideas, and by the time we got to Newfoundland we had invented a thing called the acoustic torpedo arrester, which was called a CAT. Our engineer officer invented a long line that dragged a great big tin can and inside it he put a klaxon horn, which would make a big racket...to attract the torpedoes [away from the ship]."

His worst experience? "When I was seasick... Then I wanted to die. The action stations bell rang and I prayed that the torpedo would come right through my bunk." Despite Westgate's one rough crossing, prairie boys generally fared better than most out in the mid-Atlantic. Perhaps it was their immunity to agoraphobia (a fear of open spaces) that made prairie volunteers competent seamen.

Two of the three Doig sons in Winnipeg left the family construction business early in the war and joined the RCN. "Most of us from the prairies had never seen the ocean," recalled Harold Doig. "And then we got onto ships for the first time...bobbing up and down constantly out in the middle of nowhere. In the early years we were running a convoy and saw a lot of action. Some got used to it... But others? My kid brother joined up when he was twenty-one. And when he came back off his first convoy at twenty-two, he was grey. His hair had turned grey around the temples just from the action he had seen."

Roy Harbin had to get his parents' permission to join the Navy at age seventeen. By 1943 he was a stoker "getting ten cents more than a seaman." Next it was off to Halifax for torpedo school where he learned electrical wiring, then to Newfoundland where he went on active service as an electrical artificer. He spent fifteen months aboard the frigate HMCS *Montreal*, first doing escort duty with convoys, then patrolling back and forth in the English Channel looking for submarines. The one U-boat that *Montreal* sank, Harbin says, "we never got any credit for. We dropped charges all night and then...we picked up survivors... I think we picked up eighteen survivors.

"I'd never shot a .45 in my life, but they gave me a big .45 and then they gave me the two guys in the sick-bay to guard," Harbin laughs. There was no need for the gun. There was little animosity between the crew and the prisoners. Harbin and his mates offered cigarettes and cards at one point; in fact, when a crew member guarding a group of prisoners dozed off and a Canadian officer approached, the Germans woke up the guard so he wouldn't get into trouble.

"These prisoners were awfully happy when Canadian ships picked them up because they had heard Canada was wonderful. [But] when we dropped them off in Plymouth you can bet there was some pretty unhappy people. The British marines, I guess they were closer to the war than we were, and they came along and they're just butting them along with their bayonets and so on, and they just hustled them right off. The captain died on our ship. I guess he may have been coming up when we were still dropping charges, because he was bleeding from the ears and the nose."

Nineteen-year-old Cliff Perry left his job at a Toronto printing firm to join the air force in 1940. But lacking the senior matriculation then required by the RCAF, Perry settled for signalman in the RCN. After some months of duty on a minesweeper running from the west coast to Alaska, he took further training and got his commission in 1943. Then, because it meant a chance to go overseas, he volunteered to join the (British) Royal Navy.

At first, Perry served aboard ships escorting convoys to Murmansk. Later he served on motor torpedo boats patrolling the English Channel just off the French coast. Their mission was to act as the first line of defence for convoys in the Channel and to attack anything moving along the French coast.

"I didn't realize it at first," recalls Perry, "but it became obvious afterwards that we were preparing for D-Day... We went out at dusk, came back at dawn. We did that for nearly a year and a half... There was rarely a night went by where we didn't have some kind of activity... Everything from being shelled from shore if we got too close [to] aircraft attacks, bombs dropped, torpedo bombers, submarines..."

One night, Perry's ship, a destroyer, sank two German E-boats and took some prisoners, including the commander of one of the E-boats. Perry was assigned to look after the German captain, who had sustained a wound to his chin. He wrapped a towel around the man's face and gave him a shot of morphine. But the blood continued to drip from the wound and on to a set of binoculars that hung around the commander's neck. Perry removed the glasses to make the wounded man more comfortable. The next morning, when the German prisoners were put ashore, Perry discovered he still had the binoculars.

"Look, we're in trouble," he reported to his captain. "You're not supposed to take anything from any prisoner. But I've got these goddam binoculars!"

"I never want to see them," replied the captain. "I never want to hear about them. I don't want anything to do with them. Get out."

Perry still has them today.

The bitter battle of the Atlantic was long, brutal, and costly. One of its worst incidents came between Christmas and New Year's Eve 1942, in a cat-and-mouse game between a large convoy of freighters and tankers, westbound from Britain to Newfoundland, escorted by four destroyers and five corvettes. The convoy was attacked by wave after wave of U-boats in a five-day fight. Fourteen of the convoy's forty-six ships were sunk and more than 100 merchant seamen died. As many as twenty-five U-boats were involved in the battle, making this the hardest-hit convoy the RCN ever escorted in the long Atlantic struggle. The four destroyers—*St. Laurent*, *Chilliwack*, *Battleford*, and *Napanee*—dropped countless depth-charges, but owing to wartime security procedures it was not until some years after the war that they were credited with destroying a single U-boat.

The contribution to the war effort of Canadian merchant seamen is seldom acknowledged. While their best-known work was done on the Atlantic convoy route, Canadian merchant seamen were involved in one of the early crucial moments of the war. In the spring of 1940, when Hitler's blitzkrieg pushed the British Expeditionary Force into the sea at Dunkirk, two dozen Great Lakes freighters were sent to England to assist the evacuation across the English Channel.

When the war began, Canada's merchant navy consisted of 37 ships and 1,400 merchant seamen. By the end of the war, it had grown to 180 ships and 12,000 mariners. Canada lost 67 merchant ships during the war, and of the 7,705 seamen credited by the Department of Transport with sailing in dangerous waters, 1,146 were killed and 198 taken prisoner of war.

Alan Erson, born in Dublin but raised in Canada, joined the Canadian merchant navy in 1943. He became a radio operator and served on three different ships. One of them, the SS *Bridgeland Park*, was in a huge convoy of some 900 ships en route to England in February 1945. The ship, which was carrying a cargo of lumber and was considered unsinkable, was positioned in the rear right-hand corner of the convoy, known among merchant seamen as "Coffin Corner."

There was a Greek freighter directly in front of Erson's ship. When the Greek ship reported trouble with its steering gear, it moved out of its convoy position, and the SS *Bridgeland Park* moved up. When its steering gear had been corrected, the Greek ship pulled back into what had been the *Bridgeland Park*'s position—coffin corner.

"Right away—boom! A whole pack of subs attacked," Erson remembers. "They sank about six ships all around us. There was a tanker beside us and a torpedo hit it amidships. I can still see those poor guys, swimming in that boiling oil. I said to the captain, 'Can't we do something for them, stop and pick them up?' He said, nope, his orders were to keep going. The navy would pick them up... How long could you last in boiling oil and freezing water? I don't suppose any of them survived."

Moving from one merchant ship to another and from one merchant navy to another was common. Martin Walsh was a merchant seaman from Dunnville, Ontario. For almost three years, he was a stoker on coal-burning ships. "I fought the Nazis with a shovel."

In 1943, while in New York, he and three other Canadians volunteered to join the Polish merchant navy aboard the SS *Baltyk* for a trip to the United Kingdom and back. Instead, they were shanghaied aboard another Polish ship (the SS *Narwyk*) that was off to the Middle East. Eventually they wound up in Egypt, where Walsh celebrated his eighteenth birthday on June 13, 1943. He didn't get home until February 1, 1944.

"If you serve in a military unit or with your fellow countrymen who have similar interests, you can lean on each other in a crisis because you are part of a unit," Walsh said. "On your own it's not easy."

Hoping to join the merchant navy as a radio operator, Jerry Thornton took a radio course in Toronto. He was still seventeen when he got his licence, but he couldn't get a job on board a Canadian merchant ship. When he discovered that British Marconi needed operators, he joined them and spent the rest of the war, from late 1940 on, serving on various British merchant ships.

"It was a convoy coming up the African coast, near the Canary Islands, that scared the living daylights out of me," Thornton recalls. His convoy was subjected to four days of submarine attacks that trip. "Four days. We lost twenty-five ships. The captain said that there must have been a torpedo shot at us and it went right underneath us... The four ships on our left-hand side, the three ahead of us and the four on our right-hand side all disappeared, every one of them got it.

"The ship just ahead of us and on the left-hand side was coming back from Australia loaded with women and children and it got hit. It didn't sink, they managed to get into Gibraltar, but the screams and the yelling... It was fierce, it really was... We slowed down to see what we could do to help, but the escort came along and told us to get moving, no stopping, because you are a dead duck once you do that."

Torpedo attacks were only half the battle. The merchant ship *Point Pleasant Park* took a torpedo hit in the crew's quarters. Paul Tooke was the third officer on board and remembers that the explosion killed ten men and trapped twenty-eight others as the ship went down. As the survivors got free and into lifeboats, the U-boat surfaced. Hatches flew open, machine guns blazed, aimed at the wounded ship's waterline. The survivors had only minutes to evacuate. Tooke's lifeboat travelled some 350 miles before being spotted by a South African Navy trawler. A few weeks later, he was back at sea on another merchant vessel.

Dave Broadfoot also joined the merchant navy. He left school and began looking for work in the shipyards of Vancouver. When war broke out he decided to join up before he was drafted. The Royal Canadian Navy rejected him because he was under age at seventeen and had no parental consent ("I never got my parents' consent for anything," Broadfoot admits. "Even becoming a comedian was a secret.")

After six months of coastal experience aboard passenger boats along the British Columbia coast, he transferred to ocean-going merchant ships. For the next three years, he travelled extensively on various tankers and freighters, seeing the world and maturing in the process. He doesn't feel strongly about the attempts to obtain veterans' benefits for merchant seamen.

"The fact is that I only went into the merchant navy because I couldn't get into the regular navy... I joined knowing that I was going to be a civilian. There was no illusion about that. And I was paid way better than the sailors, the regular navy," he says. Yet he acknowledges that had his ship been hit, the pay differential would be of little value.

At fourteen, Francis Martell of Arichat, Nova Scotia, used his older brother's birth certificate to get into the merchant navy as a mess boy, later becoming a cook's helper. By the end of the war he was earning the munificent sum of $80 a month, plus $40 danger pay.

(The Canadian Merchant Navy Association, however, maintains that no merchant navy officer under the rank of captain or chief engineer received as much pay as the RCN equivalent "even in 1944, and that the 1940 rates for all merchant navy ratings were much lower than RCN rates until 1944.")

After forty-two years in the Canadian merchant navy—six of them during wartime—Nova Scotian Bennie Amirault protests the contention that "we chose merchant ships to avoid serving in uniform, or so that we could pick and choose so-called safe trips under strong convoy." Through much of his experience aboard the merchant ship *City of Delhi*, Amirault remembers very few trips travelling in the relative safety of an escorted convoy. The *City of Delhi* often carried explosives across the Atlantic, and "we didn't always sail in convoy. We had plenty of alerts. We had to look for protection only from our own gun crew. We'd have been no match for an armed raider or a submarine...

"The sailings were long and very lonely... We had to rely on luck, good navigation skills, and help from Heaven." (Luck eventually ran out for the *City of Delhi*; shortly after Amirault joined another ship, the *City of Delhi* was torpedoed and sunk off the coast of Italy.)

"Theirs was an occupation noted in peacetime for hardness and monotony, yearned for only because of the sense of freedom it gave," wrote Joseph Schull in *The Far Distant Ships*. "Now was added the prospect of death by freezing water or flaming oil in a life unrelieved by uniforms, recognition, or the shoreside amenities for naval crews. And freedom was gone; behind the merchant service stood the shadow of compulsion. The ships had to be sailed and these men had to sail them."

Of all the armed services, perhaps the Royal Canadian Air Force was the most far-sighted. Interest in commercial and leisure aviation had grown considerably in the 1930s, but a few people recognized that aircraft would also change the future of warfare. In June 1939, former First World War flyer and president of the Canadian Flying Clubs Association Murton Seymour lobbied the Canadian government to expand flying club activities in elementary flying training for defence purposes. By August, the RCAF was moving to "war stations."

Although it was very much smaller than the Luftwaffe, the RCAF—with 4,061 officers and airmen and 270 aircraft—formed the Home War Establishment, with Western Air Command based in Vancouver and Eastern Air Command in Halifax. Soon after September 10, 1939, the defence of Canada began with patrols of the northeast Pacific and the northwest Atlantic. The heaviest action came in 1942–43, when U-boat activity moved to the coastal waters of North America.

As well, when war was declared, civilian and military flyers across Canada were charged with the additional task of training air crew. Their job was to recruit and train a continuous flow of qualified air crew to take back the skies over Europe, North Africa, and the Pacific. It took time, but the British Commonwealth Air Training Plan eventually graduated enough pilots, navigators, gunners, bomb-aimers, and ground crew to make a significant difference to the war overseas.

Because of the RCAF commitment to the BCATP, in the early months of the war only three RCAF squadrons could participate in overseas duty. But by the end of the war, forty-eight RCAF squadrons were serving in western Europe, the Mediterranean, and the Far East.

On May 23, 1940, Squadron Leader F. M. Gobeil, commanding a Canadian squadron in the RAF, scored the first RCAF victory of the war when he shot down a Messerschmitt 109 over Berck, France. Other Canadian airmen were soon in the ranks of Churchill's "few" in the Battle of Britain. The first RCAF squadrons were formed in January 1941 and took part in their first offensive operations over German-held territory in April. Canadian bomber crews attacked the freight yards at Schwerte in June, the first RCAF bomber crews to make an attack on Germany itself. A year later, on May 30, 1942, sixty-eight RCAF crews took part in Bomber Command's first 1,000-bomber raid of the war.

Eight of the seventy-four Allied squadrons which gave aerial support to the Dieppe raid belonged to the RCAF. Despite opposition from senior British officers, including Arthur ("Bomber") Harris, a unique Canadian bomber force, No. 6 RCAF Group, was formed. By the end of the war Canadian squadrons were sending out more than 200 heavy bombers on each raid with a payload of 900 tons of bombs.

Ralph Wood captured some of the feelings of bomber crews in the last entry in his navigator's log: "Op No. 77, Berlin, 3 November '44. My last operational trip... I could write pages about our feelings, our twitch, and our relief when we got back... I've never felt so keenly about a trip in all my life. There were numerous fighter flares and fighter con-trails all the way there and back. Saw one jet fighter. The moon was rather bright. The raid was a wizard, though. Andy [Lockhart] and I exchanged congratulations and shook hands on it before we got out of the kite. Gosh, we were a couple of happy kids. Moncton Express III came through with flying colours."

Wood, who came from Woodstock, New Brunswick, was one of the earliest products of the BCATP, graduating from No. 2 Air Observer School in Edmonton in late 1940. After bombing and gunnery training, advanced navigational training, and a hurried wedding to his fiancée Phyllis, Wood went overseas as a Canadian in the RAF in the spring of 1941.

He had some close calls. On one occasion, in 1942, he had a rash on his thigh and the medical officer took him off the scheduled mission because he felt the rash would be irritated by wearing a parachute. The aircraft he would have been in exploded on the way to Germany. Nobody survived. A month later, on a training exercise in England, engine troubles forced a crash landing. The pilot was killed, another crew member was seriously injured, but Wood escaped unscathed.

Two years later, he was reunited with an old Moncton friend, Andy Lockhart, by then a flight lieutenant. Together they completed fifty missions in Mosquitoes. One of these, in October 1944, involved mining the Kiel Canal, an extremely dangerous low-level job. Both men were awarded the Distinguished Flying Cross.

Another Canadian who shone in the RAF was Everett L. Baudoux, who had earned his private pilot's licence in 1936. Baudoux didn't wait for Canada to declare war on Germany to join the air force; he went overseas and joined the RAF in 1938. By January 1940 he was a full-fledged pilot/navigator, flying Hudson bombers. During one of his 100 missions, many of them attacks on German shipping, Baudoux "shot down a Messerschmitt 109 with a Hudson. But," he adds modestly, "there were three of them attacking me and one fellow got careless."

In 1941, before the United States was in the war, Baudoux was sent to Portland, Oregon, on a clandestine operation to fly one of the first B-17 Flying Fortresses back to England. He was later posted to Gibraltar as a squadron leader. It was often depressing work.

"I had lost seven crews in about ten days. I can remember coming back off an operation myself, dog-tired, sitting in the office at nights trying to write to mothers and wives about how their son's life was worthwhile—that kind of stuff... I was twenty-three, and I thought, what the hell am I doing here? What is mankind doing? It starts to get to you."

Bob Scott's job was to keep the aircraft at RCAF Bomber Command stations Middleton St. George and Croft flying every night. Scott had graduated from the University of Saskatchewan with a BSc in mechanical engineering in 1936. By 1942 he was overseas maintaining Wellington and Halifax bombers.

"The biggest problem," wrote his daughter Jennifer Wilder, years later, "was when planes went down and didn't return. He never really knew if they were actually shot down or whether it was a defective plane and something his crew had overlooked before the planes left on bombing raids..."

Early in 1945, Scott was on loan to the U.S. Army Air Force and was sent to do intelligence work behind enemy lines in France. He related a story about his experiences to his daughter. "Trying to find some place to stay overnight, he turned into an alley and was about to knock on a door when a horrible sensation swept over him and as he turned he faced a German soldier, six feet tall, with a dagger raised in his hand, coming down on him. As he looked up, he realized it was a poster, not a person. The poster was there to let people know that the Germans were everywhere, and to keep their thoughts to themselves and be quiet. This scared him badly."

One night in December 1943, a Halifax crashed and burst into flames near the field where Scott was working. Scott was one of the first to arrive at the accident. He immediately took charge of the rescue. Seeing one member of the crew trapped inside the rear turret, he entered the burning fuselage. Although at first he was driven back by the heat and smoke, he succeeded in reaching the turret and in passing the injured airman safely through a hole in the rear. He ensured that there were no further members of the crew left, before he made his way out. Scott received the Order of the British Empire.

A young country-schoolteacher-turned-wartime-navigator flew aboard some of the bombers that Bob Scott worked on. Alan MacLeod had left his schoolhouse in Prince Edward Island to join the RCAF in 1940. His 431 (Iroquois) Squadron was based at Croft in Yorkshire. MacLeod survived thirty-two bombing missions in 1944, over France, Norway, and Germany, but "we didn't realize, nobody realized, the casualties. Thirty per cent of Bomber Command air crews were lost— the highest in World War II except for the U-boat crews... It's all well and good to say that when you go out at blackout time for six or eight hours over Europe that you are just going to work, because that's what you are trained for. But a lot of guys don't come back and you never know which one it's going to be...

"We came home one night with thirty holes in the fuselage, big ones—six inches in diameter... That's when you know the guys that you are meeting are trying to kill you. That's what it's all about."

No. 427 (Lion) Squadron also flew from Croft in Yorkshire. Among its RCAF bomber pilots was a young, slight fellow from the West. Bob Garvin says the only reason they accepted him at the recruiting centre in Saskatoon was because "they let me weigh in with my pants and shoes on." After a stint as an instructor at Hagersville, Ontario, Garvin was posted to Leeming Bar station to fly Halifax bombers. By this time—fall 1944—Bomber Command was sending crews in at low altitude to mine German-held harbours in Norway and Denmark.

"We would fly between 50 and 150 feet off the water...at night...to stay under their radar. Then we'd drop our mines, usually by parachute... The worst part was the weather. We lost a lot of crews. The loss ratio was anywhere from twenty to thirty per cent... One night we lost three out of four planes." Flight Lieutenant Garvin survived nine mine-laying missions and earned a DFC for displaying "the greatest determination" in accomplishing these missions.

Determination seemed to drive young Don MacNeil too. Originally a boy drummer in the Pictou Highlanders, he wasn't allowed to join the air force when the war broke out unless he had a college education; so he took engineering at Dalhousie in Halifax and joined the RCAF in June 1940. Although his heart was set on becoming a pilot, when he

finished Initial Training School in Regina, he was chosen to become a
WAG (wireless/air gunner). When he arrived in Britain for operational
service, he asked to remuster as a pilot. That meant going back to
Canada for pilot training. He was sent overseas a second time in 1943.
Eventually he was posted to Coastal Command.

MacNeil flew B-17s, chasing German submarines in waters around
the British Isles and along the convoy lanes to Murmansk. With its
capacity for 2,100 gallons of fuel and depth-charges attached to its
wings, the Flying Fortress was good for fourteen-hour sub patrols.
MacNeil remembers a lot of boring trips, spiced with a few hair-raising
experiences, including a mission on which he had to bring home his B-
17 with only two of four engines operating.

Another distressing experience was serving on a "committee of
adjustment" which consisted of pilot officers who took turns writing
letters to the families of comrades killed in action. "It took a lot out of
a person, at age twenty-one or twenty-two, but you did it because it
had to be done," he says. "I couldn't do it today."

For a while, he was based at Wick, Scotland. On the way home from
missions near Norway, he would fly over a lighthouse at Noup Head,
on the western tip of the Orkney Islands. "It used to be wonderful to
see this damn little lighthouse there. They had two families that were
the lighthouse keepers," he remembers. He would fly a couple of circuits around and wave at the people.

One night, when another such run was scheduled, he and his crew
put together a couple of boxes—spam, candy, whatever surplus supplies they could get hold of—and on their way home dropped the two
boxes at the lighthouse. The crew put their names and address in the
boxes, and a week later they received a telegram from the two families,
thanking them for the supplies.

Thomas William Watson travelled a long way from his native Yukon
during his wartime service in the RCAF. Soon after he arrived in
Bournemouth, England, for combat posting, Pearl Harbor was
bombed and, says Watson, "Everything changed." By the end of
January 1942, his No. 232 Squadron was on the opposite side of the
globe—in Singapore, then Java, New Guinea, India, and Burma.

On a typical series of missions in March 1942, Watson recalled,
"We'd been strafing the Jap landings every day... Sometimes you'd

never get out of your cockpit. You'd just re-arm and go back and strafe them when they were landing on the east side of Batavia [on the island of Java in Indonesia.] I made four runs on them...a Hurricane with twelve guns, each shooting 1100 rounds a minute... Eventually, I was shot down... I crash-landed in a rice paddy with my wheels up, flaps down... I got out of the plane and started running..."

Four days and 100 kilometres later, Watson caught up with his squadron in the town of Bandung. He was later shipped out to Perth, Australia, where he met Rowena Neal, a Canadian girl who had evacuated to Australia from Kobe, Japan, when the war broke out. When they met, Watson asked where she was from.

"Halifax," she said. "You?"

"The Yukon." And they laughed. A year later they were married. And at the end of the war he was awarded a DFC for a service record that was "an outstanding example of courage and tenacity."

Don Warner joined the RCAF in the summer of 1941 and qualified as a pilot. After being posted overseas in 1943, he spent the next two years flying various kinds of aircraft, including Hudsons, Venturas, and Flying Fortresses. The only one he did not like was the Beaufort torpedo bomber, which he still remembers as "a dreadful aircraft." He and his crew of three were assigned to Beauforts on training missions, dropping dummy torpedoes into the water from a low altitude.

"One day, I was out on patrol and flying quite low, about 300 feet or so. Suddenly the right engine acted up. I'd been told if that happens, don't fool with it long. You have to make up your mind within seconds...because a Beaufort will not fly on one engine. Bottom line.

"I fooled with it for the merest of seconds and decided the engine was gone... So I just told the crew we're going to ditch. We're coming down into the fucking water! I had no experience ditching. Cardinal rule was—you don't land along the trough of the waves, you land across it. I pulled out of the dive and had the luck of the gods... I pulled the perspex above me out so I could climb out after the crash. That's the last I remember."

Warner was knocked cold when his head hit the sighting device. His crew managed to inflate the rubber dinghy and haul him free. The Beaufort sank in a minute. The dinghy was spotted by a fishing trawler and then a navy vessel took them to the Isle of Arran. Warner needed

145 stitches in his head. He was in hospital for seven weeks, but it was nearly six months before he could fly with confidence again.

Later, when he was posted to Transport Command, he and his crew were ordered to deliver one of the dreaded Beauforts to Rabat, Morocco. They hit a bad storm, and Warner decided to try to fly under it. By the time they were out of the storm, fuel was so low he knew they wouldn't make Rabat. They were about forty miles north of Lisbon, Portugal. Their options were to head for Spain (where they could be shot down), land in Portugal, or try to reach Gibraltar.

"I knew in my heart of hearts I was not going to risk my life or the crew in a Beaufort again. It's once too often... So I decided to come down in Portugal."

Warner landed the plane on a beach near a hotel. There was a lagoon between the beach and hotel and very soon "I saw a horde of people massing on the other side of the lagoon. Some of them got into little boats and started towards us...Guess who was in these boats? Two or three of [the hotel's] porters. A guy came up to me and said, in broken English, 'Bags for hotel?'

"We had just landed, and so I had my bagful of civvy clothes and civvy shoes, because we thought we'd be in Rabat for a week. So he takes my bag. When I got to the hotel, everything was gone out of my bag except my shoes. He stole everything—underwear, ties, socks, shirts... The reason he didn't take the shoes, they were too big for him."

A man from the British embassy came to see them and told them they would be interned. He took their clothing sizes, explaining that they would be there for some time and would need civilian clothes, and asked if they needed anything else. "I said, 'If you can get me a cornet or a trumpet, I'd appreciate it. If I'm going to be here a few weeks, I could practice.' You know what he did? He actually got a cornet to me."

They were interned ("I'm embarrassed to tell you") at a tourist hotel at Caldas da Rainha, some fifty miles from Lisbon. "Everything was paid for," he chuckles. "We didn't even sign chits. We went down for breakfast, dinner, and supper, the beds were changed, two in each room, adjoining. We had the freedom of the town, but we weren't supposed to go more than a quarter of a mile or something outside the town limits." They were interned for seven weeks before being sent back to Britain.

Archie Van Hee was born in Belgium in 1909, but he grew up in Canada. By the time he was twenty, he was consumed by flying, earning his air engineer's papers and commercial pilot's licence by 1930. He already had 2,500 hours of flying logged by the time war broke out and he was soon an RCAF instructor. By 1943, Squadron Leader Van Hee commanded fourteen PBY (flying boats) patrolling coastal waters for the Home War Establishment in Eastern Air Command. Based at Yarmouth, Nova Scotia, his No. 160 BR (Bombing and Reconnaissance) Squadron provided cover for Britain-bound convoys.

"In 1943, when matériel was really being shoved into Britain," recalls Van Hee, "very seldom was there a convoy of less than a hundred ships. I remember escorting one with 200 ships... Each of us recognized the responsibility of getting these convoys safely overseas for the big show."

Among Van Hee's colleagues in the RCAF was Toronto-born Larry Foley. As a youth, Foley had dreamed of flying P-38 fighter planes. But after receiving his wings as a navigator and his officer's commission in 1942, he was posted to the Home War Establishment's No.162 BR Squadron in Yarmouth. Soon, Foley was navigating flights of PBY Cansos, hunting U-boats, guiding convoys, and escorting troopships.

"You'd take off at four in the morning and rendezvous at first light. I don't know how many times I was an escort for the troopship *Louis Pasteur*, but the captain was never where he was supposed to be. I don't think he trusted anybody."

The PBYs carried four depth-charges, each weighing 250 pounds, "and the pilot set the distance between the charges and the depth at which they would go off," explained Foley. "The routine was...you'd dive on the sub, level out as close as you could, trying to straddle the sub, to drop the charges on both sides of it."

Neither pilot Van Hee nor navigator Foley ever engaged a U-boat, but the repetitive attack manoeuvres that each of their squadrons conducted eventually paid off. During the spring of 1944 (when Foley's squadron was posted closer to Europe), the crews of No. 162 Squadron distinguished themselves. In just eight weeks these former HWE

Canso crews sank five U-boats and received some of the air force's highest citations.

The squadron's most celebrated attack occurred on June 29, 1944. Nearing the end of a twelve-hour patrol, a Canso flown by Flight Lieutenant David Hornell and Flying Officer Denomy spotted a U-boat on the surface about 200 kilometres north of the Shetland Islands. They attacked, but the U-boat crew fired back stubbornly. One of the Canso's engines was hit, and burst into flame. Co-pilot Denomy kept the crippled plane flying as Hornell pressed the attack, straddled the sub and dropped a stick of four depth-charges just fifty feet above the surface of the water. The sub sank, but the air crew had to ditch their plane. For the next twenty-one hours, Hornell and his seven crewmen struggled to stay alive aboard a dinghy in the North Atlantic waters. Three of them, including Hornell, died. Hornell's posthumous Victoria Cross was the first awarded to a member of the RCAF.

"I didn't have any sense of our value at the time," says Foley. "But...in later years, because I knew David Hornell and admired him just as a guy in my squadron...I understood the value in what we did..."

Archie Van Hee flew 2,000 hours during the war, but never saw a sub. He too feels "we made a difference, because a submarine can't do very much harm to a convoy if it has to stay fifty or a hundred feet below the surface."

As the war in Europe drew to an end, Van Hee was finally able to write to family members in Belgium. He soon received an answer in the mail from his sister, Maria. She described the joy of witnessing Canadian troops liberate Bruges and Ostende. And she told Archie how proud she felt "to have a brother in the RCAF who is helping toward final victory over the Germans."

The enemy sometimes tended to under-estimate Canadians. Lord Haw Haw, the British fascist who became the Nazis' chief English-language broadcaster, is said to have put this challenge to the Allies in the war: "Let the Canadians come. Give them a bottle of whisky and a motorcycle and they'll kill themselves."

Canadian motorcyclists met the challenge by the thousands. They became dispatch riders of the Royal Canadian Corps of Signals

(RCCS). As DRs they worked in reconnaissance, intelligence, and provost duties, escorted convoys, controlled traffic, delivered emergency parts and medical supplies, and even carried war correspondents' stories out of battle zones. In fact, Canadian dispatch rider Brian O'Regan managed to get Bill Grant's famous film footage of Canadians storming ashore at Juno Beach to the censors so quickly that it was in Ottawa within three days of D-Day. (American film footage first appeared days later.)

Not only at Normandy but during the invasion of Sicily, Italy, Holland, Belgium, and Germany, DRs rode their Nortons, Indian Chiefs, and Harley-Davidsons through dust and mud, often drove alone at night without lights, navigated across unmarked no-man's-lands, managed their own mechanical repairs, and dodged sniper fire from church steeples and rooftops throughout the war.

Among many exceptional Canadian military motorcyclists was Corporal Lionel Speller. In their book *The Winged Wheel Patch*, Ken Messenger and Max Burns describe Speller's efforts during the futile defence of Hong Kong in December of 1941. Throughout the campaign, Speller, riding his BSA motorcycle, repeatedly covered rough terrain, apparently steering with one hand, while returning Japanese sniper fire with the other. Speller received one of the few Military Medals awarded Canadian DRs.

Most dispatch riders, however, refuted Lord Haw Haw's propaganda in relative anonymity. Before the war, the name Tony Miller was revered on the motorcycle racing circuits of North America; he regularly won top honours at races from Wasaga Beach, Ontario, to the Daytona 200 in the United States.

In 1938 Miller lost his right arm in a racing accident, but still enlisted in the RCCS when the war broke out in 1939. In fact, so did the entire Canadian membership of the British Empire Motor Club. And while Miller never got overseas as a combat dispatch rider, he became a lieutenant-colonel in charge of DR instruction at the Barriefield Training Centre near Kingston, Ontario. He prepared hundreds of motorcyclists for duty overseas and even modified Harleys for wartime conditions.

Lieutenant-Colonel Miller was also the only serviceman in the Canadian army not required to salute.

Norman Campbell served the RCAF as a civilian, "but I did have to swear allegiance. [I was in the] government meteorological service...sending up radiosonde, a sounding device that transmitted back signals of temperature, humidity, and pressure...for pilots."

His first posting was the RCAF station at Fort Nelson, B.C., a key staging airport along the air route used by P-38 fighters flying from North American stations to the Soviet Union. Towards the end of the war, Campbell was posted to a weather station on Sable Island, off the coast of Nova Scotia, famous as "the graveyard of the Atlantic" and the home of hundreds of wild horses.

"One day, an RCAF Canso came landing on the lagoon at the centre of the island... They started to taxi up onto the shore," Campbell recalls, "but the wheels oozed down into the sand and they were stuck... So we got some of the wild horses that had been tamed to be in a team, to help pull this thing out.

"Anyway, the crew had to stay with us overnight. We stashed them in the weather house, which had an upstairs and an extra bathroom... and we fed them what food we had. The food...supplied by our benefi-cent government was powdered eggs, but they weren't whole eggs, they were powdered egg yolks...and salt cod that was like a piece of baseball bat or a board, you had to saw it. No delicacies of any kind, just miser-able stuff, but we shared it with them..."

The next morning, "they revved her up and they were able to take off. They had been down in Bermuda and were on their way back to Halifax and they'd had to land with us because of weather."

That afternoon, Campbell says, they looked up, "and there was this plane, coming over, buzzing over us. They circled around and came down low and something comes out of the plane, diving down on a parachute. It's a big wooden case. It was filled with fresh tomatoes, steaks, onions, all kinds of things from the RCAF mess. And they sort of waved and went away and left us with this wonderful food. They just flew back and dropped this stuff as a thank-you."

Despite many acts of heroism and kindness, the first three years of Canada's war were marked more by setbacks than victories, by trials more than triumphs. As 1942 slipped into 1943, an unspoken ques-tion haunted the Canadian mind: when would the bad news ebb and the good news start to flow in?

3

"An Appetite for Battle"

The RCAF and the Royal Canadian Navy were kept busy after Dieppe, but Canada's Army was idle, stranded in Britain, bored with endless training and itching to get into action. The waiting had been "too long for the many who had rushed to recruiting offices in September 1939, in the first flush of desire to fight Nazi Germany," wrote war correspondent Lionel Shapiro.

There seemed to be nothing for Canada's soldiers to do. Neither Britain nor the United States was yet ready for the Big Invasion—the one action that would be needed to break the hold over Hitler's Fortress Europe. And the Canadians were excluded from North Africa.

Mackenzie King's government was taking a lot of flak over Canada's inactivity. So when the invasion of Sicily and Italy was being planned, King demanded that Canadians be allowed to participate. General Sir Bernard Montgomery, head of the planned operation, felt no need for Canadian support. And General Andrew McNaughton, commander of Canadian forces in Britain, wanted to keep Canada's land forces whole and united, rather than have part of the force sent to Sicily to fight under "British" colours. King had to lobby Churchill through Vincent Massey (Canada's High Commissioner in Britain) to get his way. Montgomery was furious and announced that if McNaughton tried to land in Sicily without permission, he would have him arrested.

In the end, the 1st Canadian Division and 1st Canadian Tank Brigade joined Montgomery's Eighth Army for the invasion of Sicily and did themselves proud. Whether they meant to or not (and King was not regarded highly by the Canadian military at any level), they helped boost the Canadian prime minister's standing.

Lionel Shapiro was part of the Sicily operation and later wrote: "I knew the Canadian was a well-trained soldier... I knew he was an intelligent soldier... I did not know that he possessed so voracious and rollicking an appetite for battle."

The Allied invasion of Sicily began on July 10, 1943, with 160,000 men—British, Canadians, and Americans—14,000 vehicles, 600 tanks, and 1,800 guns. Ross Munro, Canadian Press correspondent, scooped his colleagues with his report on the invasion, which ended: "With their initial success behind them now, and some blood on their bayonets, Canadians were prepared to go into really tough battles."

The thirty-eight-day battle took its grim toll: of the 31,158 Allied casualties, there were 562 Canadians killed, 1,664 wounded, and 84 taken prisoner. But when it was over, Italy was, to all intents and purposes, out of the war. Before the Sicilian campaign ended, Benito Mussolini was kicked out and 137,000 Italians were taken prisoner—many of them willingly. Canada's army was on the move and the Allied struggle was looking better.

Two weeks after the Sicilian triumph, the Allies—again with Canadian involvement—tackled the more formidable task of invading Italy. That campaign, against the tenacious German troops, dragged on until April 1945.

One of the bitterest military encounters that first winter in Italy was known as the "Christmas battle"—the battle for the Adriatic seaport of Ortona. General Montgomery wanted to take Rome by December 1943, and Hitler was equally determined to defend all territory north of Gaeta on Italy's west coast and Ortona on the east. The battle for Ortona lasted a month. The Canadians formed the spearhead of Montgomery's offensive, the fiercest fighting since El Alamein.

In a gully outside Ortona, Captain Paul Triquet of the Royal 22nd Regiment led an already battered infantry company into a snare of tanks, machine guns, snipers, and artillery. When they were completely encircled by the enemy, Triquet told his men: "There are enemy in front of us, behind us, and on our flanks. There is only one safe place (to be), and that is the objective." He got there with seventeen men and four tanks and won the first Victoria Cross in Italy.

Henry Beaudry was positioned on a hillside near Ortona. Born on the Poundmaker Reserve near Hague, Saskatchewan, Beaudry, a full-blooded Cree, had joined up after seeing a poster that read: "Join the Army and See the World." Until then, North Battleford was the biggest city he had ever seen.

In 1943, he went to Sicily and Italy as an ack-ack (anti-aircraft) gunner with the Saskatoon Light Infantry. Near Ortona, "we got stuck... I was trying to hitch this trailer onto a truck and a sniper hit me. I could feel the bullets going through my hand. I couldn't stop the bleeding." After a month in hospital behind the lines, Beaudry became a trooper in an armoured regiment.

A year later, in a village in northern Italy, Beaudry and his fellow soldiers found themselves in a building surrounded by Germans. "They threw their grenades that we called potato-mashers," he remembers. "They come and roll along the floor. We picked them up and sent them back and they'd blow themselves up. All night like that." Towards morning, Beaudry and the other Canadians ran out of ammunition and were captured by the Germans.

The Italian campaign was also the first taste of combat for Ottawa native Harry Pope. In the spring of 1942 he had graduated from Royal Military College as a lieutenant, but it wasn't until the following summer that his infantry unit, Voltigeurs de Québec, was posted overseas and used as reinforcements for the Royal 22nd Regiment in Sicily.

On May 17, 1944, Pope was leading his platoon in his first attack against the Germans in Italy. Trying to take a hill, he kept having to jump into shell holes (made by Allied artillery). He leaped into one occupied by the first German soldier he had ever seen. The German surrendered and presented Pope with his gun. Pope thought it was a Luger, but later discovered it was a Very pistol (a type of flare gun).

A few moments later, another German soldier loomed fifty yards in front of Pope, who promptly killed him with one shot. Two days later, Pope was captured while trying to retrieve two of his own men. He escaped after a few days and spent the next seven weeks with Italian partisans and British paratroopers operating behind German lines. Harry Pope was awarded the Military Cross.

The 4th Reconnaissance Regiment (Princess Louise Dragoon Guards) went through some tough slogging in central Italy too.

Fighting twenty-five or thirty miles ahead of the infantry for three or four days at a time, "the Recces" conducted surprise attacks against small groups of German soldiers, then lived off the Germans' rations until returning to Allied lines. As Major Harold F. Parker of Saint John, N.B., commander of a "Recce" squadron, put it, "We keep on going until the enemy shoot at us. Then we know they're there."

A war correspondent for *The Toronto Telegram*, Bert Wemp, travelled with the Recces and claimed "they are the most amazing and daring soldiers I've ever contacted." They were resilient too. In one engagement, Wemp reported that five of Parker's men, "Lieutenant R.W. Stewart, Sergeant Geoffrey Farrow, Sergeant Louis Clarke, Thomas Avill, and Jack Leider were in the leading carrier when a German 75-mm shell hit it and went straight through. The force of the blast blew the carrier to the side of the road, but by some miracle all escaped... Then the rescuing carrier went through seventeen machine-gun nests and made it without further casualties." A few months after this encounter, Major Parker was killed.

Another dangerous job was that of a forward observer. The average lifespan of a forward observer with an armoured unit was said to be twenty-four hours, but David Armour, who joined the Italian campaign at Ortona as a forward observation officer with the 5th Canadian Armoured Division, survived the entire campaign. In fact, he stayed with the unit all the way through Italy, France, Belgium, Holland, and into Germany.

Forward observers needed a variety of skills. On one occasion, the Canadians and the Italian Partisans liberated a town in the northern plains near Venice. The following morning, Armour decided to climb up the local church tower and asked the local priest to come up with him to help spot German gun positions and plan his counter-fire.

"So we went up in this square belfry. This priest was simpatico to us, but he couldn't speak English and I couldn't speak Italian. But it occurred to me that he could probably speak Latin. All my family, through generations, have spoken Latin. You know, we learned it at school and I could speak it conversationally at that time.

"So I started speaking to him in Latin and he beamed. I told him I'd like him to draw me a panorama on each wall of what he knew about German positions, you see. And I showed him how to do a panorama, drawing arrows down like this and shading it and all the rest of it. So he went ahead, and he was a whiz. He put in four different German batteries that I was able to destroy."

Nursing Sisters of the Royal Canadian Army Medical Corps were also in Sicily and Italy, ministering to the wounded under dangerous conditions, especially during the Ortona campaign, when casualties were constant. The first Canadian nurses arrived in Italy in November 1943, after heavy air attacks in which ninety-nine Nursing Sisters were rescued by lifeboats and taken aboard escorting destroyers. The 5th Canadian General Hospital was also greatly handicapped by the loss of its equipment in Augusta harbour in Sicily as a result of enemy action.

Somehow, the nurses kept a sense of humour under trying conditions. Peter Stursberg, a CBC war correspondent, interviewed several Nursing Sisters in Sicily. Sister Elizabeth Lawson of Saint John described the air raids that occurred, when the nurses were off duty and playing bridge. "We all dived under the table. When it was all over we were as mad as anything because our hands were mixed up." Sister Trennie Hunter of Winnipeg told him, "You ought to see my bedroom. It's so nice and it would be so quiet if there weren't forty-nine others in it." Sister Margaret Stanley of Brandon, Manitoba, added, "We all go to sleep at the same time as otherwise we would be stepping all over each other."

George "Pinky" MacDonald, born in Stellarton, N.S., was determined to get to Italy. He likes to point out that by enlisting in the army on September 7, 1939 (Canada didn't declare war until September 10), "I beat Canada to it. Mackenzie King, too." He took anti-aircraft artillery training. After sitting in England for a year and a half he got fed up, so he stowed away on a British troopship, hoping to get to Italy. When he was discovered, he was thrown into the brig and threatened with a court martial. The ship docked in Algiers, North Africa, and after a lot of yelling and scolding MacDonald was released "without prejudice." The brigadier-general in charge decided the paperwork involved in a court martial would be too much trouble.

MacDonald got to Italy, where he joined an ack-ack outfit (4th Battery) attached to the 5th Armoured Division. He went with them through northern Italy and France to Holland, landing there the day The Hague was liberated. The only wound he suffered was a knife wound, inflicted by an anti-Allied Algerian native who stabbed him seven or eight times. But MacDonald got even: he picked up a big branch, swung it like a baseball bat, and got him. "It was a beaut. You could hear his nose crack."

The resounding successes in Sicily and Italy helped pave the way for the D-Day invasions in 1944, the most ambitious and daunting invasion in the history of warfare. Its success would tip the scales in favour of Allied victory.

The invasion involved 175,000 Allied troops, 4,000 invasion ships, 600 warships, and 10,000 planes. Five divisions (two American, two British, one Canadian) launched the seaborne assault. The Canadian sector, code-named "Juno," was in the centre of the British front.

For once, all three Canadian services were fighting together. Of the 15,000 Canadian troops that hit the Normandy beaches on D-Day, one-third were brought in by RCN landing craft, while RCAF bombers and fighters flew overhead and Canadian destroyers and minesweepers were at work in the Channel. Canada suffered 1,074 casualties on D-Day—including 359 killed.

Commanders and chiefs of staff can plan strategies, generals can cope with tactics, analysts can examine and interpret. But to the average soldier, war is the particular hell that is within his range of vision. He seldom has a sense of the whole picture. To him, D-Day and the days that followed were a fearsome, somewhat traumatic experience which—if he survived—would stay with him all through his life.

Joe Oggy remembers his first inkling that something big was up. As he and his infantry unit marched through the streets of Southampton on June 5, there were weeping women on the sides of the street. The night before, their officers had issued them live ammunition. On board the ship that took them into the Channel, Oggy and the rest of the Queen's Own Rifles got a hearty breakfast of bacon and eggs. He remembers thinking, "The condemned man ate a hearty breakfast...and by the time we landed, we'd puked it up." Even then "we didn't realize that this was really going to be D-Day."

Oggy was second-in-command of an infantry section of the Queen's Own Rifles, in the first wave of landings on D-Day. They scrambled down nets from the ship to the landing craft. On the way in, Oggy stood up in the landing craft to give his crouching men a blow-by-blow description of what was going on. There were bullets and rockets flying in all directions. He saw a Spitfire blown up, quite possibly by a poorly aimed Allied rocket.

"We were told, you have fifteen minutes to live. Kill or be killed. If there's a retreat off this beach, the Queen's Own Rifles will be the last to leave," Joe remembers. But first he had to get there, through water up to his shoulders.

"I managed to get into the shoreline and I rolled against the sea-wall, and I thought, 'What am I going to do now?' because boys are lying there dead and wounded in front of me, fifteen feet from me. This one fellow, I'll never forget, he was an Indian boy, he tried to get up and every time he tried to get up, they put more lead into him. I kept hollering at him to stay down. I was protected by the wall; they couldn't get at me. So finally, he just didn't move. He was dead."

After some risky manoeuvring, Oggy crawled through a hole in the six-foot-thick wall—opened by a navy shell—but once through he was within the sights of a machine gun in a pillbox on the other side of the wall. Then one of his men, "Stumpy" Gordon, arrived.

"I said, 'I'm scared, Stump...'

"He says, 'Jesus, I am, too.' He took his water bottle off and gave it to me, ran to the pillbox, which I couldn't see, took off a grenade, threw it through the hole, and then another one, then came running back and says, 'Gimme my fucking bottle, you old fart,' and he says, 'Come on, let's go.'" Stumpy Gordon was wounded, but he made it.

A little later, when there was a moment to reflect, Oggy scraped the mud off his wristwatch. "It's over fifteen minutes," he remembers thinking. "And we're still alive, a lot of us. Thank God. And God help those that are on the beach."

As he advanced through the town of Bernières-sur-Mer a little later, his heart went out to the dead and wounded.

"You saw guys lying on the road, snipers picking them off...and you kinda thought, well, you felt sorry for them, you thought of his mother or his wife or sister. Then you thought to yourself, you're lucky. By the end of the day, you thought, I'm gonna die ten times tomorrow, and the next day and the next day and the next. There's no end to it... But somehow you managed to get through it."

Despite their inexperience at amphibious landings of this magnitude, Allied invaders did have a few things going for them. On Bill Warshick's LCT (landing craft tank) he and his signal corps with the Royal Canadian Regiment had "a veteran Royal Navy commander at the helm... He told us that this was his fifth landing. He'd been at all the landings in North Africa and Italy... And he said, 'Don't worry. I'll get you guys in high and dry.'

"And he did," claims Warshick. "He kept his word. I remember I walked ashore and there was maybe two inches of water over the ramp...not even enough to get my boots wet... Apparently it was thirty days before they could get his craft afloat again...it was stuck so high on the beach."

Royal Navy gunners were equally dedicated, to a fault. RCAF airman Frank Vines piloted one of the scores of Dakotas disgorging paratroops in the skies over Caen on D-Day. Vines recalls that it was "pitch-black as we dropped the paratroops about twelve miles inland. But the Allies were bombarding the coast with battle-cruisers and battleships. It was like watching lightning below us with all these bloody great guns going off.

"The Royal Navy were pretty touchy too, shooting at anything that flew over. We got shot up. A 20-mm shell went right through the can area and blew it apart. Nobody got hurt." But the shell had damaged a cable in the DC-3's flap controls leaving Vines no alternative but to forgo the planned route over Holland in favour of the most direct way home. He consequently ran the gauntlet "straight back across the Channel, over all the warships. We were hanging on for dear life, but got back okay."

Allied air crews flew 14,000 sorties on D-Day. Along with the Dakotas was a stream of Horsa gliders carrying paratroops of the 6th Airborne Division to Normandy. "The glider stream was forty-six miles long," remembers Ren Henderson, "with 460 gliders and tow planes." Henderson was a pilot instructor who had been given an overseas posting in 1943 and was flying glider escort in a Spitfire on D-Day.

"We had probably twelve or fourteen squadrons up that morning. We picked up the glider stream at a place called Littlehampton, England... It was an incredible sight," Henderson says. "There were something like 8,000 vessels of every description, all headed in one direction across the Channel. We could have bailed out anywhere between the south coast of England and the coast of France, and wherever you landed you couldn't have been any more than 300 yards from a ship. There'll never be another sight like it."

The 1st Canadian Parachute Battalion, which dropped with the British 6th Airborne Division on D-Day, suffered heavy casualties but performed its assigned tasks, which included demolishing two bridges and capturing a strong point near Varville.

Toronto native Jimmy Wilson went ashore with the Stormont, Dundas, and Glengarry Highlanders from eastern Ontario, popularly known as the Sand, Dust, and Gravel brigade. He remembers trying to read *The Murders in the Rue Morgue* during the Channel crossing and "as we got closer, you could hear rumbles...the heavy battleships lobbing shells in on the beaches. I was standing in the back of the ship, just looking around, seeing thousands of men... Suddenly you realized that you're part of history... It's very emotional."

In addition to all their other gear, Wilson's company also had collapsible bicycles aboard the landing craft. Their mission, after landing, was to ride the bicycles to Carpiquet airfield, some nineteen kilometres inland, and take it. But the bikes were useless. "We were pinned down by shell fire, and we just dropped the bikes," he says. They had only gone a few kilometres. They didn't get to Carpiquet for several days, by which time it was taken.

"The bicycles were the first thing to go," agreed Gordon Clarke, who had joined the Stormont, Dundas, and Glengarry Highlanders in Peterborough. "It was obvious that we weren't going to bicycle anyplace and who the hell wants to be carrying a useless bicycle around? So, D-Day, we went to Bernières-sur-Mer, just inland from the beaches. A few shells came into the orchard and our first casualty was a chap named Box. We did have a couple of casualties on the beach. The landing craft hit some mines and I remember a couple of our contingent were wounded from the shrapnel."

Clarke himself was wounded—the first of three times—on the way to Caen, when a piece of shrapnel went through his thigh. "In those (early) days we had no forward operational first-aid posts, so you had to go back to England and, man, was I upset about that," he laughs.

Right after Caen, Jimmy Wilson was wounded in the upper arm by a shell burst. "The fellow with me was killed by the same burst," he says. "His name was George King and whenever we got mail call he was 'King, George.' Don't know where he was from. He was black, nice guy."

D-Day was Newfoundlander Gordon Drodge's nineteenth birthday. He was a gunner in a Sherman tank. He was seasick all the way across the Channel. He remembers the infantry boys with their bicycles on D-Day, because "they rode on the back of our tanks, some of them."

Drodge's tank came ashore in the second wave. They saw "a bit of action" on D-Day. The next day, a German 88 ripped into his tank just as he was bending down. It "came so close to my back it put a ridge across my back but didn't break the skin..." The shell killed another gunner in the tank and wounded the major in command of it.

Later, in Belgium, though he was still only a corporal, Drodge was given command of a tank. He had a brand new crew, and his tank was eighth in a row pursuing German tanks. Drodge says the statistics on the number of Canadian tanks destroyed by the enemy are wrong by one: his tank inadvertently disabled the Canadian tank in front of it. His gunner had his hand on the trigger of the 75-mm gun that was aimed straight ahead. The safety-catch was on, but the gunner was so nervous that his knee accidentally jogged the safety-catch and the gun went off. The tank ahead of Drodge's was knocked out of action. Nobody was injured, and everyone assumed the tank had been hit by a German bazooka. After wrestling (briefly) with his conscience, Drodge reported the true facts to his lieutenant, who dutifully passed along the information to the major. But the major had already made his report, attributing the incident to enemy fire. "So," Drodge explained with a laugh, "[the major] says to the lieutenant, 'I've already reported it, one of my tanks was bazookaed. As far as I'm concerned, that's it.'"

When ack-ack gunner Alan Skaife landed on D-Day, it was well after eight o'clock and there wasn't much return fire. In March 1942, his outfit, the 4th Light Anti-Aircraft Battery, had hit the first enemy aircraft to be brought down by Canadian artillery—a Messerschmitt 109E. The 4th was attached to the Stormont, Dundas, and Glengarry Highlanders on D-Day. Skaife's worst moment happened soon after the landing—"the first time that I saw somebody killed... It was an 88 that hit him and...he was just no more." Later in the European campaign, Skaife was hit in the leg by shrapnel and evacuated to England.

Hubert Thistle wasn't as lucky. He had started his military service with an infantry regiment, the Sherbrooke Fusiliers, but the unit was later converted to an armoured regiment. On D-Day, Bert Thistle was the wireless operator in a tank. Their objective was the Carpiquet airport and then Caen. On D-Day+1 Thistle's tank crew ran into heavy opposition.

On June 18, his parents in Newfoundland got a telegram from the Department of National Defence informing them that their son was "officially reported missing in action" on June 7. Not until that October did they receive further word: there was "every chance that your boy is a prisoner of war but it may be well over two months before you have any definite word."

In the days that followed D-Day, Allied servicemen continued to pour across the Channel. Joe Baker landed on D-Day+3 with the 69th Anti-Aircraft Battery, attached to the 3rd Canadian Infantry Division. He had already seen action in battery positions around Britain, most notably on the nights of November 14 and 15, 1940, when the Luftwaffe destroyed Coventry. In France he saw action at Carpiquet, at Caen, and in the Falaise Gap. The first time he was wounded was near Ghent, in Belgium. He got a piece of shrapnel "right near my pacemaker," but he was out of action only for a few days. His second wound (in the arm) was inflicted at Nijmegen, Holland. This time he was evacuated to England, but once again returned to his outfit.

Sergeant Air Gunner Bill Gibson flew his first combat operation as tailgunner aboard a Lancaster bomber on D-Day+3. His bomber squadron then flew a mission each night for a week—seven trips in seven nights.

"We flew in support of the landings, bombing air fields, railway yards, V1 sites. And we were on the raid to Cambrai. That was a horrible trip...a horrible target, the worst I was ever on. It was terrifying. My hands never left the guns that night."

On their ninth bombing mission, "all hell broke loose," as a German night fighter came at Gibson's Lancaster head-on. "His cannon shells went from our wing tip, right down the wing, through the cockpit, over the navigator's head, through the radio, under the mid-upper gunner's leg, and took the bottom out of my tail turret. I could see the ground down between my feet."

When the pilot ordered the crew to bail out of the disabled plane, Gibson and another gunner had to get their parachutes, which were stored by the main door. "We only had time to open the back door and go under the tail, and I snapped mine on so fast that when it opened I only had one clip hanging on to my parachute and I was spinning around like a top."

The whole crew managed to parachute out safely. But Gibson got tangled up in his parachute lines, landed on the sloped roof of a little French farmhouse, and rolled off. His pilot came down on the same farm, but crashed into "I don't know how many cases of empty wine bottles... God almighty, the noise!"

Gordon MacLeod landed on D-Day+5. MacLeod had joined the militia in Nova Scotia in time to act as guard of honour during the royal visit to Canada in 1939. The 4th Anti-Aircraft Battery, to which he was attached, like Baker's 69th, had distinguished itself in Britain long before June 1944. During a two-month period in 1942, the 4th shot down sixty-one enemy aircraft, a record that no other Canadian unit even came close to matching.

D-Day+5 was not as terrifying as D-Day itself, but it was still dangerous. "The first night ashore was pretty scary. You could hear the Tiger tanks rumbling and...they were burying men." But he and his unit survived the trek all the way up into Holland and through to the North Sea, where on VE Day "we sat in this big POW camp. The prisoners were all gone... We listened (on radio) to the celebrations in London that night...and we said, 'Here we are, and we don't even have a glass of beer.'"

John MacCormack of Halifax landed with the 1st Anti-Aircraft Battery in France a month after D-Day. For the landing "these absolutely huge rafts...came alongside the ship and then the guns and vehicles were lowered down onto the raft... When my jeep was going to be taken out of the hold I went down to oversee it being taken up. It got about six inches off the deck. These were English soldiers looking after this aspect of the operation, and you know how the English like their tea. Well, just as it got about six inches off, somebody yelled 'Tea!' The guy pulled the lever, my jeep went down on the deck and bounced about five times."

On the night of August 7, Canadian, British, and Polish forces prepared to launch a huge attack to take Falaise, south of Caen. Lieutenant MacCormack gathered his gun crew to fill them in on their part in the attack: "I said this attack will really shorten the war, it's an important thing... And so one of the fellows said, 'Well, I guess we'll be in the history books.'"

The next morning, the United States Army Air Force was sent to bomb ahead of the Germans, but missed the target and dropped bombs on the outskirts of Caen, where MacCormack's gun crew was now located. "Five of those guys that were in that gun crew...were killed," MacCormack says, "including the guy who said, 'We'll be in the history books.'"

Ervine Morris remembers that air attack, too. He had started in artillery with the 45th Battery in Lindsay, Ontario, but switched to the 2nd Field Survey Regiment. Morris describes the "short bombing" by the Americans as "the most devastating experience."

"There were six sections in the company plus the headquarters section... Two sections were sent out to do a job and for some reason they bivouacked in an ammunition dump, and they (the American bombers) dropped a bomb in that dump and obliterated them. [When] we fell in on parade the next morning, one man stood up out of that section."

Five days after the main Canadian assault on Juno Beach in Normandy, Andrew van Rassel came ashore with the 7th Canadian Reconnaissance Regiment (17th Duke of York's Royal Canadian Hussars) and an assortment of armoured cars, scout cars, and Bren carriers. By fall 1944, van Rassel's unit was in Holland working to clear the Scheldte estuary so that Allied supplies could come into the Belgian port of Antwerp. For a Dutch-Canadian the liberation march was especially memorable.

"I had been in touch with a branch of the family in England before landing on the Continent," remembers van Rassel. "When we got to Nijmegen, I began searching for my cousin Thea Van Eck. I couldn't find the address, so I found out I was near a police station. I asked if anyone knew the family... There was a funny response. I could sense the suspicion. Who knows? I could have been a German in a Canadian uniform... So this one guy goes off. And he returned with the head of the political police there... Dick Van Eck, my cousin's husband! They had nothing but subsistence rations and rented accommodations, but there was still lots of tears and hugs and kisses all round... The Dutch considered us Canadians as their liberators."

After VE Day, van Rassel was posted to Utrecht, where he met two of his father's sisters. Soon after, van Rassel saw the name of another uncle, Gerrit van Rassel, on a storefront; two of his cousins were the proprietors. Finally, on a road near Amsterdam, he met the daughter of another uncle; she was in the Dutch paramilitary force and was posted to a Canadian headquarters as an interpreter.

But you didn't have to be of Dutch descent to be warmly welcomed in Holland. The people of the Netherlands had suffered under German occupation and the bitter winter of 1944–45 had caused widespread hunger. The arrival of Canadian troops in the spring of 1945 was an event of immense importance. They were regarded as avenging angels, and the friendship forged between the Dutch people and their Canadian liberators was to endure for many decades.

The violence and destruction of the war was too much for some people to grasp. Hector Gaudet landed in France with the 4th Anti-Aircraft Battery a few days after D-Day. "Some women met us and they had fresh milk. We had no money, but they gave us the milk." Later, during the liberation of Belgium, Gaudet was driving a load of rations when a V2 rocket "lit" near him and demolished half a house. When he entered the house he found a ninety-one-year-old woman unhurt but obviously shaken. He spoke to her in French.

"What happened?" she asked.

"I don't know," Gaudet said.

"There must have been a heavy wind or something," she said. "It took half the house away."

Hector Gaudet sums up his feelings about the war this way: "It's an experience you couldn't buy for a million bucks...and you couldn't sell it again for a nickel."

4

Home Rules

Wherever you lived in Canada, the war seemed thousands of miles away. No bomb ever fell on Canadian soil, no troops ever invaded Canadian shores, no rockets ever whizzed over Canadian heads during the night, no enemy tanks ever thundered through Canadian towns or villages.

The closest the war ever came to Canadians was the menacing activity of German U-boats in the Gulf of St. Lawrence—and most Canadians knew relatively little about this until after the war was over—and the brief appearance of a Japanese submarine that fired some shells at a lighthouse on Vancouver Island.

Nevertheless, the home front faced its own hardships, and even though these were insignificant in comparison to what Canadian armed forces overseas were encountering, they seemed bad enough at the time.

In newspapers and magazines, on the radio, on movie screens, in speeches by political leaders, on posters and bank calendars, on stamps and envelopes, in greeting cards and comic books, and on candy-bar wrappers, Canadians were badgered, cajoled, threatened, nudged, scolded, exhorted to do or not do an ever-growing list of things. Save... be careful what you say... don't travel if you don't have to... sacrifice... scrimp... dig deep to finance the war... write often... send parcels... knit socks... save tinfoil... re-use everything... wear last year's clothes... buy bonds... walk, don't drive... be kind to men in uniform... do volunteer work... roll bandages... support the war effort... don't listen to defeatist talk... use less sugar, gasoline, meat, butter, rubber... take a job in a war plant... join up. Canadians called it patriotism; when the Germans did it, it was called propaganda.

Hardly a day went by without some heart-tugging story demonstrating that somebody, somewhere, had it worse than you. One example, under the headline "Mother Misses Her Nine Sons," appeared in an Alberta paper.

"Taking the place on the farm of nine sons who have gone into the war effort is no small job, Mrs. W. W. Roberts of the Woolford district, southwest of Lethbridge, Alta., has discovered.

"Five of the Roberts boys are in the armed forces, three of them overseas and the other two completing their training in Canada before going to a theatre of war. Four other sons are working in small-arms factories, two in Canada and two in the United States.

"Mr. and Mrs. Roberts felt the absence of their boys considerably, but the mother decided to take on the extra work. For months past, she has ridden a tractor, doing plowing, combining, putting up hay and hauling grain to elevators. She has not neglected her other work, but raised a large garden, many fine turkeys, chickens and pigs, and then canned hundreds of jars of home-grown fruits and vegetables."

Canadians were urged to save fat and bones "and help smash the Axis." Instead of frying food, an ad suggested, you could imagine the satisfaction it would give you to pour that hot fat right down the back of Adolf, Tojo, or Benito. The ad explained the connection: "Fats make glycerin, and glycerin makes high explosives to sink their submarines, destroy their aeroplanes and tanks. Bones produce fat, also glue for war industry."

Another ad announced that "Canada Needs Tin," and still another reminded everyone that government regulations required "the return of your old toothpaste or shaving-cream tube with your order for a fresh supply of these toiletries."

"I'm patriotic!" announced the delectable young lady in a black nightie, sitting up in bed. "Since rubber and metals are needed to win the war, I roll my curls in Kleenex tissues. They're comfortable to sleep on. They help prevent hair ends from breaking."

And of course, there was the Victory Bond campaign. A big double-page spread was illustrated with drawings of a young woman in a war plant, a farmer bringing in his crop, a newsboy hawking papers, and a mother looking adoringly at a photograph of her son—in uniform, naturally. Scattered across the ad are small news clippings with appropriate headlines: "Both on War Duty Buy Victory Bond"... "Lost Sailor Son's $1000 Buys Bonds"... "Newspaper Boy, 13, Sure He Can Pay for Bonds"... "Rejected by Army He Buys Bonds Same Day"... "Reduces Dress Budget to Save for Bonds."

The one thing that was not in short supply was work. Shipyards that had lain idle during the Depression years employed tens of thousands of men and women constructing warships of one kind or another. Automobile plants were turning out armoured vehicles and military trucks. More than 300 aircraft a week were produced, along with millions of rounds of ammunition and thousands of rifles.

Thousands of young people left home to work in factories. Bert Merrill was not yet seventeen years old when he left his New Brunswick home for Amherst, Nova Scotia, where he got a job at Robb Engineering Works, on a munitions line producing shell casings.

"The lower floor level where I worked had an all-male staff," Merrill recalls, "while the upper floor was mostly females, with the occasional male supervisor. Liaisons between the two floors during break periods and toilet breaks were not uncommon, particularly during the graveyard (midnight to 8 a.m.) period."

Merrill roomed with a woman whose husband was overseas with the army. He slept in the living room on a bed-chesterfield in a corner just outside the landlady's bedroom.

"At the time, I had no difficulty with the arrangement but an unsolicited visit one evening from my landlady convinced me that she was prepared to initiate me into the facts of life. Fortunately, I was able to establish there was no special interest and that I really was more interested in a neighbour's daughter who often visited."

Many of the workers were women, which created debate, some of it acrimonious. "Not only do the women in our armed services not receive equal pay for equal work," said MP Dorise Nielsen, in the House of Commons, "but all women in employment have suffered this liability. In urging the government to make it the law of the land that there shall be equal pay for equal work, I would remind them that this principle has been acknowledged by the great trade union groups in this country."

At least one poll asked whether women in war plants should receive the same pay as men. Seventy-nine per cent of those questioned felt that women should get the same pay as men, sixteen per cent thought they should not, and five per cent were undecided.

Newspapers and magazines abounded in ads coaxing women to pitch in by taking jobs, thus freeing men to join the armed forces. Some ads were government-sponsored, others were tied to some commercial product, but the message was essentially the same: get involved in war work. One such ad asked: "Are civilian jobs really important?" The answer was an unequivocal "Yes!" and the details were spelled out—how to apply, where help was needed, etc. "The humblest job in a home front service is as important as victory itself," the ad stressed.

Whatever misgivings might have been felt about unequal pay, such ads apparently worked. By the middle of the war one out of every four persons directly or indirectly making Canadian war munitions was a woman.

Canada's labour minister, Humphrey Mitchell, said, "I do not think we could win this war without the women."

Some people didn't think women should work at all. In 1942, *The Globe and Mail* in Toronto printed this letter from a reader: "Being a mother is a 24-hours-a-day job. Right now I'm itching to go out and work and I flatter myself that I could be used very advantageously in several branches of business, old as I am, but I can't bring myself to leave the youngest, who is 11. How these young women can leave two or three of pre-school age and not much more is beyond me. That is where the government should step in and forbid these weak-minded or avaricious girls to work unless competent care is provided and paid for by the mother first. We don't need the government to provide shelter and care for these poor little waifs. Let the mother pay for them out of her fat cheque..."

And an MP from Quebec read into the House of Commons record an article by a Jesuit priest on the subject of young women in war plants: "There is a marriage that will never take place: that of the young lady who has ruined her health working in a munitions plant in order to earn some money for the purchase of clothes with a view to getting married. After six months of slow poisoning, she is debilitated, sallow-complexioned, exhausted, underweight, uncurable, and she has not one cent for medical treatment. She has been a habitual visitor at hospital dispensaries; her suitor no longer sees her, offended by her new manners that are too vulgar, and the parish priest has heeded her despairing cry which she would direct at all Canadian women for the charitable purpose of warning them.

"Gullible girls will no longer believe the deceitful propaganda of newspapers which show smiling, well-dressed, elegant young ladies among shells, at work benches or tending greasy machines. Why, they dirty their faces like men, and it is uglier because it's least expected; that is not a proper environment for them..."

The naysayers were fighting a losing battle. By late 1943 more than 250,000 women were employed in war production. The work was often difficult, dirty, and wearying, but it also brought companionship, money, and independence.

When it came to women in uniform, the debates sometimes got hotter. The government seemed to sense the fact that the country might be divided on the matter of women in the services. Certainly the recruiting posters and ads for women reflected two different approaches.

An army poster for men would show a handsome, determined-looking young man, rifle gripped in one hand, the other arm outstretched with an index finger pointing toward a distant, dark cloud in the centre of which could be seen an ominous black swastika. "Lick them over there!" the heroic figure is saying, and across the bottom of the poster is an additional slogan: "Come On, Canada!"

But the recruiting posters for young women were rather more subdued. One, for the Canadian Women's Army Corps, featured a drawing of two attractive young girls in civilian garb looking in at the window of a CWAC recruiting office. "Come on, Peg—it'll be thrilling," one girl is saying to the other. At the bottom is the reminder: "This is Our Battle, Too!"

Another recruiting poster, a joint effort on behalf of all three armed forces, shows a pretty, smiling girl. The heading reads: "They called her Frivolous Sal," but the copy tells us that "Sal" is now wearing the uniform of one of the armed forces, "and she was never happier." We are further assured: "It's done Sal a world of good. Balanced meals, regular hours, new self-discipline and the right companions have worked wonders. Best of all she has the satisfaction of knowing she's doing her duty. Nothing takes the place of that."

Not everyone believed the image of self-discipline and duty. One Wren said her boyfriend wasn't happy about her joining up, but his reaction was mild compared to that of some of the people at a drop-in centre where she had been working evenings before enlisting. "They seemed to think that all women in uniform were prostitutes," she said.

Wren Thelma Ransom encountered "amongst some very old-fashioned people the idea that...if these were nice people they wouldn't be either working in war plants or in the service."

On the other hand, Margaret Los, who served in the Women's Royal Canadian Naval Service from late 1942 until the service was disbanded after the war, was encouraged to join. "I swear I'm the only one whose mother told her to join.

"They started recruiting for girls in the service in late 1942 for the navy. My mother had been widowed early and she made great sacrifices to put my sister and me through school and by this time she was well into her sixties, and I thought, 'Oh dear, I guess I shouldn't go.' [Her sister had left home by this time.] One day my mother said to me, 'I don't know what's the matter with my children. I've got wimps for daughters.' She said, 'If it had been me, I would have joined the first day they announced it. I don't know what I did wrong.' And I said, 'Do you want me to go away from home?' And she said, 'I want you to live a life.' So I went and joined the navy."

She was twenty years old at the time and, like all Wrens, she took her basic training in Galt, Ontario, in a building that used to serve as a reform school for girls. "When I told my mother where I was going, she said, 'Well, I never thought you'd end up there.'"

From there, she was sent to St. Hyacinthe, Quebec, to train as a radio operator. The behaviour and attire of the Wrens were always scrutinized by the nuns of the area. "We were right on the Yamaska River, and we used to go swimming there," Los recalls. "The nuns were always looking to make sure we had a brassiere on under our bathing suits. If we didn't we couldn't go swimming.

"I couldn't ride a bike, so my girl friends decided they were going to teach me... But the nuns wouldn't let you wear shorts; you had to wear a skirt. Well, to this day I kill myself laughing when I think that the shorts we wore, like Bermuda shorts, were 'sinful.' [Instead, I was] riding around with a skirt that was blowing up in front of my chest and I couldn't let go of the handle to grab the skirt because I was very much a beginner...

"The nuns," adds Los, "had jurisdiction over the morals of the town. When we went bicycling we were in town."

After St. Hyacinthe, she was posted to Moncton, where there was a big manning pool for the British Commonwealth Air Training Plan. "They used to have a big dance with big bands every Friday and Saturday...tea dances on Sunday...and something going on Wednesdays. And the CO had a shuttle bus going between our place and them all the time. A lot of our girls married English men and went over to live in England."

Elaine Leiterman joined the Women's Division of the RCAF in 1943, when she was seventeen. She had been born in the gold-mining community of Porcupine, in northern Ontario. "My father was an accountant in the mine office. I was born in the morgue because there was no hospital at the time," she says. Leiterman became a radio-telegraph operator and served at stations in Quebec, New Brunswick, and Nova Scotia. Perhaps her greatest challenge during the war was overcoming the anonymity of serving at home in the forces. "Every now and then you got lonely and missed your family. I had come from a very sheltered family and I'd never really been on my own, so I missed that, especially when they wrote and said they were moving to B.C.

"Each station you arrived at, you were a number in a blue suit, and that was the thing you had to overcome, that sense of being nobody. Gradually you became an individual and you were somebody, a person."

Shirley Smith lived in Sarnia, Ontario, during the war. "In the summer of '42," she recalls, "everything was swell and all my friends were kids...but suddenly too many of the kids had been killed... It seemed their deaths surrounded me."

When her cousin next door, Bunt Murray (an RCAF air gunner), was found alive in a POW camp in 1942, "my decision to enlist was firm." At Rockcliffe training station, Aircraftwoman Smith, Second Class, got her first issue running shoes, smock, overalls, and blankets and began work as an assistant in the equipment section. The loneliness she felt is reflected in her first letter home on August 23, 1942:

"Dear People... Please write. I'm not homesick, but I could easily be if I did not remember why I came in the first place... The other kids were given lists of things to bring such as hangers, mirrors, cup, etc. but I'll get along...

"Please send some of my lipsticks, especially 'Red Dice' not 'Suez' or 'Blush Rose'... Send the bath brush, underwear, p.j., bedroom slippers etc. but nothing I couldn't wear with a uniform on."

Smith wrote 160 letters home between that first day at Rockcliffe and her eventual posting and service at No. 5 Service Flying Training School (in the BCATP) at Brantford, Ontario. For several years, she worked in the equipment section as storekeeper and remembers, "It was the first time I was an individual and treated as one."

Grace Collyer of Toronto was twenty-eight when she signed up for the Canadian Women's Army Corps in 1941. She acknowledges that, in the beginning, some civilians tended to look down on women in uniforms.

"I must admit that the girls in uniforms weren't behaving the way they should have, at first, because they really didn't know. They [soon] smartened up and they realized the fact that their uniform meant something and that they had to live up to it a bit. A lot of them were just really in it for a lark, and I think they found out that it wasn't a lark, it was serious business. But they matured, most of them did, and I think that the ones who were overseas definitely did, and they turned out to be much more mature and better people for the experience."

When Collyer became a captain in the CWAC, she was assigned to recruiting work. "I was made out to be the damnedest liar that ever was. But these girls would come in and they'd say, 'Will I have to go overseas?'

"'Oh no, you won't have to go overseas, no, no,' I'd say.

"'Will I have to live in barracks or will I be able to live at home?'

"'Oh no, we won't have any barracks. You'll be able to live at home, just like you are now, but you'll be working at something different.'

"This is what I was told to say, so I said it. Well, of course, I met some of these girls when I was in England. They said, 'Oh no, you don't have to go overseas.' I really lived to regret those statements I used to make."

Kay Cochrane started her nursing studies in Winnipeg, graduated in 1940, but waited a long time to become a lieutenant in the Royal Canadian Army Medical Corps. She had just turned twenty-one in 1940 when the army decided a nurse had to be twenty-five. The age requirements kept changing, and Kay kept working, first in Ottawa and then in Bermuda. Finally, she managed to become attached to a London, Ontario, unit, No. 24 Canadian General, and went to a big base hospital in England, just before D-Day.

Her boyfriend, reporter Ron Poulton, got an eye injury while in training and wound up in a hospital where Cochrane was in training. "She heard I was there and she came down to see me. Well, I had a vision from then on of this angel in white," he laughs. "I was in a lot of pain at that time and there she was. So we started writing letters all the way through the war."

The war brought together many couples who would never have met otherwise. Peggy Tucker was a nurse at the Hospital for Sick Children when she met Arnold Lonsdale of the RCAF at the Active Service Canteen in Toronto.

"He was in the service, at Manning Depot, and he came up to see what this place was," she says. "The story goes that he came up the stairs and looked around and saw there were about 500 men to 100 women, and thought, 'That's enough of that.'

"One of the hostesses grabbed him at the top of the stairs and said, 'Where are you going?' And he said, 'There's too much competition here for me,' and she said, 'Just a minute, I've got a great girl for you.' And then she hauled me out and introduced us and we danced that night... He was a wireless operator in the air force. And we had fun and got engaged about a year later and he went overseas."

After service in Vancouver, Victoria, and up the Alaska coast, Lonsdale was shipped overseas to India and Burma, serving with No. 435 Squadron, doing parachute drops of supplies all up the Burma Road.

It was to be a long separation, but like so many thousands of others, Peggy Tucker kept busy. Besides her duties as a nurse, she did volunteer work for the Red Cross, packing POW boxes. Another useful occupation was knitting. "You never sat down without a pair of socks in your hand. One brother was in the army, another was in the navy and Arnold was in the air force. So the only variety you had was the colour of wool you knitted."

The war also tore couples apart. Patricia Barnett was a young woman working in the Bank of Montreal in Vancouver in 1941, when "my closest friend and I were invited to attend a dinner and dance aboard the USS *Arizona* when it came into Vancouver for a short stay. We had a wonderful evening on board, escorted by handsome young officers. Everyone was dressed to the nines. We had a tour of the ship, a beautiful dinner, and danced until the wee hours. Later, a group of us went ashore and on to a nightspot in Chinatown. It was a very memorable evening.

"The young officer who had been my escort wrote to me several times after they left Vancouver. In what was to be his last letter, he said they were in a beautiful warm place, enjoying the beaches. Days later we heard the awful news about Pearl Harbor and that the *Arizona* had been sunk with 1,200 men lost. It gave the horror of that bombing a very personal meaning to me."

When the war started, Lois Daley was fifteen years old. When she finished school, she moved to Montreal and eventually found work as a stenographer. But a social life was nearly impossible without frequenting bars. So, after many months of loneliness, "I volunteered to be a hostess at Air Force House. This was a beautiful three-storey house on Sherbrooke St. W., opposite the Ritz Carlton Hotel. I worked there three nights a week and Saturdays... My duties were to dance, share stories, and entertain the men. The rules were very strict. As a hostess I was not allowed to drink or date the men. But we could meet after leaving the house. In the three years there... I met thousands of men from all over the world. Even though it was an exciting time, it had sad moments as well. Some men would go overseas, never to return..."

During the war years, romance was in the air waves, too. Gracie Fields insisted that there'd be bluebirds over the white cliffs of Dover, and Vera Lynn vowed that there would always be an England. The Andrews Sisters, in triplicate, exhorted millions not to sit under the apple tree with anyone else but them. Bing Crosby promised to be home for Christmas (if only in his dreams).

Less romantic, but equally popular was Kay Kyser's recording of "Praise the Lord and Pass the Ammunition," which sold a million copies. And to keep up morale on the home front, there was "We Did It Before (and We Can Do It Again)," "The Woman Behind The Man Behind The Gun," "This Is The Army, Mr. Jones," "Say A Prayer For The Boys Over There," "I'm Getting Corns For My Country," and the ever-popular "Rosie The Riveter."

The movie industry, ever alert to the direction of emotional winds, produced a steady stream of romantic adventure-cum-propaganda films, such as *Mrs. Miniver*, *The White Cliffs of Dover*, and Noel Coward's *In Which We Serve*. (The Coward film was loosely based on Mountbatten's pre-Dieppe naval exploits and Lord Louis worked with Coward on the film—even as he was plotting the Dieppe debacle.)

There were anti-Nazi movies, like *Casablanca* and *The Hitler Gang*, and anti-Japanese movies such as *Thirty Seconds over Tokyo* and *Blood on the Sun*, and plenty of pro-Allies films: *The Moon Is Down* (Norway), *Mission to Moscow* (the USSR), *Dragon Seed* (China), and *Uncertain Glory* (France).

No Hollywood star fought the war more relentlessly than Errol Flynn. He starred in six war movies, including the infamous *Objective Burma*, which caused a mild international incident because it neglected to mention that the British were of some slight assistance to Flynn in that particular battle.

Even Tarzan got into the war. In *Tarzan Triumphs* (1943), Johnny Weissmuller, as Tarzan, defeated a bunch of German paratroopers who landed in the African jungle. He was aided by a perceptive pachyderm that shoved one Nazi over the edge of a cliff and by Cheeta, the chimpanzee, who wielded a mean tommy-gun against the invaders.

For Canadians, there were three feature movies of particular interest, if only because they were filmed in Canada and acknowledged Canada's part in the war. The first two opened early in 1942.

The first was *Captains of the Clouds*, which dealt, rather fancifully, with the British Commonwealth Air Training Plan. Filmed on location at Uplands Air Base near Ottawa, at Trenton Central Flying School, and near North Bay, it presented James Cagney as an over-the-hill bush pilot whose cocky manner and lack of discipline (besides his age) render him unacceptable for combat in the RCAF. In typical Cagney fashion, he shows 'em. Canada's most revered air ace of the First World War, W. A. ("Billy") Bishop, now an Air Marshal, appeared as himself and handled his acting chores with aplomb.

A British film, originally titled *The 49th Parallel,* was released in North America with the title *The Invaders.* It was the story of six survivors of a German submarine, sunk in Hudson Bay. The crew try to flee across Canada to the pre-Pearl-Harbor sanctuary of the United States. The impressive cast included Laurence Olivier as a French-Canadian trapper, Leslie Howard as an easy-going humanist, Raymond Massey as a Canadian soldier on leave, and Anton Walbrook as the leader of a Hutterite colony in Manitoba. Except for some interiors, filmed in England, most of the movie was made in Canada. The feature received quite respectable reviews but somehow failed to capture the interest of large audiences.

The movie *Corvette K-225* was released in 1943. It was a wartime sea melodrama starring Randolph Scott and featuring Canada's role in fighting the Germans at sea. Parts of it were filmed in Toronto.

The National Film Board did its share by turning out sixty short documentaries under the overall title *Canada Carries On.* The familiar and effective voice of Lorne Green was used to narrate at least twenty of the series. In 1941, one of these films, entitled *Churchill's Island,* won an Academy Award, the first Canadian film to be thus honoured.

In late 1942, the NFB found itself in the middle of a political brawl between Mackenzie King and Mitchell Hepburn, provincial treasurer and former premier of Ontario. Both were Liberals, but Hepburn despised King and made no secret of it. One of the *Canada Carries On* series, *Inside Fighting Canada,* contained a passage about Canadians being united behind "the leadership of William Lyon Mackenzie King" and "disciplined for war."

Hepburn was outraged and banned screening of the film in Ontario, which he could do because the Ontario Censor Board came under his jurisdiction. After some intense political argument, Hepburn backed down and the film opened, without cuts, on New Year's Eve 1942.

Canada's crusty film commissioner, John Grierson, found Hepburn's actions extraordinary. "It would be strange to Canadians if in a survey of Britain's war effort special care were taken to omit the name of Mr. Churchill."

*

The NFB claims that Canadians were united behind Mr. King in the war effort may have been a slight exaggeration. There were, for example, the conscientious objectors, who wanted no part of the war.

Of the several hundred thousand Canadians who requested "postponements" under the National Resources Mobilization Act of 1940, some seventy-seven per cent did so because they were engaged in farming or other essential industries. Only four per cent (fewer than 11,000) were conscientious objectors. Prominent among the latter were Western Canadian Mennonites, who believed firmly in the scriptural teaching that he who lives by the sword will perish by the sword. The Mennonites asked the government to allow them to do "alternative service." By late May 1941, the government had worked out a system by which Mennonites, Quakers, Doukhobors, and other (acceptable) conscientious objectors could serve their country without taking up arms. Most worked in agriculture, a very small number (fewer than 200) worked in service camps.

John S. Reddekopp spent time in one of these camps. The Reddekopp family (originally from Germany) had farmed in the vicinity of Hague, in central Saskatchewan, for several generations. Like his five brothers and three sisters, John was raised in a strictly Mennonite household. In the fall of 1941, he was one of the Mennonite conscientious objectors called up to do his "alternative service." He had, first, to satisfy a board about his religious convictions.

"One day in the mail I get a letter and a ticket telling me to board the train in Hague," recalled John, "to be shipped via Calgary to Banff, Alberta." There, at "Camp 1," he joined about fifty other Mennonite COs cutting down and burning diseased trees in the bush near Banff and Tunnel Mountain. "There's a zig-zag walk right up to the top for tourists to walk on. That walk has to be maintained and repaired, so I was working probably about a month on Tunnel Mountain...

"We felt our country had an obligation to be at war but it didn't apply to us," said Reddekopp about his alternative service. "I wouldn't want to speak for everybody else, but I felt more Mennonite than Canadian... The government was considerate in giving us this alternative but the service we were rendering was not very productive. It was more or less...an excuse to let us boys escape service in the army, because lots of that work was serving no purpose."

Not all Mennonites became COs. Early in the war, Kornelius Krahn and two other Mennonites from Arnot, Manitoba, went to Winnipeg and signed up for the Royal Canadian Army Medical Corps.

During most of the war, Mackenzie King had recurring problems with conscription. The issue exacerbated the rift between French- and English-speaking Canadians. The latter regarded the former as slackers, and the pejorative word "Zombie" came into use to describe the home service conscripts who chose not to volunteer for overseas duty.

In a 1944 article in *Saturday Night*, Eric Koch, himself a relative newcomer to Canada, tried to analyze the motives of the Zombies, as well as to pinpoint who they were.

"If the public were better informed about the background and attitudes of Zombies, they would not assume, as they largely have done, that they are all French-Canadian... The only official figures available are those given out by Mr. King and General McNaughton [by then minister of national defence]. According to these, 25,000 out of 60,000 draftees are French-speaking, a figure only a little larger than the proportion of French-Canadians in the total population." But Koch was spitting against the wind. Many Canadians continued to think of Zombies as French-Canadians.

For many Canadians, memories of the war years are dominated by rationing, which went into effect in April 1942. The first consumer product to be rationed was gasoline, but the program was soon expanded to include meat, sugar, coffee, tea, butter, beer, wine, and whisky.

Even though he was only nine years old at the time, Norman Griesdorf remembers rationing. He and his parents were living in Vancouver, where "we had two cars. We had a Standard, one of the small English cars, and my father had a bigger car. I remember siphoning gasoline from one to the other, because you'd be allowed a coupon to get gasoline but I think the gasoline had to go in the car that the coupon fit... I can still taste the gasoline."

"I remember the food rationing books and the round, blue tokens for meat," recalled Elspeth Read, who was nine and living in Toronto when the war started. "With all my relatives in England and Scotland...my mother packed up and mailed whatever parcels of food she could. I'm sure not all that food arrived safely. Some packages are likely at the bottom of the Atlantic."

For the most part, rationing was not so much a hardship for Canadians as a nuisance. Once again, advertisers pitched in with slogans and reminders. "Bovril helps your meat ration." "When the Japs give in, we'll get more tin—Clark's Soups." "Liberty Subscribers—Due to government restriction of paper production, a limitation has been placed on the number of copies of Liberty printed each week."

Seagram's King's Plate ran an ad with this notice: "Wartime requirements have made it necessary temporarily to use a different bottle for this brand. There is absolutely no change in the quality of the product."

In addition to food rationing, there were even restrictions affecting the manufacture of clothes: no more than nine buttons on a dress, no hem in excess of two inches, no cuffs or flap pockets, no double-breasted jackets. War meant regimentation—even for civilians.

Marie Dee, then living in Vancouver, remembers the shortages. "Whenever nylons came in, there used to be a battle royal. You know, 'Eaton's have nylons,' and everybody would rush down to get them."

For about 7,000 British children, war meant evacuation. The bombing in Great Britain prompted many British families to send children to Canada for safety. In some cases an entire school was evacuated.

The staff and pupils of St. Hilda's School, Liverpool, moved to Erindale, Ontario. This was an Anglican High Church school consisting of five nuns, seven teachers, and 100 or so pupils, from the age of six to fifteen. There were even three five-year-old boys who came with their older sisters.

As Isabel Adamson remembers it, the parents of the evacuees had only a week to decide whether or not to send their children overseas, but "the school was offered the use of the home of Mrs. W. W. Evans in Erindale for the duration. The children were in Canada four years and some of the parishioners at the local Anglican Church (St. Peter's) took them during the holiday period... My parents took two Scottish girls for the holidays, so they got to know them and love them."

Bill Brydon, who was nine years old when the war started, was an evacuee. He lived with his parents, an older brother, and two older sisters in Hepburn, just outside Newcastle.

Brydon says he doesn't know why he was evacuated; perhaps it was "because my father thought we'd lose. Or, did he think we were coming of military age? He had spent four years in France in the First War, and it was bloody hell for him... I've never figured it out exactly, except the authorities said we had to be evacuated, whether you went to the country in Scotland, or wherever."

Bill and his fifteen-year-old brother, Fenwick, were evacuated in 1940 via Glasgow. "Thousands of kids, all over the place, and there were vicars and priests and all kinds of people who were in charge of the various groups. We boarded late at night and the next thing we heard was when the engines started in the morning, before dawn. We all rushed up on deck. It was astonishing. It was just dawn, and our convoy was fifty ships strong. All you saw was fifty ships and we were out to sea. We were supported by a battleship and six destroyers. A lot of the boats were evacuee boats but a lot were cargo and whatever.

"And I remember, halfway across the Atlantic, there was a ship that couldn't keep up. I don't think it was an evacuee ship but a freighter. It just couldn't keep up. You had to do a certain amount of knots and they couldn't wait. Apparently it was sunk. The submarines were just waiting for that."

About twelve days later, they landed in Halifax. "I remember our first introduction to Canada. We got on this train, this long train, all the kids, and we were greeted by all the wonderful Canadians, coming out with candy from the towns. They had sodas and candy bars and flags, and we thought, by God, this is heaven, you know. We were having chocolate and candy and sodas all the way across to Toronto."

In Toronto, Fenwick, Bill, and hundreds of other children were taken to a dormitory at the University of Toronto where they slept on bunks for one night. The next day, the group was split up, although the two Brydon boys were kept together. About twelve of them went to Brockville, Ontario, and were temporarily put up at an orphanage.

Some of the children already there were either physically or mentally handicapped. "That caused us great concern," Brydon says, "because when we went to school [everyone knew] we were from the children's home and everyone thought we were retarded."

Waiting to get a permanent billet "was a little depressing at first." People came in ready to accept one of the British children. "They looked you over and said, 'I'll take this one or that one.' But my brother was a little older, several years, and they didn't want the older kids. So each time they said, 'I'll have that one' (me), I said, 'Well, I have to go with my brother.'"

Finally Mr. and Mrs. G. W. Brooks of Brockville took them both, and "we lived with them for four years. Very nice people. They had no children; she had been unable to have children. We got along very well with them, and we became Canadian kids, that was the whole thing."

The Brydon brothers went back to England about six months before the war ended and got the shock of their lives. "My mother said, 'What are you going to do?' It never occurred to me that at thirteen I wasn't going to go to school. I thought that was automatic. But you got a job at thirteen at that particular time in England. She said, 'Well, we're going to try and get you a job.'... So I started to work at thirteen in a factory."

He kept remembering the "opulent" food in Canada. "I've often thought that Canadians thought they were rationed. When we were in England, between 1944 and 1949, I remember one egg a week. All our butter ration went to my father. Sugar rations, you know, there was only enough for one person. The bread was almost black...

"I think the experience had always stayed with me, the Canadian experience, and when the time came I said, 'I've got to get out of here.' There was no real opportunity, especially if you were without education. Your options were very limited." In 1956 Brydon emigrated to Toronto, where at first he sold shoes, but later became an actor.

In summer 1940, when the SS *Antonia* set sail from England, there were fifteen youngsters from the Yorkshire resort town of Scarborough on board. Because the nearby port of Hull had been severely bombed, Margaret (Maggie) Beal's father, a gentlemen's outfitter, felt that the family should play it safe and send Maggie to Canada.

The *Antonia* crossed the Atlantic unescorted, docking in Halifax ten days later. Maggie Beal and two of her closest girl friends were together as far as Winnipeg, but then one of them, Jeanne Gaunt, went on to

Vancouver, where she had relatives. Beal's other friend, Olga Burrows, remained in Winnipeg. At first they stayed in a building that had been a school for the deaf (and was later turned into an RCAF base). Later, Beal was taken in by a family who lived in Tuxedo, a suburb of Winnipeg.

Beal's memories of the family she stayed with are not warm, but she made the best of it, attending Kelvin Technical High School, singing in the school choir, and getting along well in her studies. "If you said, 'Were you homesick?' I'd probably say no," she says. "But I kept this little diary...and I reread it three or four years ago... There's lots of places where I put, 'And I went to my room and had a good cry.'"

In December 1940, she was chosen (she still doesn't know how) to speak on a radio broadcast to her mother and father back in England on Christmas Day.

"It was CKY, in the old telephone building at Portage and Main... We got up on Christmas morning and took a taxi and I went and talked to my Mom and Dad as the kid from Manitoba, for just a couple of minutes. Years later, I found out that my mother and father had a totally horrific experience, because they had to go to Leeds to do it, which is sixty miles away [from Scarborough], and Daddy had given up the car. There were no cars, and they ordered a taxi that didn't come and they started walking and they sort of thumbed a ride. It was a milk truck that took them to the station, and it was cold and everything was awful and they had a pretty tough Christmas."

During that broadcast, Beal recalls, "I fell in love with the microphone." In 1960, when she was living in Ottawa and doing radio work (as Maggie Morris), she was signed up to appear on the CBC panel show *Flashback*, which ran for six years. She moved to Toronto to do that series. In 1963, for Mother's Day, the program secretly flew her mother over from England to be a surprise guest on *Flashback*.

Joyce Gordon's childhood experience was the opposite of Bill Brydon's and Maggie Beal's. Born in Montreal in 1934, she was less than five years old when her parents moved with her to England—in June 1939. Her father was unemployed, and the trip to England was a chance to look for work. He got a job with Shell Oil in England, at a refinery an hour's ride on the train from London, due east along the Thames.

Joyce quickly became aware of the war because "my father was an air raid warden, so he was issued a tin helmet and we had a shelter in the garden which we used to sleep in at the very beginning of the war. We did everything proper. You know, you never went anywhere without your gas mask and you slept in the shelter... It wasn't one of those dugouts, it was just sitting on [the ground]. It was a square structure built just twelve feet from the house, so if the house blew up I don't know how protected we were. Stupid. The doorway faced the house. So how protected could you have been?"

Eventually they stopped sleeping in the shelter. Gordon's mother simply shoved her under the kitchen table during air raids. And she remembers "standing at the back door with my father, looking towards London, where you could see the glow in the sky. Every night there would be a siren and then there'd be an all-clear and it became normal for me... When the war ended and there were no more air raid sirens, [it felt as if] something was wrong. It was so eerie, because when you grow up with that happening all the time, that's normal."

She remembers that, in 1941 or 1942, she and her mother planned to return to Canada—without her father. "I remember being on the boat train with her, our baggage was all headed for Southampton and she and I were being evacuated back to Canada. And I remember my mother saying, 'We can't go, we can't leave your father.' We turned around and went back. And my mother must have told me, or I must have heard it, that that ship went down; it was torpedoed and everybody was lost. How much of this is fabrication, how much of it is my mother's exaggeration of the drama of it all, I don't know." The Gordons didn't return to Canada until 1947.

She found adjusting to Montreal difficult. "I was a freak, I looked like Alice in Wonderland. I had long straight black hair and lisle stockings and the other kids were wearing silk and make-up. I can remember them all crowding around me at recess saying, 'Isn't she cute? Say something, say something.' In two weeks my English accent went in self-defence, because at that age you want to be like everybody else... That was a major adjustment, you know, it took a year or two to adjust to."

Years later, after she had become an actress, Gordon volunteered for two LSD research sessions at Toronto Western Hospital. The first one, she remembers, "was absolutely terrifying." She blocked out the whole experience, but she was persuaded to take part in a second experiment.

"So we had a smaller dose and the young psychiatrist who was administering all of this gave me a dose of something so that I would experience whatever it was, but the subjectivity of the fear would be cut down. And I had a flash of being in the water with a bunch of children... I connected it (with the ship that had supposedly gone down) and there was a tremendous sense of guilt. All I was saying on the tape-recording of this LSD session was, 'It had nothing to do with me, it had nothing to do with me, it wasn't my fault, it wasn't my fault.'

"So obviously, somewhere, that left a pretty permanent scar in terms of feeling responsible and guilty that I survived and all those other children didn't."

Although Canada never endured anything like the Blitz or the wartime privations that Europe suffered, many people feared enemy action. In Windsor, Ontario, in 1942, Mayor Arthur J. Reaume sent a telegram to J. L. Ralston, minister of national defence, asking for immediate action on his city's appeal for "a protective guard on her traffic arteries between Detroit and Windsor." His request was prompted by the appearance of a Nazi swastika on a downtown Windsor building.

It was not clear whether the appearance of the swastika was a tasteless joke or an indication of Nazi sympathy. But the mayor was convinced the appearance of the hated symbol indicated the "presence of bold subversive elements." Protective guards had already been posted on the American approaches to the bridge, tunnel, and ferry that linked Detroit to Windsor, and the Windsor mayor felt Canada should have its own guards. His request was ignored.

In British Columbia, the fear of Japanese infiltration and sabotage became marked after Pearl Harbor was bombed and the United States entered the war against Germany and Japan in 1941. These fears were augmented in 1942, when two Japanese submarines surfaced along the Pacific coast; one launched a small seaplane to ignite forest fires in Oregon, the second fired shells off Estevan Point on Vancouver Island.

The provincial government of British Columbia pressured the federal government to take steps to prevent the creation of a Japanese fifth column. This led to the forced relocation of 23,000 Japanese Canadians away from the British Columbia coast.

By 1944, Mackenzie King's government, which had quickly caved in to British Columbia's demands to move the Japanese, was admitting that "the people of Japanese race have committed no acts of sabotage." But by then it was too late, the damage had been done.

At the same time, a real threat to Canada's safety went more or less undetected on Canada's other coast. German U-boats, operating in the Gulf of St. Lawrence, managed, between May 1942 and the end of the war, to sink a total of twenty-eight vessels in the St. Lawrence River and around the Gulf. Five of these were Canadian freighters or tankers, six more were Royal Canadian Navy vessels (corvettes, minesweepers), and the remainder were freighters of foreign (Allied) registry.

Very little information about these sinkings was carried in the Canadian newspapers, mostly because government wartime censorship deemed it best for the country's security to suppress the news of such losses, presumably to prevent panic and protect morale.

Other, more trivial stories were kept under wraps during the war, in the interest of "national security."

In July 1942, residents of Meaford and St. Vincent, Ontario, began hearing rumours that the government of Canada was planning to expropriate a block of land six miles square "for military purposes." Farmers, fruit-growers, fishermen, and resort owners in the area attended an emotionally charged meeting at Meaford Town Hall, at which they were informed by government representatives that the army had urgent need of land for training grounds for heavy tanks and artillery. The people were assured a fair price would be paid for the land.

On July 22, the Owen Sound *Daily Sun Times* ran an editorial praising the farmers for giving up their homes "for their country." The editorial ended: "Of course there is one bright ray in the future—many of the farmers will, in all probability, be able to buy their farms back after the war is over, probably at a considerably reduced price. Many of them will be little damaged, although idleness alone will not help them."

At first it was believed that 40,000 acres would be taken, but in the end only 16,000 acres were expropriated. The lives of 105 families were seriously affected. Within two weeks of the first rumours, the area was officially taken over. The prices paid to the farmers remained a well-kept secret.

Four rural schools did not open that September. Four churches were also taken: United, Baptist, Anglican, and Disciples of Christ. Although the government promised that they would be closed, boarded up, and protected, this did not happen and they were damaged by artillery fire. The graveyard at Mountain Lake, which contained the last resting place of the pioneers of the Mallory settlement, who came to the township in the fall of 1835, was, however, respected.

On October 1, 1942, the Meaford Tank Range officially opened. Three military tanks came to Meaford by CNR flatcars. Students in the public and high schools were dismissed early to witness the event. These giant tools of modern war were thought to be too heavy for the Syke Street bridge in Meaford and were driven across the river at a shallow place.

The little ray of hope referred to in the Owen Sound paper's editorial was soon extinguished. According to Helene Weaver of Owen Sound, "Some people believed that the war would soon be over and that they would return to their homes. After the war there was a movement to return the land to the people of Canada as a park but it was thought that it could not be rendered safe from unexploded shells." The land remained as the Militia Training and Support Centre after the war. In 1993, a $100-million expansion program was undertaken to construct facilities to feed and house 2,500 troops.

Rationing, evacuees, conscientious objectors, Zombies, fears of a fifth column—Canadians remember all these from the war years. Yet for many, the hardest part was waiting for and dreading news from overseas that a loved one had been killed or was missing in action.

Velma Hill was working as a postal clerk in the village of Little Britain, Ontario, during the war. "I saw the tears of disappointment when family members and loved ones discovered an empty mail box, and I saw the tears of joy when a long-awaited letter arrived from overseas."

One night in November 1944, she was working alone in the post office. After sorting the first-class mail, she began to unload another mailbag which included magazines. "I cut the cords on a roll of *Maclean's* magazines. As it opened out, my eye caught a familiar name in the middle of the picture on the cover... My thought was, 'Oh no! That's my brother's initials (Everitt Ivan Hill).' The room started to swirl and I came close to blacking out. It was a picture of my brother's grave. He had been shot by a sniper near the church wall surrounding Notre Dame in Caen. The grave was covered with flowers. This was the November edition of *Maclean's* and up until then our family's only information of Everitt's death had been a short, curt telegram informing my parents that he had been shot, 'killed in action.'"

The photo, taken by Canadian Army photographer Lieutenant Ken Bell, showed a Caen woman placing flowers on the grave. The epitaph, translated from the French, reads:

Rest in peace under the beautiful sky of France,
Son of Canada and glorious martyr.
You have given your life for our deliverance—
May your name be forever blessed in Heaven.

Others had to wait years before they learned where their sons, husbands, or brothers were buried. Sergeant Ross Johnstone from Coldwater, Ontario, was shot down and reported missing in action during a bombing mission over Germany in 1945. His sister, Jessica Moon, knew nothing further about her brother's fate or his place of burial for almost half a century. But in the summer of 1992, a freelance writer named Moreland Jones was taking a drive through southern Bavaria with his wife. They saw a sign pointing to a military cemetery and decided to explore it. They found the graves of numerous Canadians, including one marked "Flt. Sgt. Ross Johnstone, Air gunner, age twenty-one, Coldwater, Ontario." They took a picture of the headstone, and although they were total strangers, they managed to track down Jessica Moon and bring her the picture of her brother's grave.

The suffering and death of so many young men put the troubles of the home front into perspective. War, after all, was total war. Victory depended on victory on every front. If Churchill could vow to fight on the beaches and on the landing grounds and in the fields and in the streets, the least Canadians at home could do was fight on the home front. And, like the others, that front eventually triumphed.

Canadian sailors and Wrens dance on the deteriorating deck of a troop ship bound for Britain, early in the war. *Margaret Los Haliburton*

A convoy bound for England assembles at Bedford Basin near Halifax in the early spring of 1942. *National Archives of Canada PA-112993*

Murray Westgate served at HMCS *Fort Ramsay*, Gaspé, when U-boats were attacking Allied shipping in the Gulf of St. Lawrence. *Murray Westgate*

Halifax bombers shown on a British airfield preparing to form up for a bombing raid over occupied Europe. *Canadian Forces Photographic Unit PL-40474*

Col. (later Brigadier) J. K. Lawson commanded the Canadian troops in Hong Kong—the very troops he had advised were not combat ready. *Department of National Defense PMR 77-537*

Returning from a raid over Germany this Lancaster crashed at Eastmoor in 1944. This photo was taken by RCAF photographer Victor Albota. *Victor Albota*

Some of the healthier-looking Canadian POWs (captured in Hong Kong) were assembled for this Japanese photo, released at war's end. *Canadian Forces Photographic Unit PAC PR480/RE 91-7029*

Dead Canadian soldiers and a disabled Canadian tank on the pebbled beach at Dieppe, after the disastrous 1942 raid. *Department of National Defense PMR 86-285*

This captured German photograph shows Canadian POWs being marched through the streets of Dieppe following the failed raid. *Department of National Defense PMR 86-320*

Ross Munro of Canadian Press was one of the most respected of all war correspondents. *Ken Bell, National Archives of Canada PA-136206*

On D-Day some Canadian infantrymen had to carry bicycles ashore, in addition to their other gear. Their hapless mission was to ride to a German-held airfield some 18 kilometres inland. *G.A. Milne, National Archives of Canada PA-135963*

Canadian soldiers (Queen's Own Rifles) stand in front of this battered German stronghold at Bernière-sur-Mer on D-Day. *National Archives of Canada PA-137013*

Canadian artillery pounded out a path for advancing infantrymen through Normandy on D-Day and later. *Ken Bell, National Archives of Canada PA- 115569*

Corporal Joe Oggy went in on D-Day with the Queen's Own Rifles. Before landing they were told: "You have 15 minutes to live." *Joe Oggy*

British evacuee Margaret Beal was chosen to broadcast from Winnipeg to her parents in England on Christmas Day, 1940. She later became famous as TV panelist Maggie Morris. *Winnipeg Free Press*

Nurse Peggy Tucker met Airman Arnold Lonsdale at the Active Service Canteen in Toronto early in the war but they didn't marry until he got back from overseas, in October, 1945. *Peggy Tucker Lonsdale*

Actor Errol Flynn "fought" in every theatre of war—all in glamorous Hollywood films.

Wren Margaret Los, photographed while serving in Moncton, New Brunswick. She was among the first Canadians to hear of Hitler's death. *Margaret Los Haliburton*

Seeing this November 15, 1944, cover of *Maclean's* showing a French woman putting flowers on the grave of Canadian soldier Everett Ivan Hill (inset), was how his family learned where he was buried. *Courtesy* Maclean's

5

First In and Last Out

In many ways, prisoners of war experienced the longest war. A flier could think in terms of completing a tour of duty; a sailor could expect his ship to put into port from time to time; a soldier hoped that reinforcements would one day relieve his outfit, so that he could get some rest. But a POW had to live, day after day, week after week, with the knowledge that only the end of hostilities would save him from the rigours of captivity. And he had no way of knowing when that might be.

The first time Canadian troops were thrust into combat was in December, 1941—the day Franklin Delano Roosevelt defined indelibly as "a date that will live in infamy." He was speaking of the Japanese attack on Pearl Harbor. But on the very same day, Canadian troops experienced their baptism of fire in Hong Kong.

When Hong Kong fell on Christmas Day 1941, after a long and pointless battle involving two Canadian infantry battalions, the Royal Rifles of Canada, from Quebec, and the Winnipeg Grenadiers, 1,192 soldiers became Canada's first prisoners of war.

Among them was Sidney Skelton from Ontario. He and his Royal Rifles saw action and defeat at places called Sugar Loaf Hill, Stanley Mound, Stone Hill, and Palm Villa. They fought back, retook ground, but were finally overrun by the Japanese. Skelton was severely wounded in the fighting and his wartime diary paints a desperate picture of his mental state just before capture:

"Death and blood all around me... They just got Jack next to me. We were talking when suddenly a shell made a mess of him... Noise all around... They are coming closer... Oh God, it doesn't seem that I can stand it any longer..." On December 23, Skelton and two others encountered a machine gun nest. His two buddies were killed and Skelton became a POW. The Japanese put him to work in a coal-mine; he spent nearly four years in captivity, during which time his weight plunged from 145 pounds to 89 pounds.

The hapless prisoners were treated abominably. "We were the first in and the last out," says a veteran sergeant who became a prisoner after Hong Kong.

They were starved, they suffered an endless assortment of ailments (from dysentery to diphtheria), they were denied medical attention, they were forced into hard labour. They were beaten for any mistake or misstep. Indeed, beatings became commonplace. Some prisoners were beaten to death. A few who tried to escape were murdered.

Even the medical officers who were included among the prisoners were mistreated. Dr. John W. Crawford, the senior Canadian medical officer, was slapped and beaten when his men died of diphtheria because they had been given no serum, or of starvation because they were denied food.

A British army doctor, Major William Stewart, was in Singapore during those dark days. When Singapore fell, he escaped and headed for Australia, but the ship he was on was sunk by a German raider and he wound up in Japan, as did many of the Hong Kong captives.

Major Stewart later made a report to the Canadian government that revealed details of the ordeal of Canadian prisoners of the Japanese. Men who dared to go on sick parade were invariably suspected of malingering. "These men are here to work, not to be sick," the major was told by the Japanese. Often, the "malingerers" were slapped around. Sometimes an imprisoned medical officer who dared to speak up on behalf of the ailing Canadians was struck.

In Stewart's POW camp, more than 100 Canadians died of various ailments—all attributable either to malnutrition or to inadequate (or inept) medical care. Stewart described his time there as "a daily night-mare."

In addition to four doctors and two dental officers, the Canadian contingent in Hong Kong included two nursing sisters—Kay Christie and May Waters—who worked at the Hong Kong hospital. With the surrender, both nurses became prisoners of war—the only Canadian women ever to achieve that dubious distinction.

On Christmas morning, "Japanese troops burst in and began bayoneting the patients on the floor," nurse Kay Christie told author Bill McNeil. "I remember one of these young fellows, a young Canadian lad of about seventeen, who tried to escape and those soldiers went after him, constantly sticking their bayonets in his arm. This went on until he just played dead and they finally stopped sticking him. His arm had to be amputated when he was returned to the British Military Hospital."

Starting early in 1943, more than 1,100 Canadians were shipped to slave labour camps in Japan. They were forced to work without adequate safety devices in shipyards, foundries, and coal and iron mines. At one camp alone, 77 men out of 376 died.

Muriel O'Brien Whomsley of Beaverton, Ontario, was only four years old when her eighteen-year-old brother, Gerald O'Brien, joined the army. He was captured at Hong Kong, and his family were not sure that he was alive until 1945.

She says her brother had "horrendous nightmares" for years after the war and suffered from deep depression. He rarely spoke of his experiences, but she remembers some things which he reluctantly divulged about his time as a prisoner of the Japanese: "They were awakened very early in the morning, still dark, to go and work in the mines, and returned late, dark again—never seeing light. They were fed one bowl of rice daily and had to drink their own urine to survive."

"Beatings had become commonplace," wrote Kildare Dobbs in *The Star Weekly*. "Some who were savagely flogged lived. Others, like Riflemen J. Mortimer, E. Doucet, H. Matheson—to name only three—were beaten to death. One sergeant was tortured, four escapees murdered. These atrocities were in addition to those committed during the siege and surrender—when wounded were bayoneted, nurses and civilians raped, mutilated and murdered, and prisoners massacred by their Japanese captors."

All told, 254 Canadians died in Japanese prison or work camps. As for the survivors, unlike other Canadian veterans, the Hong Kong veterans did not immediately receive medical and pension compensation. Some were denied hospital treatment because Canadian doctors were ignorant of the tropical diseases the vets had contracted in captivity. Others were accused of malingering or faking illness. And still others were labeled "crybabies" when they complained of mental problems because of their prolonged captivity. Almost from the day they returned to Canada the Hong Kong Veterans' Association fought for treatment equal to other returning vets. In 1951 the federal government offered Hong Kong vets one dollar for every day they spent in forced labour; each survivor received about $1,300 in compensation. Fifty years later, the HKVA goal of full disability has still not been achieved.

Yet the ordeal of Canada's Hong Kong vets is not totally forgotten. Eve (Arnoldi) Armour served as a Wren from 1942 until after the end of the war. In 1945, she was in charge of the signals station in Victoria. One day she heard a signal that a ship was due to arrive carrying British and Canadian men who had been prisoners of the Japanese.

"It was a gorgeous sunny day and the seagulls were screaming and the band was playing and everybody was lined up... The Yanks were on the two top decks and the British and Canadians on the two lower ones and everybody was cheering as the ship came in...

"Then they lowered the gangplank and the first Canadian [emerged]... I'll never forget it...he was just a walking skeleton. And as he came down the gangplank...he tripped, and then just ahead of him there were two stretcher-bearers with, it looked like a corpse, and he tripped on this thing and that boy let out this groan and his face was...a kind of yellow-green colour.

"Well, when the second boy tripped...the matelots [sailors] just broke through the shore patrol and the shore patrol lifted their arms and they went up that gangplank and they carried every single boy down with all their stuff.

"But, you know, the band stopped playing, there was just a hush. The Americans, you see, didn't know what condition these boys were in, because the British and Canadians—especially the British—were the worst off, I think. [They] had been prisoners for four years... I understand that three or four boys died that night."

She cannot get through the story without breaking down.

Diana (Warren) Taschereau (whose father, Leslie Warren, served in

Singapore and Sumatra and died of malaria in India) was in England at the war's end:

"One of my saddest...memories was the sight of POWs from Hong Kong after VJ Day... I was on a medical ward and as they arrived I was transferred to a surgical ward... Most of them, I gather, succumbed in the camps to the routine treatment of the Japs. Those few who I nursed were just stunned. They were mentally slow, unable to move much nor respond. Feeding them was agony. Such a long time to try to get them to swallow a mouthful, and yet they were so starved."

Winston Churchill, who had been persuaded against his better judgment to beef up the Hong Kong defences with two Canadian battalions, later paid a brief tribute to the colony's defenders in his lengthy history of the war, published in 1950: "Their tenacity was matched by the fortitude of the British civilian population. On Christmas Day the limit of endurance was reached and capitulation became inevitable. Under their resolute Governor, Sir Mark Young, the colony had fought a good fight. They had won indeed the 'lasting honour' which is their due."

But Churchill's words were little consolation to the families of those boys, both Canadian and British, who were so rashly sent to death or captivity.

On the other side of the globe, about 8,000 Canadians were taken prisoner by the Germans during the Second World War. Although they were not treated quite as harshly as the POWs in the Far East, many suffered and died.

The worst treatment of the prisoners occurred towards the end of the war in Europe, as the Germans grew desperate. Even so, earlier in the war, immediately after the Dieppe raid, there were ugly charges and countercharges between the Allies and the Germans about the shackling of prisoners. That it was done by both sides is undoubtedly true; what remains in dispute—even after all these years—is who did it first.

In the weeks immediately following VE Day, when many Canadians were liberated and returned home, Canadian newspaper headlines illustrated the point: "Montreal Airman Chained By Nazis" or "This Winnipegger Survives Hell of 'German Culture.'"

The Winnipegger was Lance-Sergeant Saul Stanley Tishler, a paratrooper taken prisoner in December 1944. "One day in midwinter," Tishler wrote, "everyone was awakened at a very early hour and told he is going to march out. The Russians are close. At first we are told we are going 70 kilometres and then take a train, but no one believes it. It started on February 9, and when it ended some 50 days later, a total of 730 kilometres were marched.

"Food? It wasn't there. Eleven loaves of bread, two and a half pounds of meat, one pound of cheese, and some fat was the complete diet of this march of death; the normal consumption of a family of three for a week, if they only ate once a day.

"How did they exist on this? Some did, but many died. Died of exposure, malnutrition, meningitis...and many other causes. There was no medical attention to speak of. Some died simply because they didn't want to live any more. Is it possible, you ask? I say yes because I saw it."

The Montreal airman was Warrant Officer Lorne Goat. RCAF airman Goat was shot down in a Wellington bomber in August 1942, when he was still a sergeant. He was sent to Stalag 344 at Lamsdorf, south of Breslau, and found himself among 1,000 British and other airmen. Goat kept a diary, which recorded how in October 1942 the prisoners had their hands bound by ropes, which were replaced by chains in December.

"As the Jerry guards became scarcer, we used to be able to get out of the chains more frequently. If the guards did come back when we had them off, we'd create a panic by yelling 'air raid' or 'fire,' and slip them back on in the confusion."

He, too, took part in a long and painful march as the war neared its end, as did Warrant Officer Welland Phipps, of Ottawa, an RCAF flight engineer who was shot down in April 1943. But Phipps and another man, Flying Officer Hugh Clee, of Vancouver, managed to escape from the marching column after it had been moving east for three days.

"Food was the grimmest part of the march," Phipps said later. "We had virtually no rations and lived off whatever we could pick up on the way. I lost between twenty-five and thirty pounds in weight."

Stephen Bell, who was taken prisoner at Dieppe, spent time in various different camps—in France, Poland, and Germany.

After several days in one POW camp in France, he and other prisoners were herded aboard boxcars, 125 men or so to a car, where "you couldn't even sit down," Bell recalls. "Sweat just dripped off the end of your fingers. No place to relieve yourself. We went through France, Holland, Belgium, into Poland. Six days and five nights. Whenever they stopped, they opened the doors and took the dead guys out, and put in two buckets of water. Before we got on the train, they gave us [each] half a loaf of bread and one tin of meat. For six days and five nights."

Like other prisoners, Bell helped dig tunnels and worked on many elaborate schemes to escape. He escaped five times and was recaptured four times.

One time, he was almost free when a bullet hit him in the back. His life was saved because he was wearing a webbing belt, which slowed down the bullet.

In February 1945, Bell, together with Murray Deneau, who was from the Essex Scottish Regiment, escaped from a forced march in Germany. They slipped away during a Russian artillery attack when the guards scattered for cover.

It was thirty degrees below zero; there was a foot of snow. Starving, freezing, and soaked, they lived on frozen apples and frozen cabbage leaves. Finally, desperate for food and shelter, they knocked on the door of a house. A woman of sixty or so came to the door. Bell, whose German was quite fluent by this time, explained they were two escaped Canadian soldiers, hungry and tired.

"I told her, I know you can turn us in for the reward," he says. But the woman invited them in, gave them "the best potato soup I ever tasted in my life" and hid them in the basement. Her husband was sick in bed.

"The next day, she asked would we mind if she brought a friend over to see us. We didn't care. She brought this woman over [who] had letters from Gravenhurst, Ontario. Her son was a prisoner of war in Canada, and wrote home to say how well he was treated, the bacon and eggs, the steaks, and Eaton's catalogue—you could order a radio, you could order a chesterfield. She had two or three letters that she read to us in German. She had never seen a Canadian before, but she was so thankful that her son was in Canada, and not a prisoner in Germany."

Later, Bell and his buddy made contact with a column of advancing Russian tanks. The Russians had never heard of Canada, "so we said we were Americans."

Otto Sulek was in a POW camp when the Germans surrendered. Born in the Sudetenland, Czechoslovakia, he fled Nazi occupation in 1938, first to England, then to Canada. In 1943, he joined the RCAF and became a mid-upper gunner on a Halifax bomber. On his twenty-first operation—laying mines near Flensburg on January 12, 1945—he had to bail out over Denmark. He was captured by the Germans the next day and spent the rest of the war as a POW. He was at a camp at Moosburg, in Bavaria, at the end of April when the German war machine toppled. Just as the American tanks were rumbling towards Moosburg, the Germans turned the POW camp over to senior Allied prisoners.

"Soon the Yanks were into town. Suddenly German soldiers came running toward camp, but SS troops were shooting at them. We cut holes in the fence and let these soldiers in. They were fifteen- to sixteen-year-old boys. As a last gesture the SS blew the bridge over the Isar at the far end of town. By 1100 hours it was all over... All over town white flags, bed sheets, tablecloths—anything white—was hoisted... The town was surrendering."

Sulek made it back to Bournemouth in May and got his first change of clothing in four months, "and some decent food, which my stomach could not take yet."

When ack-ack gunner Henry Beaudry was taken prisoner in December 1944, near Ortona, Italy, he and several other Canadians were sent to a camp about thirty miles outside Munich. In February 1945, both captors and captives were starving. The Germans turned them loose.

"I had a friend in the prison camp. We couldn't understand each other," Beaudry says. "He was a Mongolian. Our skin was the same. The Germans used to tease us."

Beaudry and the Mongolian changed uniforms because Beaudry was cold, while the other man was less affected by cold weather. "The

Mongolian had a sheepskin lining in his jacket and it was warm, but mine was just a thin khaki jacket."

Beaudry and his friend were released when the Germans ran out of food, and got to the American lines. "The Americans kept asking me questions. They thought I was a Russian and this other guy was Canadian. And he didn't even speak English." Once the Americans were convinced Beaudry was a Canadian, they sent him to England and "that's when I...got back into a Canadian uniform."

Tail gunners who survived downed bombers were few and far between. George Hutton is one of the few. He joined the RCAF late in 1942, trained in Quebec, was sent to England, joined No. 425 (Alouette) Squadron in 1943, and flew twenty-three missions. During the return from the last one, he was shot down over Hanover in January 1945. One wounded member of the crew went down with the aircraft, the other six, including Hutton, bailed out.

"Jeez, I was caught within fifteen minutes (of landing)," explained Hutton. "There was a home guard guy and the Gestapo chief of Bielefeld (about fifty miles from Hanover). The two of them caught me and messed me around a bit. They kept saying to me, 'Americanish or British schweinehund,' and I'd say Canadian. Every time I said Canadian, they'd belt me. It took me three cracks on the head to smarten up."

Hutton remembers spending time in solitary confinement at an interrogation camp in Frankfurt. "Thirty-seven days by my count. By the interrogator's count I was there seventeen days.

"It was electrically heated, believe it or not. They put you in and you had a pot to go in. Every so often you'd awake, you'd hear the door and there would be black bread in there and there would be a jug of coffee made of acorns. But they'd turn on the heat, you see. The heat would be on for two hours and you'd get up and you'd almost strip naked. Then you'd hear a click and the heat would go off. So every half hour you'd put your clothes back on and then the next half hour you'd be [trying] to keep warm."

Eventually, Hutton ended up in a prison camp at Barth, on the Baltic Sea. "That's where we stayed until the Russians came through." There were about 10,000 prisoners there, he recalls—about 8,000 Americans and the other 2,000 would be RAF, New Zealanders,

Canadians, Australians, too. All air force, except when the war was closing, when the Russians were advancing, then they started bringing in army guys who were caught before Dunkirk...

"Sand, colder than hell, and right on the Baltic. We used to say we could see Sweden, but we couldn't... Cold all the time...and you were hungry...

"You got one-sixth of a loaf of black bread a day and you got at least three cups of ersatz coffee, and occasionally you'd get horsemeat stew, maybe once every eight days. You'd get it [the day's ration] around noon... You were supposed to get a Red Cross parcel, one a week. I think all the time I was in there, up until the war ended, I got about four parcels."

Not long after he arrived at the Baltic camp, Hutton got into tunnel-digging. "I wasn't too good at trying to escape... The aim was to keep as many guards as you could busy. But none of us Canadians [made it]. One guy in Barth claimed there was at least 100 tunnels started in that prison camp. Now, that's from '39 to '45. The odd guy tried to get out in the garbage pail or in a manure wagon or something like that. From our prison camp, there was about four who made it. But they made it to Hamburg or somewhere and then they got a boat that took them to Sweden. [If you got caught] they put you in solitary confinement.

"Towards the end of the war there was a waiting list to get into solitary confinement...because solitary confinement was right close to the Germans' mess, the cook house, so they were fed better. Oh, Jeez, I was twenty-seventh on the list when I got liberated."

Each afternoon, during the outdoor exercise periods at 4:30, they could hear the roar of artillery as the Russians got closer. The Germans "started to tell us, 'The Russian hordes, the Russian hordes.' And, boy, when they came through, they *were* the Russian hordes... They are human beings, they are uneducated, they are dirty and when they advanced they came just like locusts... They were savages," says Hutton. He claims they raped "anybody that was a female."

By the time the camp was liberated by the Russians, Hutton's weight was down to 100 pounds. He tried to eat but couldn't keep anything down. In London, awaiting transportation back to Canada, he went into a pub with some buddies, had one drink, and passed out.

"The American military police come around and they say, 'Oh, we'll have to get the RAF or the RCAF.' And the next thing I know I'm in an ambulance and they take me to this English doctor. So I'm lying on this cotton-picking stretcher and he's listening to my heart and taking my temperature and all this stuff and he says, 'Canada, you've got walking bloody pneumonia.'

"And I says, 'What the hell is walking pneumonia?'

"He says, 'You're too stupid to know enough to lie down.'"

Hubert Thistle was taken prisoner after D-Day. At one point, he was with a large group of POWs being moved in railway boxcars—twenty-three days of travelling across Europe, "all over the country because the bridges, railroads, everything was blown out." As usual, the biggest problem was food.

"They'd throw a couple of loaves of bread in, and you'd get a chunk off it, dry black bread. They had a big garbage pail that you could shit or piss in, you know. Once a day, two guys would volunteer, when the train stopped, to take it out and dump it. They'd volunteer just to get out and stretch their legs."

They ended up in a camp near Leipzig, Germany, where "we used to get the odd Red Cross parcel," Thistle remembers. "We were lucky if we got one a month. That's the only thing that saved us. In the Red Cross parcel was cigarettes, some kind of meat, dry biscuits, powdered milk, stuff like this... I don't think they dished them out. I think they did two for me and one for you."

In the end, when the western Allies were closing in from one side and the Russians from the other, the German guards at Leipzig simply threw away their weapons and Thistle and his fellow POWs walked out. "We were pretty weak and worn out, and my boots were worn right down to the leather, no socks, just a piece of something wrapped around my feet.

"The first guy we saw, you won't believe it, was an American reporter, a war correspondent out in the front line, in his convertible yet. He shared some cigarettes with us and told us where to go to this town. He said the front-line troops were dug in there... We went there and they shared stuff with us. Then we had to report to the MO. By now I had big blisters on my heels and he ordered me back with other guys in a Red Cross van."

On D-Day+1, the Halifax bomber that Tom Guy was piloting was hit and shot down over France. For a time, with the help of the French underground, he managed to elude the Germans, but before the month was out, he was a POW. He wound up in a camp in eastern Germany for the bitter winter of 1944–45. In late January 1945, as the Russians were advancing from the east, Guy's German captors forced all 1,500 air force prisoners to march for three weeks.

"I think it was nineteen or twenty below and it was very cold," Guy remembers. "We crossed the Oder River. The German civilians were fleeing the Russians. Even their little children were bundled up, you could just see their little noses sticking out of their wagons... It was so cold. We used to stop at various farmhouses or state farms. The rations were practically non-existent. That is to say that for 1,500 people they might have 100 loaves of bread or something of that nature, plus an odd tin of soup. It was pretty tough."

Throughout the war, POWs and their captors carried on a risky, sometimes deadly, cat-and-mouse game. The prisoners often felt duty-bound to attempt escape; the captors were determined to thwart these attempts.

Steve Mitchell, with the 2nd Canadian Infantry Division, was wounded and taken prisoner at Dieppe, and after some time in a hospital was sent to Stalag 9C. Having been a trombonist before the war, Mitchell joined a prisoners' band formed by a British bandmaster who had been captured at Dunkirk.

Whenever the Germans made periodic room checks to look for escape tunnels, everyone was ordered out of the room during the search except the band members, who were seated atop an escape hatch, playing "The Blue Danube"—a perennial favourite with the German guards.

Many of the most famous stories come from Stalag Luft III, the setting of *The Great Escape*. Several Canadians were involved in that event. Flight Lieutenant Tony Pengelly from Toronto created maps and forged documents. Another Torontonian, Ray Silver, was one of those who drew lots to determine the "lucky" fifty who would go. He lost—but lived.

Stalag Luft III was a large and busy place. When it opened in 1942, it held several hundred Allied prisoners. By February 1945, the population was more than 10,000. In the decades since the war, there have been many books and magazine articles on the place, usually written from the limited perspective of a small group of Allied prisoners who had little knowledge of the adventures of other groups.

One of the more recent such books, published in the United States in 1988, was called *Stalag Luft III, The Secret Story*. It was written by Arthur A. Durand, a member of the U.S. Army Air Force and a lecturer on history and military affairs. Going through the book's 412 pages, one would never suspect there were ever any Canadians at Stalag Luft III, except for a passing remark attributed to Friedrich-Wilhelm Von Lindeiner-Wildau, commandant at Stalag Luft III. The commandant is quoted as saying the Canadians were "rather pleasant fellows."

Late in 1944, along the border between Belgium and Holland, the mechanized infantry of the North Bay Algonquin Regiment was pursuing the Germans. Among the Algonquins was rifleman Fred Weegar. One night he was told, "We're going in on a little night attack, the armour can't come in with us. They said there's nothing in there, just some second-rate German troops, blah, blah, blah. I'm saying there's tank motors over there and they aren't Shermans. No, no, they said, there's no German armour around here for miles and miles.

"So we get in this little town in the middle of the night, nice and quiet. German troops are walking up and down the street with their girlfriends and what have you... Then all hell broke loose, and there's Tigers and self-propelled guns. We're in the middle of it, and our tanks can't come in. Three companies all told. There had to be fifty or sixty captured, including me... One thing about Canadian forces that was terrible was our Intelligence. They were bloody awful to say the least."

In one of the POW camps, somewhere in northern Holland, the German sergeant who was head of the guard came from Woodstock, Ontario. "He had taken his wife over to Germany in 1939 for an operation and they conscripted him. Both of them were of German descent. She wanted to go back to Germany for this operation and he took her. He never got out again. Oh, he hated them with a passion. He was an older man, he had to be in his fifties then. This is why he was on guard duty at this camp. An awful nice man, spoke perfect English. I never saw him again after we left there."

The last camp Weegar was in was Luft 8C, near Frankfurt, "right across the road from Stalag Luft III—you know, 'The Great Escape.'" He says it was a "retaliation camp" for non-commissioned officers, corporal and up.

"This was in December. They'd roust you out for roll-call at two o'clock in the morning in the snow, because there were reports that we had their prisoners in Italy in tents, blah, blah, blah. It was a pain in the ass. They'd throw all your straw ticks out and you'd sleep on the bare boards, and there weren't many of them. You wound up with one for your calves and legs, and one under your ass, and one under your head. All the rest were burned to get some heat in the bloody place...

"In 8C, there were many men who had been prisoners for years— English and a lot of South Africans, who had been captured in Benghazi and Tobruk and El Alamein. Such men were always attempting to escape and asking others, 'Do you want to sit on the escape committee?' 'Forget it,' I said. 'You want to be here another ten years?' they said. But we knew the war was over. It was just a matter of time. Even the Germans knew it. But these guys had been POWs for years, they were so used to the German army being powerful, they couldn't see it. Every place they'd been, they had been overrun."

When Fred Weegar got back to Canada, not long after VE Day, he was sent to the Canadian National Exhibition grounds (still an army installation then). An officer lined them up one day and announced over a microphone, "You've got two choices. You either sign up to go fight the Japanese, or you're gonna be sent up to one of those training units and you'll be there for the rest of your goddam life!"

At this point, a general arrived and asked the officer, "What do you think you're doing?"

"Getting volunteers from these men."

"These men are POWs, just back," said the general. "Don't you know the Geneva Convention? They cannot fight in any other theatre of war. They're through. I want every man here out, with his discharge papers in his hand, paid, before 12 o'clock."

Added Weegar, "You never saw the army move so fast in your goddam life. We were out that day."

*

Back home, Canadians played host to about 30,000 Axis prisoners of war. One Canadian encyclopedia refers to them as "German and Italian prisoners of war." But unless you count fifty to seventy-five Italian merchant seamen who were held in Canadian POW camps (mostly in Espanola, Ontario) after their ship was captured near Quebec City in 1940, they were all German. However, Canadian officials made no distinction between POWs and internees, who were Italian Canadians suspected of enemy activity.

For reasons best known to the government of Canada, Alberta played host to the greatest number of German prisoners of war—about 26,000 of them, mostly in camps near Lethbridge and Medicine Hat. In Ontario, as well as Espanola and Gravenhurst, there were POW camps at Bowmanville, Kingston, Monteith, and Kitchener. But even their combined population couldn't match that of Alberta.

From time to time the newspapers carried stories about the coddling of enemy prisoners. One of them, published just as the war in Europe was ending, told the story of four German officers, inmates of a POW camp near Montreal, who went to a tavern and had a few beers. They were hustled out by Veterans Guards just in time to avoid a riot. The Germans, it seems, had been allowed to go into Montreal because one of them wanted to have new eyeglasses fitted. Their "guard," who had joined the Germans for a beer, was later arrested.

John Melady tells the story of a POW who heard a cheering crowd in Gravenhurst, Ontario. The townspeople were celebrating VE Day. The prisoner asked one of the guards what all the noise was about and the guard told him the war in Europe was over. The prisoner asked: "Who won?"

Although there were probably various exceptions, German POWs in Canada had a somewhat easier time than Canadian prisoners in Germany—in some cases, even easier than Canadian civilians. Austrian Frank Hofer was a POW at Espanola, Ontario, beginning in 1940. The prison camp was set up in an abandoned pulp-and-paper mill and Hofer remembers "the treatment was very fair... We had lots of food in the camp... I would definitely say we ate better than many of the people in the town." Occasionally, during road construction, Hofer and his fellow prisoners gave their sandwiches to the Canadian truck drivers to help feed their families.

This was an unusual example of camaraderie. POWs were usually treated with contempt by civilians. When the first German prisoners left the train at Gravenhurst on their way to the POW camp nearby, townspeople taunted them as they were marched through the streets. Knowing the POWs were within earshot, the English pianist aboard the SS *Sagamo* played "There'll Always Be an England" whenever the steamer passed the camp. And on at least two occasions early in the war, local cottagers helped track down and recapture German POWs.

Perhaps the biggest difficulty faced by many German prisoners was the fanaticism of the Gestapo prisoners among them. These hard-line Nazi supporters dominated their less enthusiastic fellow prisoners. No talk of defeatism was tolerated. The Gestapo men even managed to censor whatever news was available, so that the "weaklings" would hear no news of German setbacks overseas. In some cases, defeatists or, heaven forbid, anti-Nazis were dealt with severely. A few dissidents may have been murdered.

In late 1944, when he was eighteen years old, Torontonian Jack Stoddard was called up to serve in the armed forces. He didn't report for duty until January 1945. He took his training at Camp Borden, in the Armoured Corps, but once the war ended, he wound up as a guard at several POW camps.

He remembers that at Seebe, Alberta, a small camp with perhaps 500 prisoners, a lot of them were SS troops. The prisoners did their own cooking and he adds, "I'm still envious... When I'd go through that kitchen, I'd think, oh, I wish I could sit down and have a meal there. It was just lovely. I can still smell the meat being cooked on the great big stove. And our stuff was just...no comparison."

During the winter of 1945–46, Stoddard was transferred to the Ontario POW camp at Monteith, which had previously been an internment camp. He remembers it as a bigger camp. He recalls being assigned to meet a trainload of prisoners in the dead of winter. "Three o'clock in the morning the train was due in Monteith, thirty-five below zero, and that's Fahrenheit, oh, cold, cold, cold.

"They came in off the trains and they were herded into this great big building where there were all these tables set up, wooden tables, and they were searched. Everything they had in their possession was put on these tables—cigarettes, lighters, watches... [They had] things that they could order from the Eaton's catalogue—beautiful shirts never worn, still in their packages...beautiful dressing gowns..."

Another Canadian soldier who guarded German POWs has similar memories. He is Wendell Sharp, one of four brothers who served in the Canadian Army during the war. For a time, Wendell was attached to the Veterans Guard, in charge of some 500 German prisoners at a camp in northern Ontario. The POWs were put to work and were paid so much a cord for cutting pulpwood. They used their money to order all sorts of items from Eaton's catalogue.

Wendell Sharp was the only black Canadian at that POW camp and at first the Germans looked at him as apprehensively as he viewed them. But they were mostly Rommel's desert troops, Sharp remembers, seasoned soldiers but not arrogant Nazis. "We got along fine," says Sharp. In fact, two POWs that he knows of came back to Canada after the war and settled in Toronto.

"They spoke pretty good English," says Sharp, "and we understood each other. I got reprimanded once. We were coming out of the bush and I was eating an apple and one of the prisoners was carrying my rifle."

According to the Geneva Convention, prisoners of war could be put to work (not officers, though). Most prisoners considered work preferable to sitting around waiting for meals or lights out. The Canadian government used their work to defray the costs of running the POW camps. Prisoners who were sent to nearby farms to work—there was, after all, a severe shortage of labour—were paid fifty cents a day. But the farmers hiring the working prisoners paid out $2.25 a day.

Farmers in the Niagara peninsula area of Ontario employed German POWs to dig peat moss for the market gardens and orchards of the region. The prisoners were paid for their toil, but they never bargained for the harassment that regularly descended from the heavens. Instructors from Dunnville's No. 6 Service Flying Training School used the flatlands of the peat bog as a low-flying practice area, just to rattle the POWs. Although the practice was strictly forbidden, RCAF pilot Ted Arnold explained, "We couldn't shoot the Germans up in real life, so we decided to 'shoot them up' by flying low over the bog.

"One day Wiley Stone, an instructor friend, was flying formation with me," recalls Arnold. "Well, we went down low over the bog where the Germans were digging. But they were fed up with this, so this one chap threw his spade up at us. Wiley was flying so low that it hit his wing. It made a hell of a dent."

Some of the German prisoners in this country had dreams of escape. Such attempts were more daring and more desperate on this side of the Atlantic. An Allied POW could hope to find help in occupied France or Belgium or Holland. But a German POW in Canada had little hope of finding any underground or freedom fighter eager to give him food and shelter.

Nevertheless, because it is the nature of incarcerated men to long for freedom, there were numerous attempts to escape from Canadian prison camps. Most of them failed.

The most notorious was the case of one Franz von Werra, a Luftwaffe Oberleutnant who was shot down in England in September 1940. In January 1941 he arrived in Halifax, along with many other German POWs, and was put on a train bound for a camp on the north shore of Lake Superior. He and another German flyer managed to jump the train near Smiths Falls, Ontario, about sixty-five kilometres north of the St. Lawrence River. The other prisoner was quickly captured, but von Werra got to the river, hoping to cross it to "safety"— the United States was not yet in the war.

After a determined attempt to find sanctuary in the States, he was picked up in Ogdensburg, New York. Von Werra, who could speak English quite well, offered no resistance, but asked that he be returned to Germany. The Ogdensburg police instead arrested him and charged him with vagrancy.

Von Werra's case received full coverage in newspapers on both sides of the border. Germany demanded that he be returned, since the United States was not involved in the war. Canada wanted him back. In the end, the Germans got him to Texas, then to Mexico, then to South America. In a matter of months, von Werra was back flying for the Luftwaffe. He was soon killed in a plane crash over Holland.

Not all the German POWs in Canada tried to escape. About 6,000 of them asked permission to stay in Canada after the war. Permission was denied. David J. Carter, who delved into the subject quite exhaustively, estimates that about 1,000 of the German POWs later settled in Canada—where, they claimed, things were a lot better than they had been in Germany, even though they had been prisoners here.

6

"You'll Get Used To It"

The spring of 1940 was Britain's darkest hour of the war. The massive defeat at Dunkirk, the increasing likelihood that Hitler would attempt an invasion of the British Isles, the fear of possible fifth-column espionage—all these factors combined to prompt the British government to take drastic measures. As panic began to spread, close to 30,000 refugees from Nazi Germany and Austria were interned in Britain as "enemy aliens." Churchill had given the order to "collar the lot."

Since Hitler's rise to power, more than 70,000 German and Austrian refugees—many, but not all of them, Jews—had fled to Britain. At the outbreak of the war, the British government classified "enemy aliens" into three categories: Category A aliens were considered "dangerous"; Category B meant "not dangerous but not trustworthy"; and Category C aliens were to be exempt from internment.

However, the fears of a German invasion changed all that. Internment was not enough. To protect Britain from any fifth-column activity in the event of an invasion, Churchill wanted to get "enemy aliens" out of the country altogether. He mentioned a figure of 20,000 internees to be exiled. Representations were made to the Canadian government, through Canada's High Commissioner, Vincent Massey, asking that the Canadian government accept 7,000 prisoners of war and dangerous enemy aliens. (Others were sent to Australia.)

At first, the Canadian government was reluctant to accept, but after further discussions, agreed to take in 7,000 men (women were excluded). However, it turned out that the United Kingdom had only 3,000

102

German prisoners of war and 2,500 Category A (dangerous alien) internees on hand. Rather than admit its miscalculations, the government simply lumped Category B or C aliens in with the "dangerous" aliens and POWs.

On July 2, 1940, the *Arandora Star* left Liverpool carrying 1,600 men, a mixture of German POWs and Italian and German or Austrian refugees. The ship was attacked by a German U-boat. More than 600 people, most of them refugees, were killed.

Altogether, about 2,200 Jewish refugees interned in England were sent to Canada and served anywhere from a few months to three years in one or another (sometimes more than one) of the eight camps set up, mostly in eastern Canada—New Brunswick, Quebec, and Ontario.

Their experiences were documented in two Canadian films—Harry Rasky's *The Spies Who Never Were* and Neal Livingston's *Both Sides of the Wire*—and such books as Eric Koch's *Deemed Suspect* and Henry Kreisel's *Another Country*.

One of the first writers to speak out against the injustices was François Lafitte, whose first book, *The Internment of Aliens*, was published in 1940. "One of the very first things that our government did," explained Lafitte, "was to turn upon people originating from Germany and Austria and other countries controlled by the Nazis, label them as enemy aliens, and begin to intern them on the grounds that they might be dangerous to our cause. This seemed not only to me but to a great number of people in Britain to be a betrayal of all the values for which we were fighting. Therefore, a matter for protest."

Helmut Blume, who eventually became dean of the Faculty of Music at McGill University, was at Cambridge when he was arrested. He had just returned from a railway station, where he had gone to meet a girlfriend who had come from London to have lunch with him.

"When I returned to the college, the headmaster told me, 'There is a policeman waiting for you.' I wasn't surprised, because I thought sooner or later it probably would happen. And then I asked him (the policeman) whether I could at least have lunch with my girlfriend, and he said, 'No, I'm afraid not. I'm sure, sir...it's all a misunderstanding and you'll be back within a very short time, twenty-four hours at the most. Just take a toothbrush.'

"I got back seven years later."

Rabbi Emil Fackenheim, who had been in a German concentration camp from 1938 to 1939 before getting into Britain, was arrested in Aberdeen.

"A nice Scottish policeman comes and says... 'I am sorry, sir, but you have to come with me for a little while.' I said, 'Say no more... Just give me half an hour to pack my things.' So I was thinking, what books do I need? I still remember [taking] some philosophy books in Greek with English translation, Loeb Classical Library. [I thought] at last I'll have time to study some Greek again, you know, after those many years. So he said, 'Oh sir, you won't need all that.' I said, 'Look, you know your business and I know mine.' I took forty books and it wasn't nearly enough, you know, for the year and a half."

Walter Loevinsohn, another Jewish refugee, remembers that anti-Semitism was part of his welcome to Canada. A Canadian officer boarded the ship he was on (the *Ettrick*) and the English intelligence officer pointed out the various passengers to him. "Over there, there are 1,000 prisoners of war: soldiers, sailors, airmen; very good troops. In the stern, there are 800 Italian civilian internees: they're no trouble at all. Over there"—and he pointed to the Jewish refugees—"these people, they're the scum of Europe."

"Canadians expected very dangerous people with poison pills and daggers and everything," remembers E. M. Oppenheimer, later a professor of German at Carleton University. "So we were searched. And they found in my possession a bottle of aspirin. They took it away and they comforted me by saying—well, I don't know how comforting they wanted to be—they said, 'You won't get any headaches in Canada.'"

When he landed at Quebec City, Viennese Jew Edgar Lion remembers: "We were taken to a railway station and we had to go through some streets with a population who thought that we were German prisoners of war. [They] were cursing us and spitting at us and throwing stones. It was a very hostile reaction by the populace."

Canada was a bewildering place to most of the refugees. Eric Koch remembers a Major O'Donahoe at Camp N, near Sherbrooke, Quebec, whose penchant for slang baffled the internees. He told the assembled refugees that he wouldn't stand for any "monkey business," a phrase unfamiliar to them. Then the major announced, "If you play ball, I will play ball. If you won't play ball, I won't play ball." They didn't understand why he wanted to play ball with them. From then on, he was referred to as "Major Balls."

The internees had a big patch of red fabric sewn on the backs of their uniforms, and a thick red stripe down the right leg of their uniforms—to make them easier targets for the guards, should one of them try to escape. Very few tried—there was nowhere to go.

The refugees were in the care of the Veterans Guard, mostly First World War veterans. At Camp L, near Quebec City, Koch remembers the guards as "sub-human...without teeth, in their sixties... And they were corrupt. That was the nice thing about them, you could buy them with a few cigarettes and pornography. Oscar Cahén...was an illustrator, he had this marvellous gift with the pen, could do girls, did a few nudes. For that, guards would do anything." (Cahén went on to become a pioneer of modern art in Canada.)

The arts were well represented in Canada's internment camps: musician Helmut Blume, pianist John Newmark, architect Eric Fisher, art historian William Heckscher, violinist Hans Kaufman, Helmut Kallmann, co-editor of *The Encyclopedia of Music in Canada* and a member of the Order of Canada, and writers Henry Kreisel and Eric Koch were interned. Five of the German or Austrian Jews who were interned in Canada during the war subsequently were awarded the Order of Canada.

And then there was Freddy Grundland, later known as Freddy Grant. Freddy was nineteen years old, living with his family in Berlin, when Hitler came to power. His father was a well-to-do Jewish businessman who, naively, thought Hitler wouldn't last. Freddy thought otherwise, and begged his father to give him money to get to England. The father refused, so Freddy, who was already a published songwriter, sold whatever he had and went to England.

"The [immigration] guy said, 'How long are you going to stay?' I said, 'Oh, maybe a couple of weeks.' I knew I wasn't going to leave, because he didn't know what I knew. He didn't know Hitler was going to kill six million Jews."

Freddy established a good reputation in popular music circles in London. He wrote songs for such established stars of the time as Gracie

Fields, Jessie Matthews, and band leader Ray Noble. One of his songs ("How Can You Buy Killarney?") was recorded by Bing Crosby.

When the war broke out, he was within a week of being eligible to apply for citizenship in Britain, and on the verge of signing a two-year contract with a music publisher. When the newspapers carried headlines about interning all aliens, the publisher backed away from the contract.

Freddy was interned and sent to a camp at Huyton, near Liverpool. Before long, he was on his way to Canada, where he was first interned at Camp Q, Monteith, in northern Ontario. From there he was transferred, along with others, to Camp A, at Farnham, Quebec.

During his time in internment camps, the authorities discovered that Freddy was a musician and composer, so he was encouraged to put on shows to entertain the other inmates. This was when he wrote his most famous song, "You'll Get Used To It," which was about life in an internment camp.

> You'll get used to it, you'll get used to it,
> The first year is the worst year,
> Then you get used to it,
> You can scream and you can shout
> They will never let you out,
> It serves you right, you so-and-so,
> Why aren't you a naturalized Eskimo?
> Just tell yourself it's marvellous
> You get to like it more and more and more
> You've got to get used to it
> And when you're used to it
> You'll feel just as lousy as you did before.

The song was not only a hit in the camp show, but all over the camp—even the guards were singing it.

Freddy's father, having belatedly recognized the threat of Nazism, had left Germany and, after considerable travelling, got to Montreal. He helped get Freddy released from Farnham.

Once he was out, Freddy stayed for a time in Montreal and tried to re-establish his credentials as a musician/composer. He was invited to a party by friends who had heard some of his songs, and was encouraged to perform for the other guests, including actors John Pratt and Robert Goodier from a Montreal revue called *The Tin Hats.*

Freddy Grant sang "You'll Get Used To It," and Goodier, among others, urged Pratt to use the song. A New York producer at the party told Pratt that if he used Freddy's song, the producer would take the show to New York. Pratt, somewhat reluctantly, agreed.

Nothing ever came of the New York production, but before too long Pratt and his two colleagues were involved in *Meet The Navy,* the Royal Canadian Navy show. Pratt introduced the song—with some additional lyrics—and it became the hit of the show. Later, Pratt was vague about the origins of the song and allowed (if not encouraged) the press to credit him with originating it. In an interview, Pratt mentioned that it had been written "by a German citizen who had never taken out his papers," but he didn't mention Freddy's name.

But Freddy Grant didn't care. By the time the navy show was a hit, he was in Toronto, playing in various clubs and, later, starting a series of music schools, both in Toronto and Montreal. He remembers, if vaguely, seeing *Meet The Navy* during its Toronto run. Did he think Pratt was good in the show?

"Yeah...well, he sang my song."

Many of the German and Austrian Jews who were interned and sent to Canada look back on the experience with rather more gratitude than bitterness. Their reasoning is simple enough: however unjust it was, the "collar-the-lot" policy of Churchill got them away from the war and, eventually, gave them the chance to start new and, in many cases, more rewarding lives in Canada.

However, the first step, getting out of the internment camps, was not always easy. You had to have a sponsor, someone who would vouch for a released internee. The Canadian Jewish community was not particularly swift in coming to the aid of the refugees. And government red tape slowed down the process even more.

After the war, about half of the internees went back to Britain and the other half stayed in Canada, where many of them became successful and distinguished.

Along with the German and Austrian Jews who were exiled to Canada, there were also a few hundred Italians—the merchant seamen captured and taken to England, as well as some Category A and B refugees, including a scattering of Italian Jews.

But many Italian Canadians were also interned. Government policy, announced at the outbreak of war, gave the minister of justice authority to detain or intern "enemy aliens." This policy became especially oppressive when Italy entered the war in June 1940.

At the time, the population of Canada included 112,000 persons of Italian origin. More than one half had been born in Canada, and another 42,000 had become Canadian citizens. More than ninety per cent of those described as having Italian roots were Canadians either by birth or by choice.

The National Congress of Italian Canadians, even now, cannot state with precision how many Italian Canadians were interned. Somewhere between 600 and 700 were sent to four camps: one in Petawawa, Ontario, one on St. Helen's Island, Quebec; and two in Fredericton, New Brunswick. Not one of those interned was ever charged with any act of sabotage or disloyalty.

Oswald Giacomelli was born in Canada. He went to Italy with his family in 1930 and returned to Canada in 1939 to work on a railroad. On June 13, 1940, the police came to arrest him while he was sleeping. He was sent to Oakville, then to a Hamilton jail for two days and later to the Don Jail in Toronto, where he remained for a month. He was imprisoned in Camp Petawawa, and in 1943 he was transferred to one of the camps in Fredericton for another two and a half years. He was under arrest for more than five years.

Giacomelli, who was a Canadian citizen, recalls that one of the worst aspects of all this was the derision to which he and other internees were subjected. While he was at the CNE grounds, he and other internees were paraded on the streets while people shouted and swore at them, calling them "aliens."

Dominic Nardocchio was arrested on June 10, 1940, a few hours after Italy entered the war. RCMP officers went to his shop and took him home to tell his wife he was being taken away. From there he was brought to a city jail where there were no beds. Later the officers brought in a few men who appeared to be drunk. One of these men said, "Let's do what we're here to do," and started beating one of the detainees. The officers watched but did not intervene.

The next morning the detainees were served breakfast from rusted metal tins, then taken to a train and loaded onto five cars, each one holding about 200 people. Nardocchio was interned at Petawawa for twenty-one months.

The same day Nardocchio was arrested, so were twenty-three-year-old Anthony Danesi and his twenty-six-year-old brother Peter. Twelve RCMP officers took them into custody where they worked. Anthony says, "We were taken to our home only to find two more officers waiting for us.

"My mother at the time was over sixty years old and when she heard they were taking us away, fainted from the shock. We were told, 'Do not touch her, leave her there.' We could not even lift her up on to a chair, a small woman of 100 pounds. This to me was a very inhuman thing; even a dog would have been treated better."

The Danesi brothers spent just over two years interned at Camp Petawawa. During this period, a younger brother was called up by the Canadian Army.

These stories and many more were assembled by the National Congress of Italian Canadians in January 1990 as part of a presentation to the Canadian government, seeking redress for these injustices suffered by Canadians of Italian origin. Despite promises of action, nothing happened.

Arguably the greatest injustice perpetrated by Canada against Canadians was the forced relocation of 23,000 Japanese Canadians—many of them born in this country—and the confiscation and subsequent resale of their property after the Japanese attack on Pearl Harbor in December 1941. The fact is that just as there was anti-Semitism before Hitler in Germany, there was anti-Oriental feeling in Canada well before the Second World War.

Vancouver-born Norman Campbell was a student at the University of British Columbia in 1942 when he gradually became aware that his Japanese-Canadian friends were no longer coming to classes.

"I was sad to see my friends sort of disappearing, friends I had had in school and in university, with Japanese names, who just didn't turn up, and I never knew that they were consciously being moved into the interior. I was quite unaware of that, just didn't see them around. The papers kept it quiet."

Toyo Takata is the son of Japanese-born parents who had settled in Esquimalt, B.C., where Toyo was born in 1920. The Takatas were the only Japanese family in Esquimalt, which even then was a naval base. Toyo was the only Japanese-Canadian student in his grade school.

"One of the funny things," says Toyo, "is that when two boys would start a fight in the school yard, the kids would yell: 'Scrap, scrap, a Nigger and a Jap,' despite the fact that "there were no blacks [in the school] and I was the only so-called Jap. And I never got into fights." Years later, Toyo learned that the expression originated in the British navy and had been picked up by those at the Esquimalt base, obviously sometime early in the 1920s.

At first, *The Vancouver Sun* struck a sensible, tolerant note on December 8, 1941, the day the news of Pearl Harbor stunned the world. The newspaper ran a front-page editorial headlined "Citizens, Be Calm," which included this admirable bit of logic:

"We have in this province nearly 25,000 Japanese, many of them Canadian-born. These latter, and the overwhelming majority of the former, are intensely loyal to Canada. They have nothing to do with the policies of imperial Japan; they are not in sympathy with those policies, and if our regulations allowed it their young men would be in uniform against the Axis to which Japan belongs."

But the fear—and the racism—prevailed. The same day's *Sun* carried a story announcing "emergency measures" already being instituted by the RCMP, including internment of all "undesirable" Japanese, tying up of every Japanese-owned fishing boat in British Columbia, closing of all Japanese-language schools, and banning all newspapers printed in Japanese.

That there was fear is undeniable. Two weeks after Pearl Harbor, there was talk of evacuating masses of population from British Columbia's coast. The *Sun* again tried to argue for calm and good sense. "There is not the slightest justification of alarmist forecasts of imminent attacks on Vancouver. Spaced at intervals, perhaps months hence, we may in truth be subjected to occasional bombing attacks. We had better be ready for it. But any idea that there is cause for a wholesale evacuation, or a desertion of our cities and countryside ought to be rejected at once." Nevertheless, some British Columbians did send their children away from the coast—to Banff or farther east— just to be safe.

Letters to the editor (not always a reliable barometer of public opinion, since the paper can choose which letters to print) sounded an alarmist tone. "The threat to the B.C. coast by Japanese should not in the least be minimized. There are approximately 10,000 to 12,000 Japanese of military age, trained and able to follow the orders they have perhaps had months ago from their home office in Japan... They are only waiting for the invaders to get a 'toe-hold' here. In Vancouver and at the mouth of the Fraser there are enough Japanese to make a most formidable show in the event of attack by their pals on the other side..."

Another letter disagreed with the "Citizens, Be Calm" editorial. "This is no time for silly sentiment—round them all up and intern them, or send them back to Japan. There can be no half-measures if we expect to win this war."

The fear, justified or not, persisted. One Vancouverite (talking to author Barry Broadfoot) recalled a schoolday when the teacher dismissed the Japanese kids from the class. Then, when there were "just the white and English kids left," she told them that Japan was at war with Canada and that it was well known that when the Japanese soldiers attacked, the Japanese people in the town or country would come out and help them. The teacher advised the thirteen-year-olds to "keep a close watch" on the Japanese kids in the class.

Dick and Marie Dee, who were living in Vancouver during 1942, remember the blackouts, the fear, the rumours of imminent invasion— especially after the Japanese landed in two of the Aleutian Islands. "I often wonder," says Marie, "if they had landed in and around Vancouver, how many of those Japanese who were rounded up and taken away, how many of them would have joined the Japs. That was the scary part."

By January 1942, *The Vancouver Sun* had abandoned its calm stance and hopped on the lock-them-all-up bandwagon. "Wherever the Japanese soldiers attack," said one editorial, "there we may expect Japanese civilians to do all in their power to assist the attackers." And a couple of weeks later, when the federal government approved the idea of removing all Japanese from the B.C. coast, the paper applauded the decision in a front-page editorial headed: "Here Was a Common-Sense Decision."

"Under advice of Mayor Hume's Standing Committee on the Japanese, endorsed by the unanimous opinion of Premier Hart and the provincial government and backed by informed public opinion roused by editorials in *The Vancouver Sun*, the federal government has taken a firm step in dealing with the Japanese problem of this coast."

And so, fear triumphed over tolerance.

Dick Arai's father ran a small chicken farm outside New Westminster, B.C. Dick was fourteen years old then, and he still remembers the RCMP coming to their little rented house, not long after Japan entered the war, and telling the Arais they had twenty-four hours to pack up and be ready to go.

"I remember my Dad says, 'Well, we'd better start packing up.' We had a chicken farm, so we had to either get somebody to look after it, or get rid of it. And I remember my Dad saying, 'The chance of coming back here is going to be very small, so let's liquidate everything.' Well, I remember we got next to nothing for the chickens at that time, because [people] knew the position we were in."

The Arai family—parents and seven children—were sent to Kaslo, a village seventy kilometres north of Nelson, B.C. (964 Japanese Canadians were interned there in 1942). They were housed in an old hotel—twelve to a room. Soon, families were split up so that twelve men could occupy one room and twelve women another. Men sixteen years or older were put to work, chopping wood, clearing roads. At first, they were paid twenty-five cents an hour, but soon the RCMP decided that was too expensive, so the pay was cut to ten cents an hour.

The room in which Dick's mother lived was directly above the hotel boiler room, and fumes came up into the room. Mrs. Arai became ill from the fumes and was taken to hospital in Kaslo. When she recovered, "The doctor said, 'If she goes back to that room she's going to get the same condition again.' My father said, 'Gee, maybe we should move,' but there was no place to move to, and before he knew it she got sick again and she went back to the hospital and...she died." She was forty-nine years old.

The Arais stayed at Kaslo until spring 1945. Today, Dick says they were luckier than those who had to go to work camps in Alberta and Manitoba. Dick's family moved east to Ontario in 1945.

Vic Shoji was born in Vancouver in 1939. He was three years old when his father's packaging business was confiscated and his family was interned at Minto Mines, B.C. They were there until 1945, when they moved to Revelstoke. "I have some memories of living up there [at Minto Mines]. It was very, very small, I can only remember about a couple of dozen houses being there. It had been a ghost town when we moved up there. It wasn't fenced or anything. I don't recall any surveillance...

"Nobody had jobs up there, there was no industry there to support anybody. I don't know how we survived... But even as we got older, I never remember hearing my parents talk about it, the internment or anything like that. I don't recall any bitter words spoken from my parents about what happened to them... I don't know why my Dad chose Revelstoke, maybe it was a smaller community or he thought it would be too difficult to start over in Vancouver. People then were racially discriminating against Japanese, [but] my parents didn't talk about that at all."

Toyo Takata's family, along with thousands of others, were herded into Hastings Park (now known as Exhibition Park) in spring 1942. Takata recalled Hastings Park in his book, *Nikkei Legacy*. "For the early arrivals, the Park was ill-prepared and a chaotic mess. Women and children were assigned to the livestock building which had not been properly cleaned or made sanitary. Dried manure was scraped off to make the quarters more habitable, but the distasteful smell lingered. Ventilation was inadequate and thick dust floated in the stale air. Privacy was non-existent until they improvised with sheets and curtains; the latrines (not flush toilets) lacked partitions until they protested...

"Some white staff within the compound exploited the situation. Gambling was prohibited, but big-stake games continued openly with a member of the supervisory staff collecting a rake-off. For those willing to pay to supplement their lacklustre diet, an underground

Japanese eatery operated within, with the covert sanction of an official, since supplies had to pass inspection at the gate and coal for cooking had to be diverted from the furnace bin. A guard or two attempted to take physical liberties with women."

After leaving Hastings Park, Toyo Takata went to Slocan, B.C., a former mining town that had been turned into an internment centre. His parents, meanwhile, went to another camp at Sandon. Eventually, they all moved east to Ontario.

When the expulsion began, and able-bodied men were taken away to work camps, many Japanese Canadians realized that the best way to keep their families together would be to leave the province and go to Alberta to work on sugar-beet farms. About 2,600 Japanese Canadians worked on Alberta farms during the war. Another 1,000 went to Manitoba, where they were treated somewhat better than those in Alberta.

In the sugar-beet fields of Alberta, the work was hard, the hours were long. Every worker, young or old, man or woman, was out in the open all day, hot or cold. Worst of all was the rush to finish the harvest before freeze-up.

One of nine children, Tsutomu ("Stum") Shimizu was born in Victoria in 1922. His father died in 1940 and it fell to the mother to look after the family. When the war and the relocation split up the family, Tsutomu and three of his brothers wound up at Camp Black, near Schreiber, Ontario, north of Lake Superior. Camp Black was an abandoned work camp out in the woods. The internees fixed it up, built beds, and dug latrines.

A month later, the Ontario government moved many of the Japanese Canadians to farm areas in southern Ontario. Tsutomu and one of his brothers were sent to Glencoe. "We were housed in the fairgrounds... Farmers would ask for five or twenty men, and they'd come and pick us up. I think the farmers paid the authorities and then we were paid twenty-five cents an hour... But the month of June, we couldn't work the whole month, it just rained and rained. We were sent down there specifically to help with the sugar-beets. It's really backbreaking work. In Ontario, they only used those short hoes... A lot of us owed money because we paid room and board for a whole month without work..."

Shimizu, like many other Canadian-born Japanese, made several attempts to join the Canadian Army but was repeatedly rejected. It wasn't until very late in the war that he succeeded.

Maryka Omatsu, born in Canada of Japanese-Canadian parents, has been active in the fight for redress. In a moving book titled *Bittersweet Passage*, she writes about the struggles of her parents during and since the Second World War.

At one point, her father applied to the RCMP for a permit to travel to another town to look for work. The Mountie doing the paperwork, unfamiliar with Japanese names, misspelled his surname. "Later, when officials asked my father to show his identification papers and found the wrong name," she writes, "my father was thrown into jail, without a trial, for 'travelling without authority.'"

In Japanese-Canadian circles, the name of Tom Shoyama is spoken with reverence. Born in Kamloops, B.C., he graduated from the University of British Columbia in the spring of 1938. That summer he was one of three young Japanese Canadians who started a new Nisei newspaper in Vancouver. *The New Canadian* was published weekly in English and Japanese. Less than a year later, Shoyama was the paper's editor.

When the war started, Shoyama, like many other young Japanese Canadians, tried to enlist in the armed forces. All were rebuffed. The Japanese Canadian Citizens League appealed to Ottawa, but the King government, under severe pressure from British Columbian political and business interests, denied the pleas of Canadian-born Japanese to be allowed to take part in the war.

Even though Japan was not yet involved in the war, by March 1941 all Japanese residents of British Columbia had to be registered. Shoyama and *The New Canadian* continued to push for the right of Japanese Canadians to join the armed forces. By the fall of 1941, a handful of stubborn Japanese Canadians had succeeded in enlisting.

The day after the attack on Pearl Harbor, the three Japanese papers were shut down. Only *The New Canadian*, which was published in both English and Japanese, was permitted to continue. It soon became a tri-weekly, and Shoyama walked an editorial tight-rope from then on—on the one hand urging Japanese Canadians to continue demonstrating their loyalty to Canada, on the other trying to speak out on behalf of the Japanese-Canadian community without getting into trouble with the B.C. authorities.

There was a serious rift among Japanese Canadians. The "gambari" (holdouts) urged resistance to the government policy of evacuating male Japanese of military age (eighteen to forty-five) and separating them from their families. They demanded "mass evacuation"—keeping families together. But their stubborn stand was doomed to fail.

On the other hand, the Japanese Canadian Citizens Council, backed by Tom Shoyama and *The New Canadian*, argued that the best way for Japanese Canadians to prove their loyalty to Canada was to comply with the government's policy.

Frank Moritsugu grew up in the Kitsilano area of Vancouver and had been editor of his high-school paper. His parents were very much pro-Canada. Before he even started kindergarten in Vancouver, he remembers, "we had a piano in the house. Mom taught me to sing 'God Save the King' and 'The Maple Leaf Forever.'" Within two weeks after Pearl Harbor, at nineteen, he went to work for *The New Canadian* under Tom Shoyama. But in April 1942, Frank and the rest of his family were sent to a camp near Revelstoke, B.C. The following year, Frank got a letter from Tom Shoyama inviting him to rejoin *The New Canadian*, which had moved inland to Kaslo.

The paper was censored, but Tom Shoyama's handling of the delicate situation "was quite marvellous... He pushed cooperation with the evacuation," says Moritsugu, "which gave him room to criticize other things. He knew when he could go to bat. He learned how to straddle quite well."

Moritsugu acknowledges that later, during the 1960s, when overt dissent was tolerated, Shoyama's delicate handling of the Japanese-Canadian situation was considered less courageous. But this was the 1940s, wartime, and the situation of the Japanese Canadians required delicate manoeuvring to steer clear of the authorities and avoid being shut down. By urging compliance with the evacuation, Shoyama was able to keep a Japanese-Canadian voice alive—and, at times, to criticize the Canadian government's actions in the treatment of Japanese Canadians.

Many B.C. politicians still didn't like *The New Canadian* and took every opportunity to attack the paper and its editor. In 1944, for example, Mayor J. W. Cornett added his voice to those calling for the deportation of all Japanese. *The New Canadian*'s reply: "No matter what the lyrics, Vancouver's mayor blows a Nazi tune." *The Vancouver Sun* promptly defended the mayor and urged the federal government to outlaw *The New Canadian*.

Another staffer of *The New Canadian* was Roy Ito, who, many years later, wrote *We Went to War*, a book about the struggles of the Japanese Canadians to join Canada's armed forces. Ito was one of those who finally succeeded, as did Tom Shoyama, Frank Moritsugu, and Tsutomu Shimizu.

All this was quite late in the war, when Canada finally gave in to the urging of British and Australian military leaders to use Japanese Canadians for interrogating prisoners, handling translation, and other intelligence work. No other country in the Commonwealth had as many citizens who could speak and understand Japanese.

Tsutomu Shimizu was accepted in January 1945. He took his basic training at Brantford, Ontario, where "we were a really celebrated unit... We were called Platoon 17, the only Platoon 17 in the whole of the Canadian Army, because you usually have only sixteen in a battalion. We were a bastard platoon... We marched in the Victory (VE) Day Parade in Brantford. We not only marched, we voted in the Ontario election—but when we got out we couldn't vote."

After basic training, Shimizu was sent to S-20, the Japanese language school in Vancouver operated by the Canadian Army, for training in intelligence work. Shimizu never did go overseas, but remained in the army until June 1946. "But I sure learned a lot of Japanese," he says.

Frank Moritsugu still remembers the problems he had with his parents about wanting to join the Canadian Army. "For the first and only time my Mom asked me to write something for the paper," he says. "She wanted me to write an article [for *The New Canadian*] explaining why I was joining up... To some Japanese, what people think of you is what life is all about. She figured I could explain so others would understand. Some fathers said, 'If you do this, I will never talk to you the rest of your life. Why would you fight for Canada when Canada has done this to us?' I said, 'This was not Canada, this was B.C.'"

Many years later, he found writing about that time a much more wrenching experience. "I tried to personalize it...and I'm typing away and the tears started to come down... And I had to stop... It's weird. Then I came up with the answer. In any of us who is old enough to feel what was happening back then...there are wounds down there, and there are scabs...and we don't touch these scabs if we can help it.

"And this is the basic reason why most Japanese Canadians who went through it never talked about it, never told their kids about it... It's because, psychologically, if you peel away those scabs you might start to bleed again... That's what happened to me. I had become the kid again, and he hurt.

"The sense of betrayal by my country was so acute... I knew all about B.C. attitudes, but we kept thinking our country would not let us down. And when Ottawa didn't stand up for us...I realized how hurt that nineteen-year-old kid was... The emotion is still there. Many Japanese Canadians still don't want to go near it yet, 'cause it hurts. And they don't want to admit it."

Unlike the Japanese Canadians in British Columbia, those living east of the Rockies had an easier time signing up for the forces—at least before Pearl Harbor. David Tsubota, of Montreal, first enlisted in the Royal Canadian Navy in the spring of 1940—the only Nisei to serve in the RCN. But he was discharged three months later, apparently because of his racial origin.

Still, David persisted. He went into the army and was with the one company of the Canadian Black Watch that took part in the Dieppe raid. David Tsubota's group was forced to surrender to the Germans. He spent the next two and a half years as a POW and was shackled for part of that time. When he returned home in the spring of 1945, the scars on his wrists were still visible.

That same spring, Lieutenant-Colonel Cecil Merritt of Vancouver, an acknowledged hero of Dieppe and a Victoria Cross winner, ran for Parliament on the Progressive Conservative ticket. One of his slogans was: "A vote for Merritt is a vote against the Japs."

He won.

7

Covering the War

During the Second World War, Norman Griesdorf grew from childhood to adolescence. His father's nomadic career as a motion picture distributor kept the family constantly on the move throughout the war, from Vancouver to Winnipeg to Toronto to New York. The family was living in Los Angeles when Pearl Harbor was bombed; in fact Griesdorf remembers thinking at the time that their Japanese gardener was planting bombs in the family garden in Hollywood. Griesdorf devoured the war news. "I read the papers avidly every day, and I had maps of the European theatre showing where all the armies were and I was moving them. I had mock airplanes that were all put together and you could handle the controls.

"I could not for the life of me imagine what they were going to have in the newspapers after the war was over. I thought they might have to cut the papers out or certainly cut them down in size. I knew nothing other than war reporting." It was not such an outrageous observation for the time. Certainly, no war in the twentieth century was more fully covered by the newspapers.

There were several reasons for this. The means of communication had improved substantially between the First World War and the Second. There were also more fronts to be covered. Canada had been involved in the defence of Britain, the debacle at Hong Kong, the Dieppe raid, the invasion of Sicily and the fighting in Italy, the invasion of Normandy, the liberation of the Netherlands, and the final conquest of Nazi Germany. More Canadian newspapers had war correspondents on assignment overseas, and Canadian Press, which had been founded in 1918, was by now a full-fledged news-gathering-and-disseminating organization, supplying both metropolitan newspapers and smaller ones across Canada.

The development of radio also increased the coverage of the war. Although the Canadian Broadcasting Corporation did not have a real news department until the beginning of the war, by the time of the Battle of Britain in 1940 Canadian radio listeners had become accustomed to the dolorous voice of Lorne Green reading the CBC's National News. A Winnipeg newspaper described it as "the Voice of Doom," and the appellation stuck to Green throughout the war.

But there was far more to the CBC's coverage of the war than the reading of the nightly news. The CBC Overseas Unit, hastily organized at the outbreak of the war, was in operation by the time Canadian forces first landed in the United Kingdom late in 1939—and kept at it until the last shots were fired in 1945.

Among the most prominent CBC war correspondents were Matthew Halton, Peter Stursberg, and Marcel Ouimet.

Halton's vivid, dramatic reports from North Africa, Italy, and France made him a favourite with Canadian radio listeners. Here is part of one of those broadcasts, from Italy, in December 1943:

"For a long time today we have watched battle... It's quiet now, but you'll hear it. It's incredible that one is here watching a battle and that one should have such a dramatic view of a battle. I see I've timed this badly—I thought there'd be a lot of noises for you right now but there's nothing. Such a view of battle, and on such a gorgeous day, with a warm sun, and the Adriatic dancing in the light. War on such a day seems particularly tragic and unreal. It seems to have no objective reality, even when the enemy shells hit right on top of this O.P. [observation post], as they do sometimes..."

Halton also covered the D-Day invasion of France and managed to bum an airplane ride from the Normandy beaches back to England in order to broadcast, via the BBC studios in London, his impressions of that historic day. His report began:

"This is Matthew Halton of the CBC speaking from England. I came back this morning from France...where our assault formations are ashore and now fighting like wildcats to hold the bridgeheads...against

German generals and German armies who know that in the next few days they either throw us into the sea or lose the war."

Peter Stursberg filed twenty-two reports during the twenty-three days of the Italian offensive. Here is a portion of one of them:

"The attack on the Adolf Hitler line has begun. Canadian infantry-men and Canadian and British tanks are now storming its outer defences. Our troops are being supported by one of the heaviest artillery concentrations of this war. Hundreds of guns have been massed in the Liri Valley here for this attack, which is on a very narrow front. Just listen to those guns roar...

"We're in the attic of an old Italian farmhouse that overlooks the front... Not all the shell fire's on our side; the Germans are replying, but their crumps are some distance away and I doubt if you can hear them above the noise of our guns... Our infantry and tanks should now be assaulting the Hitler Line. The Canadians have been given the hard part of it to crack. The barbed wire in front of the pillboxes is said to be twenty feet thick..."

Marcel Ouimet, a bilingual CBC war correspondent, filed a reflective broadcast about D-Day. It began:

"June 6th—and on the sandy beach of the once-charming but now badly battered village of Bernières-sur-Mer, a Canadian soldier lands. He's had to wade in, waist-deep in the water, to lead the first column of the support company of his battalion to a dry spot.

"His battalion, the Regiment de la Chaudière, is the only French-speaking unit on the assault. The battle has progressed favourably. The other companies are well in command already. A few shells and the odd bullet still are whistling by, but who cares? François has waited four years for this moment and his first words to a friend as he passes by are these: 'C'est beau la France.'"

But vivid as these radio reports were, in the 1940s Canadians tended to rely more on their newspapers for detailed war news. Some of the country's finest journalists served as war correspondents.

A. E. Powley, head of the CBC Overseas Unit, later paid tribute to the war correspondents: "Risk was an undeniable factor. It is a necessary part of a war correspondent's job to stay alive so that he can tell his story. But that necessity frequently has to be weighed against the value of the story, and many a correspondent, whether for the CBC or any-body else, often took his life in his hands for the sake of the job to be done."

Nine Canadian newspaper and radio correspondents went ashore with Canadian troops on D-Day. They were Ross Munro and William Stewart for Canadian Press; Halton and Ouimet for the CBC; Ralph Allen of *The Globe and Mail* (chosen by lot to represent Canadian daily newspapers); Lionel Shapiro, formerly of the *Gazette* in Montreal but by now working for the North American Newspaper Alliance; Charles Lynch for Reuters; Ronald Clark for British United Press; and Joseph Willicombe for International News Service.

Working alongside and even in the armed forces became routine for many Canadian journalists. Manitoba-born Scott Young first went overseas for Canadian Press and later served as a public relations/press officer for the Royal Canadian Navy. Arthur Cole worked in the Film and Photo unit of the Canadian Army in London, a newsman whose later experience would extend to radio as well as print journalism. Clyde Gilmour worked as a navy public-relations-officer-cum-corre-spondent.

Bill Austin went from an Ottawa press gallery job for Reuters into the army, where he eventually became assistant to Major R. S. Malone when the latter was director of public relations for the army.

Austin's job included appointing field press censors (always experienced newsmen) and making sure that both censors and war correspondents understood that press censorship was not based on the merits of any story but had to do "with military information, what could be released or could not."

"No one," Austin recalls, "deliberately tried to subvert the censorship, to my knowledge, throughout the active part of the...war. If they had they would no longer have been (correspondents)... The type of people who became war correspondents, generally speaking, were experienced newspaper people who knew what they could and couldn't do."

There were times, however, when an intrepid newsman could get around the guidelines. Scott Young and Ross Munro managed to do this when they were working for Canadian Press. Young was on desk duty at the London offices of CP and Munro was about to score one of the biggest scoops of the war: the invasion of Sicily in July 1943.

"On the Sunday morning after the invasion of Sicily," Young says, "twenty-four hours after the invasion, I was at the CP desk (in London) about eight in the morning and the phone rang.

"A voice says, 'This is the Air Ministry here. We've received something that we don't think really belongs to us from Malta, from a fighter division in Malta. Some guy named Munro seems to be sending this message.'

"I said, 'Oh, well, we're expecting it. Very nice of you to call. Can I come and pick it up?' I didn't know what the hell it was.

"I walked to Fleet Street, where on a Sunday morning normally you wouldn't see a taxi for ten miles. There's one coming up the street, so I hailed him and asked him to take me to the Air Ministry." At the ministry, Scott spoke to an official who explained that a fighter pilot had brought in a communiqué that had been given to him by a Canadian journalist in Sicily. The pilot had landed in Malta and passed the report on to someone in the RAF, who had forwarded it to the Air Ministry in London. Young concealed his excitement, took the report, and went back to the CP office.

Young's cubicle was separated from the American Associated Press office by a row of filing cabinets. The two offices used the same wire service. "Next thing I know, the guy on duty for AP comes and leans over the filing cabinet and says, 'Where the hell did you get this?' I said, 'I'll tell you later. I'd like to see if I can send it.'"

A few minutes later, the censor in charge called from the Air Ministry. "He said, 'You've sent this through and I'd like to see if I can get some background on it.'

"I said, 'Well, Munro is our war correspondent, he's in the invasion of Sicily, we know that. Apart from that, I don't know. It came from the Air Ministry, so I assumed it must have been checked by the censors and I went and got it.'"

Young's reply seemed to satisfy the censor, because the story got through. "This becomes Munro's world scoop, an eyewitness account of the landings in Sicily. This is a lesson for newspapermen... He had made some carbon copies and every time he saw a Spitfire pilot he gave him one. He said, 'When you get back to Malta, see if you can send this to London for me.' It was a great journalistic tactic on his part, that and some luck—the fact that the taxi was coming along just then."

Wes Gallagher, an American war correspondent and later general

manager of AP, said: "Munro was not only the top Canadian correspondent but one of the best five or six correspondents of the war. He
combined great personal courage with extremely lucid writing and
reporting."

Ross Munro was a lanky, scholarly-looking man of twenty-nine
when he covered the Sicily landing. By that time he was already an
experienced reporter. His grandfather had started a weekly newspaper
in Port Elgin, Ontario, and Ross's father worked there for a time. His
father died when Ross was a teenager, and Ross put himself through
school. After graduating from the University of Toronto, he went to
Ottawa to cover the political scene for Canadian Press.

When the war started, Munro tried to enlist but he had bad eyesight
and was rejected. The Canadian Press was anxious to send newsmen
overseas to cover the war, so that Canadian readers would not have to
depend on the American news agencies. Ross Munro and Scott Young
were among the first CP correspondents to go to England.

In March 1941 Munro was in London when the bombing was still
regular and heavy. A young nursing sister, Lieutenant Helen-Marie
Stevens, was dining at the posh Café de Paris when a German raider
dropped a bomb that landed in the club, causing chaos and casualties.
Lieutenant Stevens worked through the night, binding wounds, impro-
vising splints, and otherwise aiding the victims. By the next day, the
press was heralding the Canadian nurse as a heroine. Ross Munro went
to interview her, and this led to marriage two years later.

Munro also went along on the disastrous Dieppe raid, one of three
Canadian correspondents in the landing party. The other two were
Fred Griffin of *The Toronto Star* and Wallace Reyburn of *The Montreal
Star*. Munro covered the D-Day landings in Normandy and sent back
numerous detailed and moving dispatches during the weeks of difficult
fighting that followed. He even found time to visit a Casualty Clearing
Station to see how Canada's nursing sisters were doing.

"Less than seven miles from the front line," Munro reported on July
17th, "Canadian nursing sisters of the RCAMC [Royal Canadian
Army Medical Corps] are working under canvas in Casualty Clearing
Stations, caring for Canadian wounded from this Caen sector.

"In one CCS up near the front are stationed eight nurses who are
the first Canadian sisters to land in France during this war. Their unit

came ashore July 13, was set up in an open field at one a.m. next day and began to receive casualties shortly afterwards..."

Scott Young also had his share of worthy scoops and unusual adventures, starting with his and Munro's flight to England "in one of those Liberator bombers with no guns that were in Ferry Command. There's no heating or anything. We had flying suits and we sat on benches along the wall," as Young remembers it.

In England, Young got a rare interview with Canadian flying ace George ("Buzz") Beurling, the legendary Spitfire pilot. Beurling had just been posted back to England after scoring a record of twenty-eight confirmed kills in just fourteen days of fighting in the skies over Malta. He explained to Young that dogfighting in a Spitfire "was like playing pool shots all the time. There's no such thing as lining up and firing at something going straight ahead. You're going into rolls, dives and spins." The trick, Young discovered, was to know "which of the guns in which wing was aimed at what [you] wanted to knock down."

Scott Young spoke to "The Falcon of Malta" at an RAF gunnery school near Norfolk. "At noon that day I met Beurling in the mess to have a drink or two before lunch. They had the scores of each pilot in the course up on a blackboard on the wall and I said to Beurling, 'Jeez, it's funny. On Tuesday your score is way down. Wednesday it's way up. Thursday it's way down. Friday it's away up. What causes that?'

"Beurling says, 'Well, the days they're down, I shoot their way, the days they're up, I shoot my own way.'"

Unlike many of his fellow CP war correspondents, Scott Young had a wife and small son when he first went overseas. After a while, the separation began getting to him. Some army and air force officers had been able to get their wives over to England, and Young pressed CP to make similar arrangements for him, but he was unsuccessful. So Young decided to make a change. "I thought if I'm gonna be over here, I want to be in uniform and doing something other than being a reporter."

In 1943 he returned to Canada and joined the navy. After training, he was recommended for a commission, but the navy wanted to put him in public relations—virtually doing the same thing he had been doing before, but this time in a uniform. He fought the idea, but the financial realities of the situation helped change his mind: as an ordinary seaman, he would be paid $1.25 a day; as a public relations officer, his pay would be $4.25 a day. He took the commission, but insisted he didn't want to sit behind a desk in London. He wanted sea duty. He got it, just in time for D-Day.

"As soon as I got there, I was put on a corvette escorting a Mulberry dock, [one of those] big concrete things that you could sail across and sink to make an instant harbour. But it was very slow going. The seventy-five miles from Sheerness to Arromanches took four days," Young remembers. "There was an awful lot of activity, you know, depth-charges going off all over the place and [the sea was] full of submarines and bodies. But one day a pigeon landed on the tugboat that was pulling this Mulberry. It was so tired it just stood there, and somebody walked up to it and picked it up and found a little note on its leg.

"The captain of the *Mayflower* [the corvette], Pincher Martin, he unwrapped the thing. It was from a spy or public-spirited Frenchman or something in France, giving some German gun positions and troop movements and so on. But Pincher Martin, before he opened the thing, [had] signalled to England and said we had a pigeon that landed on our tugboat and it's got a canister on its leg and what are we supposed to do? Immediately a signal comes back.

"It turns out the RAF had dropped about 500 pigeons over France with little notes saying, 'If you are a patriot, write down any gun emplacements or troop movements. Put them in the [canister], and let the pigeon go.' This was the first pigeon that had reported and so they were very excited...

"The signal finally came back, 'When you finally get to Arromanches, contact local army group headquarters near the beach. Take the bird and deliver it to the general in charge of intelligence.' So when we pull into this little harbour Martin said to me, 'Well, you come with me.' Pincher felt that I could deal with the kind of people we were gonna meet better than he could.

"Now, the pigeon had been living in the ward room, but for about three days it never crapped at all. This didn't seem significant at the time...

"You've seen pictures of those beaches, just beaten all to hell, you know, half houses. We finally come to a chateau-like place and into the yard. All this time, Pincher Martin has the pigeon in a cotton bag.

"So we're ushered into this room. All the walls were covered with maps and each local spy, his name was up—like, 'Pierre, we have never received any useful information from this man,' or something like that. This was combined Allied Forces Intelligence. There was a navy commodore, an air force air commodore, and an army brigadier. All were British.

"The senior officer present said to Pincher, 'I understand you've brought a pigeon here, we'll be very interested to see it.'

"So Pincher reaches into the cotton bag with his hand. The pigeon's head is down and the rest of the pigeon is straight up Pincher Martin's sleeve, so when he lifts his hand to hand over the pigeon, this pigeon lets go three days supply of pigeon manure. Pincher Martin says, 'Shit!' [waves his arm], and sprays pigeon shit all over the maps. We got out of there a lot faster than we got in."

Shortly after the pigeon episode, Young was assigned to a landing ship called the *Prince Henry*, which took part in the invasion of southern France. "And I got all the action I really wanted," Young says. Later, he was involved in missions in Yugoslavia and Greece.

Another experienced newspaperman who wound up as a navy public relations officer was Clyde Gilmour, who was born in Calgary, grew up in Medicine Hat, and worked on *The Edmonton Journal* before going into the navy early in 1942. He served on several ships, frigates, and minesweepers, and his job was to get "honest and accurate home-town stories about the guys on the ship, what they were doing."

"You'd nose around like a newsman and talk to the guys," he recalled. "First of all you had to get them at ease because you were an officer, you know. And so you'd say, 'I'm just a reporter on this and they happened to commission me, so don't call me sir. I just want to ask you a few questions and I don't even know if I'm going to write you up, until I find out what's happening.

"You'd start asking them about their background and why they went in the service and anything that had happened to them and sometimes a lovely feature story would develop. Quite a few of the stories were sent out by the CP and used all over the country. Most of them [were] anonymous, but some of them had my name on them. In which case it looked as if I was working for CP because, you know, it had the CP logo on the thing...

"In the last year, [I wrote] quite a few stories about the misgivings the guys had about their future. And I was quite glad when the navy sent that stuff out and published it; they didn't hold it back as if it would be bad for morale. The guys were worried about their future and some of the stories reflected that."

In his own small way, Clyde Gilmour was doing much the same kind of reporting that the famous American war correspondent Ernie Pyle did: human interest stories that would touch the folks back home.

One of the most respected of all war correspondents was Ralph Allen, a native of Oxbow, Saskatchewan. He started as a sportswriter on *The Winnipeg Tribune* and eventually became the war correspondent for *The Globe and Mail* in Toronto.

Allen had a special empathy for infantrymen, whom he once described as "the war's firmest realists."

"My most vivid D-Day memory," wrote Allen, "is of a soldier caught in the wire on the beach. I knelt beside him and discovered he'd bled to death. Beside him was a pack of Canadian cigarettes—open, with one cigarette out and beside it a lighter. I tried the lighter. It was clogged. This poor man had been trying to have one last smoke and the lighter hadn't worked. Nothing had worked for him that day."

Gregory Clark, one of the war correspondents for the rival *Toronto Star*, said: "You've got to love that guy Allen. He's got a marvellous irreverence for constituted authority. To him, even General Eisenhower is just another source for a story."

Clark, who was old enough to have served in the First World War, was particularly fond of the human-interest yarns that made readers across Canada love him. But the horror of war moved him deeply and this was reflected in his writing. In 1943, Clark was covering the fighting in Italy and one of his most compelling stories dealt with the personal suffering of innocent victims of war, rather than the significance of the battle.

"Somewhere in Italy, September 26—Monsters in victory and monsters in flight, the Germans have added to the imperishable name of Lidice in Czechoslovakia the little name of Rionero in Italy, and I am one of three witnesses."

Clark went on to relate a poignant account of the brutality of a party of German soldiers who came down the main street of Rionero and stopped in front of the house of Pasquale Sibilia to shoot a chicken. The Italian's seven-year-old daughter, Elena, ran in to tell her father, who came out to confront the Germans. The German sergeant shot Pasquale in the leg; the Italian fired back and hit the German in the hand. The Germans, supported by a few Italian Fascists, rounded up Pasquale and his neighbours. They slaughtered fifteen of them. Only the approach of Canadian patrols prevented further killing.

Gregory Clark's outrage at this atrocity is vividly expressed in the angry closing to his dispatch. "In victory they are monsters. Here their bedraggled and harried rearguard, with the Allies on their very tails, are capable of monstrous acts. Not to enemies, but to humble, poverty-stricken, backward, gentle folk, who until two weeks ago were their allies. When the time comes soon for squaring of accounts, and I am permitted to attend the peace conference, will you, reader, please clip this story of Rionero out and save it against the day I might in those golden hours to come be guilty of one forgetting word, one sparing phrase, one apology for the dirty savage who roves these mountains now?

"Save it and send it to me for my shame. But I went back and saw little seven-year-old Elena... The dark little cave-like house was filled with lamentation, as though Italians were Orientals, and when my uniformed figure appeared at the door and I asked for piccolo Elena, all I saw was a tiny ragged figure vanish into the inner darkness of the house. I did not ask further. I merely vowed to remember and remember that ragged little figure against the day these gray-green bastards plead before the bar of humanity."

When Clark's story reached the *Star*, editors were concerned about his use of the word "bastards," which had never before been printed in the newspaper. The matter was taken up with Joseph E. Atkinson, the publisher, who read the story and said, "Let it go."

Another of Canada's widely read war correspondents was Lionel S. B. Shapiro, who worked initially for *The Gazette* and also did radio commentaries for the BBC and the CBC. Shapiro began writing while still attending McGill University, and joined *The Gazette* soon after graduating, in 1929. By the time the Second World War started, he had been a New York and then a Washington columnist. He went to Britain in 1941 as *The Gazette*'s correspondent and remained in that post until early 1944, when he was lured away by *Maclean's* magazine.

He covered the invasion of Normandy for *Maclean's*. His piece in the August 15 issue began: "We have been in France 45 days and it has been like a traumatic dream—a dream filled with moments of elation triumphant and rampant horror, with fleeting glimpses of Norman castles rising on noble hill crests, as though out of Disney's imagination, and of men lying grotesquely in the dusty ruins of a farmland hamlet. A dream filled with the shattering cacophony of war, blending the deep-throated roars of the big guns with the piercing scream of rocket Typhoons racing low in counterpoint with scudding clouds above. A dream made fraudulent by the hush of dawn breaking over tense men awaiting zero hour to move into the blasting hell of battle. A dream embracing life, death, courage, cowardice, dust, laughter, mud, sunshine, hate and camaraderie and all the things, crazy and noble, shrewd and terrifying, that make war."

Some years after the war Shapiro wrote a novel titled *D-Day, the Sixth of June*, which was turned into a motion picture.

Margaret Ecker, a native of Edmonton, who worked for Canadian Press in Europe, was one of the Second World War's rare women war correspondents. Early in 1945, she wrote a feature piece for *The Star Weekly* about the grim work done by nursing sisters in army hospitals in Holland, where Canadian troops were so actively engaged.

"If you like your war with handsome, newly pressed soldiers, wounded but clean-shaven, attended by beautiful nurses in starched white uniforms—you'd better go to the movies instead of reading about war the way it is here.

"Over here we hear that people in Canada don't like to read gruesome stories about the war, but it would be pretty hard to sugar-coat the description of a man whose body was riddled by shrapnel or whose feet were blown off when his jeep hit a land mine."

Ecker was the only woman present at the German surrender ceremonies at Rheims. Later the same day, she did a broadcast in Paris in which she quoted General Eisenhower as saying, "I'll certainly be glad to get rid of those damn Germans."

Getting to be a war correspondent wasn't always easy, even for an experienced newspaper man. Arthur Cole, born and raised in Belleville, Ontario, was twenty-three when the war started, and already married.

By 1942 he was working for the *Toronto Telegram*. He had been in the militia since 1938 and was eligible for a commission when he joined up. He enlisted early in 1943 in the Hastings and Prince Edward Regiment and was sent first to Brockville Military Academy, where he qualified to become a full lieutenant, then to Camp Borden as an infantry instructor.

On one weekly twenty-four-mile route march (leading mostly older men) he started out with thirty-five men and came back with thirteen—the rest had dropped out. When Cole returned to the parade ground, his company commander screamed at him, "What do you mean coming in here with thirteen? You had thirty-five when you started out, didn't you?"

"Yes, sir," said Cole.

"Well, what do you mean by this?"

"What did you expect me to do, carry them in?" For his insubordination, he was paraded before his battalion commander.

"What none of these guys knew was that he was a speed cop in Belleville and he and I were great friends. He was a lieutenant-colonel now...a veteran of the last war. Anyway, he went through the routine, told me to try to contain my temper."

That wasn't the last time that Art Cole was able to take advantage of his connections. Shortly thereafter, he was put in charge of a detachment of sixty-five officers to be posted to Prince Rupert, B.C., "and I knew damned well if I went out there I'd be there for a year, at least."

Before going into the army, Art Cole had photographed the 1st Division in December 1939 and met an army public relations officer named Jeff Yates. Determined to avoid the Prince Rupert posting, he telephoned Yates, who was now in charge of the Army Film and Photo section in Ottawa and asked for help.

"He said he was looking for a photographer, and I said, 'I'm a two-way man.' Although photography wasn't really my best suit, I was willing to settle, so he said he'd go to work on it."

This was on a Tuesday and the detachment was scheduled to leave for British Columbia the following Monday. After his talk with Yates, Cole told the battalion commander he had reason to believe he was about to be transferred to Army Film and Photo, and asked to be relieved of the Prince Rupert assignment.

"He said, 'I can't take you off. We're too far along in the planning. If they really want you they can get you back from Prince Rupert.'"

By Friday, Cole was getting anxious, so he telephoned Jeff Yates in Ottawa and reminded him that in another couple of days it would be too late.

"He said, 'Where are you now?'

"I said, 'I'm in the 812 officers' mess.'

"He said, 'Have another beer and stay there, what's the phone number?'

"About fifteen minutes later, the phone rang. It was Jeff and he says, 'You're off the draft.' About five minutes after that, this adjutant...comes bustling in and says, 'You son of a bitch. Who do you know in Ottawa? You're off the draft.' Then he said, 'When you get to Ottawa, put in a word for me. I'd like to get out of Camp Borden.'"

So that was how Art Cole got to England. He remained with the Army Film and Photo unit through the rest of the war, fulfilling a variety of assignments, from photographing training manoeuvres to taking pictures of various dignitaries. Cole took pictures of the royal family on a number of occasions. One in particular he remembers was when he and fellow photographers Lieutenant Harold Robinson and CWAC Sergeant Karen Hermeston were outside Buckingham Palace, taking pictures of an awards presentation.

"The royal family were in a big courtyard, lined up beside the main door. Robbie was over at one end and I was taking pictures of some Canadians... Robbie was ten or fifteen feet in front of Princess Elizabeth and he got a picture of her. She winked at him," Cole recalls. "No, he didn't save the picture."

Sometimes Cole found himself serving as more than just a photographer. In March 1945, Major Frederick Tilston of the Essex Scottish Regiment was involved in the assault on the Hochwald forest in Germany. The tall, red-haired Tilston from Windsor, Ontario, led a company of about 100 infantrymen across some 500 yards of open ground under terrific fire, through barbed wire, and into enemy trenches. During this assault, he was wounded three times, but he was the first to reach the German lines and the first to take a prisoner. His courageous actions earned him a Victoria Cross, but cost him both his legs.

Art Cole was dispatched to photograph the V.C. recipient in hospital. When Cole arrived he found Tilston in a ward with about a dozen
other wounded servicemen. Cole introduced himself to Tilston and
pulled out his camera, but the man seemed confused and asked,
"What's this all about?"
"Haven't you heard?" said Cole.
"Heard what?" said Tilston.
"You're being awarded the Victoria Cross." With that, the place
broke into cheering and applause. Apparently no one had bothered to
tell Tilston he was being given the British Empire's premier military
decoration for gallantry.

Getting the news to Canadians back home was one thing, but getting
news to the soldier on the Continent—in Italy, France, Belgium,
Holland, or Germany, depending on the progress of the war—required
extra ingenuity. Perhaps the most remarkable journalistic achievement
of the Second World War was the establishment of *The Maple Leaf*, the
Canadian Army's own paper.

The Royal Canadian Navy had a weekly paper called *The Crow's
Nest*, whose name came from a St. John's, Newfoundland, bar that was
favoured by navy men. The RCAF had a magazine called *Wings*. The
Americans had *The Stars and Stripes*. The British had *The Union Jack*
and *The 8th Army News*. The Canadian Army had nothing.

Colonel J. L. Ralston, then minister of national defence, visited
Canadian Army installations in Italy late in 1943 and discussed the
matter with the top brass there. After various ideas were kicked
around—such as air-mailing out impressions of Canadian Press news
to be printed in Italy—Ralston authorized Lieutenant-Colonel Richard
S. Malone, the army's chief of public relations, to go ahead and start a
newspaper. Malone was to function as editor-in-chief, but the actual
job of turning out the paper would be the responsibility of a managing
editor, J. Douglas MacFarlane.

"I was in Sicily at the time," MacFarlane remembers, "attached to
General Crerar's headquarters as his—get this—personal public relations officer, and I was getting a little edgy, too, but they—they being
the big shooters—had decided that what the Canadian forces in Italy
needed was a daily paper of their own."

How does a captain in the Canadian Army in Naples build a news-paper staff? Fortunately, the army had something called "indenting," which meant that a man's official records listed his civilian occupation. MacFarlane ferreted out a staff of experienced news reporters and writers who had worked on various papers across Canada.

The Maple Leaf started out as a weekly, and the first issue was published on January 14, 1944. In an editorial in the first issue, Lieutenant-Colonel Malone said the paper would be a weekly "for an issue or two," and his word was good. By early February, The Maple Leaf was a daily paper, put out by and for Canadian service personnel. It ran news items from Canada and the United Kingdom, as well as cartoons, features, columns, sports news, and an editorial. The editorials were almost always signed: "J.D.M."—J. Douglas MacFarlane.

One thing the paper did not have in the very beginning was pictures. There was no zinc to make the necessary engravings, but "this was quickly remedied in subsequent editions," MacFarlane later wrote, "by emergency measures: a visit to several Naples undertaking establishments and the removal of the metal lining of all available coffins, ensuring a sufficient supply of engraving material until army channels could meet requirements."

The staff included Ross Parry, originally from Vancouver; Ron Poulton of Moose Jaw, Saskatchewan; Jack Donoghue of Winnipeg; as well as George Powell, Ruth Carmichael, George Kidd, cartoonists Les Callan and Bing Coughlin, and numerous others.

From the outset, The Maple Leaf reached out to the ordinary man or woman in uniform. It was irreverent, folksy, full of newsy tidbits, and fun to read. Even its headlines were irresistible: "Japs Caught With Kimonos Up." The day the Germans surrendered, the entire front page of The Maple Leaf was given over to a single word, in huge letters: KAPUT! And when the war in the Pacific ended that August, The Maple Leaf's front page, top to bottom, announced: IT'S ALL OVER!

During the Italian campaign, the paper had a daily circulation of 10,000. That tripled after D-Day, when Allied forces stormed Normandy. An edition of The Maple Leaf was soon being published in Caen, then in Brussels, then in Amsterdam, and finally in Delmenhorst, Germany. In addition, from July 1945 through February 1946 there was also a London edition, with its own staff.

The paper sometimes carried dispatches by Canadian Press or Reuters correspondents such as Ross Munro or Wallace Reyburn, but it relied mostly on its own uniformed staff.

Lieutenant J. L. McKenna, assistant editor of the paper, reported from France four days after the D-Day invasion: "The steel fist of the Allies this week tore at the earth of Western Europe, seeking to gain a grip by which the iron heel of Nazi domination may be lifted from the peoples who have been oppressed these past four years.

"It is still early to say the landings have been completely successful. Anyone who has had anything to do with amphibious landings realizes the magnitude of the task undertaken, that success cannot be guaranteed in a few days. But the fact remains that everywhere the Allies have been able to hold on to what they have gained."

That same day's issue of *The Maple Leaf* carried a story by Corporal Ron Poulton, who was still covering the Italian campaign. It began: "On a slope of one of the many hills that hump up from the green floor of the famed Liri Valley, hundreds of tank and infantrymen from an armored brigade paid tribute to their comrades who fell in recent fighting.

"To ranks grown suddenly quiet, the padre said: 'You have contributed in no small degree to the famous exploits of the Canadian Corps. And we are met together today to remember with gratitude the sacrifice of our comrades.'

"There was a silent goodbye behind the halting notes of the 'Last Post' and in the two minutes of quiet that followed. In that two minutes there was much remembering done. And many present must have echoed to themselves, in the rich language used by fighting men, the resolve voiced by the chaplain when he said: 'There is good hunting over the hills.'"

But there was much more to *The Maple Leaf* than frontline reports. There was a regular feature called "Home Brew," which ran short and sometimes startling, if relatively inconsequential, news items from across Canada.

"St. Jovite, Que.—Four Nazi prisoners were captured soon after they escaped in sub-zero weather from a lumber camp. They surrendered, saying it was too cold to be out."

"Ottawa—Army recruiting officials have related the story of a female civil servant who had to use the moss-grown office boy's excuse of visiting a sick grandmother to get time off to join the Canadian Women's Army Corps."

The "Mild and Bitter" column contained similar items from England. "Bournemouth—A motion that licensed parts of Bournemouth municipal pavilion should be closed because of 'degrading happenings' there was defeated at a meeting of the town council. One councilor reported he had seen 'drinking in the corridors and men with their arms around half-drunken women.' Undesirable women, he added, were loitering on the staircases."

The letters to the editor generally contained complaints about some aspect of overseas service. "Editor, *Maple Leaf*: I am certain that many Canadians here in Italy will agree on what I have to say. I want to know why we have to be inflicted with the same motion pictures over and over again. Right now we are seeing a circuit of films that we saw here in Italy last March. I am sure that the number of Canadians who have had occasion to see, at least six times, such old standby films as *I Take This Woman* and *Hellzapoppin* would be amazingly high...[signed] The Little Corporal."

There was even a kind of poet's corner, titled "Rhyme and Reason," to which a soldier named E. J. Caughty contributed this:

When I am in the front line
And shells go whistling by
I've often said it to myself
I'd sooner live than die.

And there were cartoons. Inevitably, the paper carried such favourite American cartoon strips as Blondie and Li'l Abner. But *The Maple Leaf* rolled its own, too. One of the popular features was "Monty and Johnny," created by Lieutenant Les Callan, who had been an editorial cartoonist for *The Toronto Star* before enlisting in the artillery and being sent overseas. "Johnny" was simply an average Canadian soldier serving in Canada's army and "Monty" was Field Marshal Bernard Montgomery, who had jurisdiction over British and Canadian troops.

One typical Callan cartoon shows two soldiers in the foreground, with various trucks and other battle paraphernalia in the background.

One soldier is saying to the other: "Then they threw everything at us. I'm sitting in the hole, see, when suddenly the major lands smack in my lap. Yep! They threw everything at us! Including the major."

But by far the most successful of *The Maple Leaf*'s cartoonists was Ottawa-born Sergeant W. G. "Bing" Coughlin, the creator of "Herbie."

"I advertised in *The Maple Leaf* that we needed a cartoonist," explained Doug MacFarlane about the birth of Herbie. "Bing saw the box ad and answered it and sent samples of his work and I took him on. Norman Smith was a draftsman in the army, did map-making and so on... I think it was through Bing that we got him, because he was from Ottawa, too... They bunked in together and Smith was a really funny guy. He would set up all sorts of situations which produced or reflected Coughlin's cartoons."

The original title of the cartoon was "This Army." But soon after, MacFarlane noticed that one character kept appearing in the background of the cartoon—a little, chinless fellow. MacFarlane suggested placing the character front and centre and naming him.

"Good idea," said the editorial staff. "What'll we name him?"

"You can name him after me," said MacFarlane. "A name I hate and dumped years ago."

"What's that?" they said.

"Herbie."

(MacFarlane had been baptized Douglas Herbert. MacFarlane's parents later added the name James, after his maternal grandfather. MacFarlane hated the name Herbert and eventually dropped it.)

After the war, Coughlin and MacFarlane assembled some of Bing's best cartoons and published a "Herbie" book. As MacFarlane wrote in the introduction, "Herbie was, in fact, the Canadian Army, the ambassador-at-large who almost missed the troop train for Halifax, got lost in the London underground and drunk in the Queen's at Aldershot, failed to salute that flag car at Leatherhead, holed up with a simply delighted English family on Exercise Spartan and was unholed by the provost. He was first in the bully-beef barter queue in Sicily, thrown for a loss by vino rosso, midwife at a bambino's birth in Italy. He stubbed his toe on a Normandy beach and became D-Day's first casualty thereby. He fought and franc'd his way through France and

Belgium, fell into an Amsterdam canal, thought V2 fluid was hopped-up calvados, was brought back to life and came home. He was strictly an army guy. He beefed, moaned, cursed and groaned. To him, all brass was tarnished, particularly any associated with hats. Anybody with hooks on his sleeve was a public menace and shoulder adornment was something to be shunned."

Even when the fighting stopped, the stories didn't. Four days after the surrender in Rheims, *The Maple Leaf* carried a story by a staffer named Sergeant Joe Greaves. The headline read "Magic Carpet Trip Thrills Thousands of Allied PW's." Here is part of Greaves's story:

"With an RCAF Transport Squadron—The big transport nosed through the heavy cloud bank. Below, the English Channel lapped at the shores of Dover's Cliffs and two sergeants peered through the foot square window. The English one said: 'That's Blighty. Five years is a long time.' And a tear stole down his cheek. The Canadian said: 'Yeah, a lot longer'n two.' Then 32 lean faces grinned as one and noses pressed against the tiny window panes for the first look in years. And 32 voices broke into song. They sang 'Take Me Back To Blighty' and 'Going Home.'

"Less than 48 hours ago they had been prisoners of war. Some had been prisoners for five years and some for four. And some had been taken at Dieppe and some shot down over Berlin. But now they were all going home.

"Every day RCAF transport planes wing over Germany unmolested, drop down on German landing strips and pick up released prisoners of war.

"When Squadron-Leader Bob Joyce, Calgary, brought his transport down on the little landing strip northeast of Hanover, the ex-prisoners of war were waiting. As the plane slid to a stop before the bomb-riddled hangar, they shuffled forward, then stopped. Waiting for someone to tell them to climb aboard, they were like children who were not quite sure if they were doing the right thing.

"Rain dropped from the grey blankets they had flung over their head and shoulders. Their uniforms were of all makes and sizes. Some wore German officers' caps and some proudly wore the forage they had when captured. But they all wore grins on their faces that stretched from ear to ear."

Joe Greaves was a black Canadian from Port Arthur, Ontario. He had been a driver in the Army Public Relations section and was driving MacFarlane one day when he asked if he might make a contribution to *The Maple Leaf.* "This was when we first started, in Naples," MacFarlane recalled. "I said we sure could use some [help] and he wound up, just like that, as a columnist and a great writer."

Besides supervising his staff, MacFarlane wrote editorials—almost daily. Some of them spoke out on serious issues, some were more or less locker-room pep talks. When the paper was established, Lieutenant-Colonel R. S. Malone had accepted Defence Minister Ralston's offer, but with certain conditions: the paper must go to the front daily (it went up with the food rations), and there was to be complete editorial freedom with no obligations to any "brass" and no directions from military or government sources. In return, it was agreed that the newspaper would not express opinions on domestic Canadian issues or comments on internal military problems that might affect morale. For the most part, MacFarlane had no problem staying within those boundaries.

In October, 1944, for example, the JDM editorial headed "Indicators" dealt with the treatment of soldiers by their higher-ups:

> As the war progresses, more attention is being paid to the big "little" men in the army. Extent of this check into the needs of the fighting man and sympathy for his problems would be enough to bring the Colonel Blimps out of their Turkish bath boiling in more ways than usual.
>
> Latest example of this change of heart by the brassier hats comes from Baghdad where Lt.-Gen. Sir Arthur Smith, of the Persia-Iraq Command, has held a "grouse council." At his invitation, representatives of the forces under his command came—some of them hundreds of miles—to present their grievances. The complaints ranged from too much bully beef to khaki trousers with not enough space in the seat.
>
> Something of a similar survey is being made among the

Canadian troops in Italy by Defence Minister Ralston, who is touring the Dominion forces in this theatre.

The troops are taking questions at the minister's invitation. He hasn't answered them all for a variety of reasons, but he has been able to clear up some points which have been bothering Canadian soldiers. Answers or no answers, the mere fact that the minister is seeking the opinion of the man in the line on problems, present and future, is a good indication.

Men in high position, no matter how able their advisers, must find out for themselves the mood and wishes and troubles of the frontline soldier who doesn't often find time and place for complaint with effect.—J.D.M.

MacFarlane proved himself not only a dynamic leader of his own staff, a man capable of turning out a superior daily paper that quickly became a valued guidepost to his uniformed readers, but also a good team player from the army's viewpoint, celebrating the military victories, generally steering clear of any controversy with the brass.

The Maple Leaf's readers were happy with it. The Canadian military leaders were happy with it. Indeed, the paper became a favourite of Field Marshal Montgomery, who made a practice of carrying some copies of *The Maple Leaf* with him when he was visiting front-line Canadian troops.

According to Bill Austin, Lieutenant-Colonel Malone's second-in-command, it was Malone who suggested this tactic to Montgomery. "Dick Malone was very close to Montgomery," Austin remembers. "He would get the papers for Montgomery, that day's paper, and Montgomery would be able to give them 'hot stuff.' [Montgomery] was told by Dick at the start, when you're going among Canadians, take along some of these."

When the war in the Pacific ended, on August 15, that day's *Maple Leaf* was unusual in one respect. Under the masthead on page 4, where the editorial normally appeared, the space was empty except for a box with a border around it, and, as usual, the initials J.D.M. at the bottom of the space. Inside the box were three words: OUT TO CELEBRATE.

RCAF tailgunner George Hutton was shot down over Hanover in January, 1945, on his way home from his 23rd mission. *George Hutton*

Wendell Sharp trained as a paratrooper but ended up guarding German prisoners of war in Canada. *Wendell Sharp*

Army Nurse Kay Christie became a POW after the fall of Hong Kong to the Japanese. *Kay Christie*

One of the thousands of Japanese Canadian families interned during the war, shown in a detention centre in B.C. *Japanese Canadian Cultural Centre*

Vancouver-born journalist Frank Moritsugu was finally accepted by the Canadian Army in1945. *Frank Moritsugu*

Japanese Canadians bury one of their own, who died of illness in a camp in Angler, Ontario. Note the white circular patches on their backs, to make them easier targets if they tried to escape. None did. *Japanese Canadian Cultural Centre*

Captain J. Douglas MacFarlane, MBE, shortly after he was made managing editor of *The Maple Leaf*, in Naples, January, 1944. *J. Douglas MacFarlane*

Female impersonator Lorne
Wickie as Gypsy Rose Lee, a
show-stopper in the RCAF
show *The Tarmacs*. *Lorne
Wickie*

Wayne and Shuster in mock German uniforms, trying to
hitch a ride to Dunkirk. They starred in Invasion Review,
a Canadian Army show that toured war zones in Britain
and Europe. *Ken Bell, National Archives of Canada*

Alan and Blanche Lund, whose dancing career blossomed in the cast of *Meet The Navy*. *Blanche Lund*

The Royal Family greets the cast of *Meet The Navy* backstage at London's Palladium. From left, Princesses Elizabeth and Margaret, Vincent Massey, King George VI, Queen Elizabeth, Billie Mae Dinsmore (in white), Robert Goodier, Phyllis Hudson, John Pratt, and Blanche Lund. *Robert Goodier*

Seen on an earlier voyage aboard *Esquimalt* is Terry Manuel, a survivor of the sinking. *Terry Manuel*

HMCS *Esquimalt* was torpedoed by a U-boat on April 16, 1945, just three weeks before VE Day. She went down off the coast of Nova Scotia. *National Archives of Canada*

Shipmates mere weeks before the sinking: Donald White (on starboard watch, top) died; W. E. Joe Pinder, front left, was on shore leave; Fred Mimee survived; Ralph Pool's body was not recovered; Terry Manuel, right, survived. *Terry Manuel*

Crowded carley floats barely hold *Esquimalt* survivors. On extreme left is Lt. Robert MacMillan, the minesweeper's skipper. *Terry Manuel*

Dead crew members of HMCS *Esquimalt* on the deck of HMCS *Sarnia*, the rescue ship. *Terry Manuel*

Abbey of Ardenne, in Normandy, was Kurt Meyer's headquarters. At left is the building where Bert Thistle and other Canadian POWs were slated to be Meyer's next victims on D-Day. *Bert Thistle*

Gordon E. Clarke, of the Stormont, Dundas and Glengarry Highlanders, went in on D-Day. Over the next months, he was wounded several times and became a POW. *Gordon E. Clarke*

Bert Thistle of the Sherbrooke Fusiliers came within moments of being slain by the brutal Colonel Kurt Meyer, who was later convicted of murdering eighteen Canadian prisoners. *Bert Thistle*

8

Something for the Boys

Next to letters or parcels from home, the best way to put a smile on the face of a soldier, sailor, or airman serving overseas was by bringing him some entertainment to help him forget the war, if only for an hour or so.

The Americans had the USO (United Service Organization), through whose auspices thousands of entertainment units toured the United States and overseas, putting on shows for servicemen and women. Inevitably, the public was aware mostly of the glamorous stars who entertained: Bing Crosby, Jack Benny, Ingrid Bergman, Glenn Miller and his Army Air Force band, Martha Raye, and, of course, the ever-ready Bob Hope.

The British had ENSA (Entertainments National Service Association), which did similar work, but with an English accent. Here, too, much of the glory went to the better-known stars: Gracie Fields, Noel Coward, Bea Lillie, George Formby, and Vera Lynn.

But the Canadians didn't fare so badly, either. During the five and a half years that Canadian service personnel were in uniform, they were entertained, at different times and in different places, by such home-grown luminaries as Wayne and Shuster, Alan and Blanche Lund, John Pratt, Bob Farnon and his orchestra, Jimmie Shields, and Mildred Morey. Others were not then widely known but would be in the future. Among these were Fred Davis, Victor Feldbrill, Billy O'Connor, Jack Kane, Ivan Romanoff, Denny Vaughan, Roger Doucet, Peter Mews, Carl Tapscott, Robert Goodier, Billie Mae Richards, Paul Grosney, and Doug Romaine.

The two biggest shows were *The Canadian Army Show* and *Meet The Navy*. But there were many other shows, too—in all three branches of the forces—some of them small, simple, and easily transportable, and featuring unknown but remarkably versatile performers and musicians.

One thing that set apart Canadian wartime shows from other Allied efforts—and perhaps made them that much more appreciated by their uniformed audiences—was that they were not only *for* the troops but *by* them. Whereas the American USO and the British ENSA used civilian entertainers, Canadian entertainment units were made up of men and women in uniform. Every singer, dancer, actor, musician, and even backstage support person was a member of the forces.

There were perhaps a handful of exceptions to this rule, but these were mostly administrative rather than performing personnel. One notable example was Jack Arthur, a veteran showman who was brought in to produce *The Canadian Army Show*. He was offered a commission as a major, but turned it down because "I don't want any goddam colonel telling me what to do."

A number of private companies also took it upon themselves to mount fairly ambitious amateur shows to entertain the troops. Among them were Bell Telephone, Canada Packers, Sun Life Assurance, and T. Eaton, as well as various service clubs and citizens' groups.

(Joseph J. Russell, a manager at Eaton's in Montreal, was founder and director of the Eaton Masquers, who performed at service camps in Quebec and Ontario from 1940 to 1945 and then went on to the United Kingdom and the Continent for another six months after VE Day.)

W. Ray Stephens, a Second World War veteran who wrote several books about wartime entertainment, summed it up aptly: "Where there were warriors, there were also the minstrels."

The value of music was also recognized by the military, even if only vaguely at times. R. Murray Paterson, who eventually went overseas with the 5th Field Regiment, Royal Canadian Artillery, was in training at Simcoe, Ontario, when a sergeant-major appeared one day and asked for volunteers among the NCOs to go to Toronto for a three-week course in playing the mouth-organ. Paterson knew enough not to volunteer for anything, but his name was chosen out of a hat, anyway, and he went to Toronto for the mouth-organ course.

"There were about twenty of us from different camps in the province... The purpose of the course was to help us when we went on a route march. We were to play a tune to help make the march a little easier and pass the time. We would march around the [University Avenue] Armouries and outside the surrounding streets when the weather was favourable. The only tune I can remember was 'When The Saints Come Marching Home.'... When the course was finished we returned to our respective camps and I have never blown a mouth-organ since."

Of those performer-musicians who never went overseas, one of the busiest and most colourful was Billy O'Connor, an irrepressible Irish Canadian who had the rare distinction, in those days, of being a second-generation Canadian entertainer. His father, Tommy O'Connor, was born in Kingston, Ontario, and worked as a pianist and entertainer. He had travelled in the late 1880s with the famous Lew Dockstadter's Minstrels in the United States and was once accompanist to Blackstone, the magician. O'Connor, Sr., passed along his talents by teaching five-year-old Billy piano when the family moved to Toronto in 1919. By the time he grew up, Billy O'Connor was already a seasoned veteran of such show business as there was in Canada.

"When war broke out, I was playing in Kingston, in Lake Ontario Park, with a seven-piece band, on Labour Day, I think it was. I ended up with a two-piece band. All the guys had left... I ended up with a bass fiddle, a clarinet, a saxophone and all this baloney, and they all hitch-hiked back to Toronto. [When] I got back in three days' time, they were all in the air force."

O'Connor was twenty-eight years old and supporting his mother. Without a band, he made ends meet by playing stags. "Guys [would be] getting their army calls, so they'd have these stags, with five or six strippers. And I'd play at four or five of those shows a night, in all the hotels on Jarvis Street and at the Royal York."

O'Connor tried to join the Royal Canadian Army Service Corps, hoping to get into *The Canadian Army Show*, which was then in rehearsal. But he was about an hour late. "They put the wicket down on the Army Service Corps, and I went home and said, 'Well, to hell with them. If they don't want me, to hell with them.'"

Two weeks later he was called up to report for active duty. No sooner had he got into uniform than he was assigned "with a bunch of guys with brooms and stuff" to go to the Victoria Theatre in downtown Toronto, to clean it up, because the *Army Show* was coming in to rehearse. "Here I am dying to get into the *Army Show*, and my job is upstairs cleaning out the booth where they had the spotlight... I'm up there scrubbing, and I was as black as could be, covered with dirt."

The rehearsal was about to be called off because the pianist hadn't shown up, when someone told the dance director that there was "a guy upstairs cleaning the booth and he plays a little piano." O'Connor was summoned, overalls, dirt, and all; the dance director gave him some hasty instructions and O'Connor played for the dance rehearsal.

O'Connor still didn't get into the show. Instead he ended up in an infantry centre in Brantford. In his spare time, he'd play the piano at the YMCA and word soon spread that Billy O'Connor was an entertainer. So he was made a lance-corporal and encouraged to entertain his fellow soldiers.

Then his real break came. He was told "the colonel" was coming home from England and O'Connor was asked to put together a little show in the drill hall. The colonel turned out to be Lieutenant-Colonel R. Y. Cory, who had been overseas with the 48th Highlanders in the First World War and was now the commander at Brantford. Cory was so impressed with the "little show" that O'Connor was soon appointed the entertainment corporal.

In December 1943, the young men and women of No. 20 Canadian Army Basic Training Centre (Brantford) presented a show at that city's Capitol Theatre called *Here Comes The Army*. The program for the benefit performance at the Capitol Theatre listed this credit: "L/CPL. BILLY O'CONNOR has written and produced the show, and many of the songs used throughout are from his talented hand. He is a tireless worker, following in the footsteps of his father who was a showman for forty years."

From then until well after the war ended, Billy O'Connor wrote, produced, and performed in shows at Brantford, often taking the shows to other Ontario locations—small towns like Delhi, St. George, and military installations like Camp Borden and the RCAF station at Hagersville.

*

The Canadian Army Show began as *The Canadian Army Radio Show*, broadcast each week from the Sun Life Building in Montreal, although much of the talent had been moved there from Toronto—music director Robert Farnon and quite a few of his musicians, tenor Jimmy Shields, comedienne Mildred Morey, and comedians Johnny Wayne and Frank Shuster.

Wayne and Shuster had started working together in high school. By 1941, they were writing and performing a household-hints radio show for Toronto's CFRB called "The Wife Preservers." Soon they were on CBC radio and building a national audience. In 1942, both enlisted in the Canadian Army and Jack Arthur, a veteran theatrical producer, arranged to have them transferred to Montreal to headline *The Canadian Army Radio Show*. The radio series ran from December 1942 until September 1943, at which time the army decided to turn it into a stage show to tour Canada.

Wayne and Shuster found themselves in unusual circumstances. They were privates surrounded by officers—most of whom knew virtually nothing about show business.

"We were the only writers they had," Frank Shuster remembers. "We sat at this meeting with the captains—everybody [else] is a captain or a major. Major George would say, 'How about a Spanish number?' All our lives there has been somebody saying, 'How about a Spanish number?' I never knew why, and we'd always say, 'What for?' So, anyway...all we did was say 'No' to the officers, like 'You can't do that. That's a dumb idea.' So are they going to promote us? Never, in four years." (In time, they became sergeants.)

In preparation for the stage show, Wayne and Shuster were sent to Detroit to see *This Is The Army*, the U.S. Army show written by Irving Berlin. They loved it, but they had their own ideas. Jack Arthur, the producer, encouraged them to write their own "bits," and he proceeded to plan the rest of the show.

"But everything he suggested was so terrible," says Shuster. "First of all, he said, 'We've got this wonderful curtain. I just bought it in New York and it cost $3,000 and it's a giant V for Victory. As you sing the last chorus it lights up, it becomes a strobe-light thing.'

"So we said, 'Are you serious? You can't, it's so corny, Jack.'... So, he says, 'All right, you sons of bitches, go and write something better.' So, we wrote 'That's an Order from the Army,' and it was a good song and a good opening."

In the end Wayne and Shuster and Captain Bob Farnon wrote most of the songs in the show, including "But That's All," "On Behalf Of The General Staff," "A Soldier, A Sailor And An Airman," and "Hi'Ya Mom." They also wrote virtually all of the comedy material for the show—not only the material which they themselves performed. *The Canadian Army Show* toured across Canada, playing in civilian theatres (with the proceeds going to the *Army Show* Fund for the welfare of troops) and in army camps.

Army types don't like soldiers, whatever their specialty, ever to forget that they're in the army. Murray Ginsberg, who played trombone in the pit band of *The Canadian Army Show*, still remembers the periodic attempts, especially in the early days of the national tour, to "smarten up" the cast and musicians.

"I remember at Camp Borden," says Murray, "we had to demonstrate for the high brass that the musicians could take a Bren gun apart blindfolded, you see. You had to know the parts so completely, you know. So who do they pick on? Jack Groob, a fiddle player. He was the last guy they should have picked in the whole company.

"They blindfold him. It was a hot, sunny day, and we are all standing around, and they give him the machine gun and the sergeant major says, 'Okay. Go!' And he was timing him to do it in ten seconds or something. About four days and ten minutes later, he was still doing it. And of course, that really blew it, you know. They said, 'This won't do, we'll have to have more training.' So we took training wherever we went. Every morning."

The show toured for six months across the country, but it never performed—as such—in England or Europe. The army decided to break the show up into smaller, more mobile units. (No one seems to know how many *Canadian Army Show* units there were overseas. Shuster remembers five, and he may be right. Probably what happened was that more were added as the war continued.) "We all went over at the same time, but a couple of units went to Italy, and some to England. Our unit was the first one to go into Normandy," says Frank Shuster.

Wayne and Shuster toured with a unit called *The Invasion Review.*

The cast included singer Jimmy Shields, comedienne Mildred Morey, and a small band.

Shuster has fond memories of one particular performance in London. He and Johnny Wayne did a comic "swami" act, in which Shuster, as the swami, sat on stage, blindfolded, while Wayne went into the audience, and held up objects proffered by members of the audience. Shuster, the swami, would "guess" what each object was.

"He'd say, 'What am I holding in my hand?' And I'd say, 'I can't see it.' And he'd say, 'Well, go into your magic chant,' and I'd go, 'Alakazam, allabazam, allaleaf,' you know a whole lot of crazy talk. And then I'd say, 'I've got it, it's a handkerchief.' Then he'd go to another place, it was something else he knows we can get.

"And the blow, of course, is he can pick anything he wants to pick, something so obscure, you know, not glasses, some crazy thing, and they're wondering how the hell is he going to get that because it's really difficult. And I'd say, 'I can't see it, I can't see it.' He says, 'Go into your magic chant,' and I'd go into the chant, and I'd say, 'I still can't see it.' And then, from behind the curtain a guy speaks out: 'Hold it up higher, I can't see it, either.' And that's the blow. It's a good blackout because nobody knows where it's coming from."

During their run at English armed services bases Wayne and Shuster remember that the V1 (buzz) bombs were constantly falling from the skies. "It's a slow bomb," remembers Frank. "You'd hear it tick-tick-tick-tick... And when the motor cut off, you knew in about two or three seconds... Boom!"

At one station the comedy duo was performing the swami sketch inside a Nissen hut in front of about 200 servicemen seated in chairs. Wayne had begun his search for unidentified articles in the audience when everyone heard the ominous tick-tick-tick-tick overhead.

"I've got the blindfold on," recalls Shuster. "I'm sitting on the stage. And it's quiet. Nothing's going on and I'm saying to myself, 'Did everybody leave town?' I don't know what's gonna happen, but I'm in show business, I'm not gonna say, 'To hell with this' and run."

Then the ticking stopped.

"What is this? What have I got in my hand?" asked Johnny. Silence. No one said a thing. The V1 exploded away from the hut. Everything rattled and shook. Without skipping a beat, Johnny Wayne said, "What was it?"

"A buzz-bomb!" exclaimed Shuster.

"Right!"

Shuster remembers the laughter. "It was great, because everybody was still alive and that's why they loved it."

Meet The Navy, the big show put on so successfully by the Royal Canadian Navy, began in the mind of Captain Joseph P. Connolly, who in 1943 was both Director of Special Services for the RCN Volunteer Reserve and a Halifax lawyer with an abiding interest in show business. Determined to put the navy on the entertainment map in Canada, he managed to get official approval to go to Toronto to start rehearsals with a small cast at the University of Toronto's Hart House. A few sample sequences were put together, and the wartime equivalent of backers' auditions were put on for admirals and cabinet ministers, in hopes of getting all-out navy and government support.

In September 1943, *Meet The Navy* opened at the Victoria Theatre in Toronto, five months after *The Canadian Army Show* had opened at the same theatre. It was an immediate hit.

Among its strengths was a cast of gifted performers. Three of its strongest members were John Pratt, Robert Goodier, and Lionel Murton, who had previously worked in a Montreal show called *The Tin Hats*. Blanche Harris and Alan Lund, billed as "Lee and Sandra," were spotted by Captain Connolly in a Montreal private club. (During the lengthy run of the show they married and later became famous as Alan and Blanche Lund.) There was a marvellous bass from New Zealand named Oscar Natzke, whose rich, deep voice thrilled audiences, and A. Cameron Grant, who seemed born to play Captain Bligh (to John Pratt's Mr. Christian) in a broad spoof of *Mutiny on the Bounty*. Ivan Romanoff led a rousing mixed chorus. Another highlight was Robert Goodier's satirical pantomime of a young woman getting up and getting dressed in the morning.

Blanche Lund remembers the era of *Meet The Navy* with pride and warmth. She and Alan Lund had been dancing together since they were fifteen. At first, they were merely dancing partners, but later they got engaged. One day Alan said, "If we get married and have children,

I'm going to hate one day to say, 'All we did was Victory Bond drives.'" Until that point, Blanche had no thoughts of signing up, but she said, "If you're joining, I'm joining." They joined the navy and the cast of *Meet The Navy* and stayed with it for the next three years, soon becoming a main attraction.

Wren Billie Mae Dinsmore had worked as a stenographer at the CBC in Toronto before joining the navy. But it turned out she could sing and dance and even play the accordion, so she became a valuable member of the *Meet The Navy* cast. She married Bill Richards, a musician in the show, and later had a successful acting career. Among other things, she did the voice of "the kid" in the long-running CBC radio series "Jake and the Kid."

But, unquestionably, the show-stopper night after night was John Pratt, a sad-faced stringbean of a comic who came out on stage alone, in a sloppy, oversized uniform, and dolefully sang "You'll Get Used To It." He had added extra lyrics to Freddy Grant's original song to include jokes about navy life.

After its triumphant opening, *Meet The Navy* began a tour across Canada, aided additionally by glowing reviews and a five-page picture spread in *Life* magazine. The tour ran for a year, going from coast to coast, including Newfoundland and Labrador. The navy elected to keep the cast together when the show travelled to England and Europe.

Bob Goodier, who became a dramatic actor after the war—he was in the very first season of the Stratford Festival—has wonderful memories of his years with *Meet The Navy*. In particular, he felt great fondness for Oscar Natzke, the big New Zealand singer.

"He called everybody 'laddie,'" recalls Goodier, "and he and I were great chums. He had a wonderful voice. I got him to grow a beard while he was in the hospital. (After one of our tours entertaining the troops, they'd give us things, like cartons of eggs and, of course, how silly people get, we were all in the back of a couple of trucks and the girls [Wrens] were throwing eggs at us, raw eggs. They hit Oscar in the eye and he was in the hospital for a while.)

"He came out with a patch, of course, and we were walking down one of the streets in London. There was Pratt, Murton, and myself walking with Oscar. I saw a chemist's shop, so I said, 'Look, I gotta get something.'... I went in and got three other patches and I gave one to

Pratt and one to Murton. We all put them on and we walked single file behind Oscar.

"Oscar didn't wait for anybody, he storms ahead and then he wonders why people were laughing like hell... Then he turned around and saw us walking with these patches on... He looked like Long John Silver for a while, with the beard and the patch."

Lloyd Malenfant, who was a featured dancer in *Meet The Navy*, started dancing when he was seven years old in Winnipeg and was in the Winnipeg Ballet when it first started. After joining the navy in 1941 and taking signals training, he spent a year or so at sea. He was on the corvette *Drumheller* when it was credited with sinking a submarine. (Once, his ship took aboard about twenty Chinese survivors from a merchant ship. "One of them was a marvellous cook and we had the best meals we ever had.")

Malenfant was in Ottawa when a concert party performed there. It was the nucleus of *Meet The Navy*. He auditioned and was accepted. He still considers himself lucky to have been in the navy.

"When I first joined the navy and I got to Halifax, this signalman came up to me one day and said, 'I understand you tap-dance.' I said, 'Well, I haven't done it for a while.' He said, 'Would you like to go in concert groups?' I said, 'That would be fine,' so I wrote home for my tap shoes because I hadn't taken them with me. I was dancing in messes all over Halifax and, you know, I was supposed to have duty watch every third night. [Instead], I was out tap-dancing. So it all paid off in the end. I feel I did exactly what I wanted to do."

During the London run of *Meet The Navy*, various celebrities made a point of catching the show. They included Noel Coward, Alfred Lunt and Lynn Fontanne, and Vivien Leigh. The King and Queen and the two royal princesses attended a matinee, escorted by Vincent Massey. One night, one of Vincent Massey's staff tried to get in to see the show at the Hippodrome with his family.

"My brother-in-law, George [Ignatieff], was third secretary at Canada House under Vincent Massey," explained Marjorie Ignatieff. "[But] tickets were hard to get. [We] had to settle for three in the gods. Very high up and cramped.

"My husband, Alec, was six feet, six inches, my brother-in-law, George, was six feet, two inches and rather bulky, so for the first part of the show they did nothing but complain and fidget. George...felt with his position he should have merited something better.

"By this time, I was getting 'browned off' (as the saying was then), when onto the stage came a long, thin streak of a chap in sailor cap, white T-shirt, and navy trousers, singing 'You'll Get Used To It.' And of course, we all started laughing. A good time was had by all."

Meet The Navy launched another illustrious career: that of Victor Feldbrill, who was to become one of Canada's most distinguished conductors. He was just nineteen and about to enroll at the University of Toronto when he got his call-up. At the army depot they looked at his file and said, "It says here you're a violinist." Feldbrill said he was.

"Well, the navy is looking for you!" was the reply.

It was the start-up of *Meet The Navy*, and Feldbrill was promptly hired by conductor Eric Wild for the show's pit band. It was a tremendous opportunity for him. When he got to London, he had a letter of introduction from Sir Ernest MacMillan (who had heard him play) to "people anywhere, and it opened a lot of doors for me."

While the show was playing in London, Feldbrill was accepted at the Royal College of Music and the Royal Academy of Music, "so all the studies I thought I would have to do at the university, I was able to do while I was there," he said.

Feldbrill remembers another incident:

"There was a member of the violin section who was a real misfit as far as being in the service. I remember the day I met him in Toronto, and he said, 'Can you believe it? I'm thirty-nine years old. If I were one year older I wouldn't have to be going through all this.' He reminded me of Edward Everett Horton. He absolutely couldn't stand this togetherness. He was born in London. So, we were in England, and he decided one day to go to the registrar to get a birth certificate, which he'd never had. It was just after VE Day and we were still doing some shows in Aldershot. He came back and he had found out that he was one year older than he thought he was. Now, here he is, sitting in the pit, and we could see him beginning to fall apart. John Pratt got wind of this. Pratt sat on the edge of the stage and sang directly to this guy, 'You'll Get Used To It.' He literally went screaming out of the pit.

"They sent him home. Next day he was gone. But that poor guy, we felt so sorry for him... It was such a shock to him. It was almost three years out of his life that he wouldn't have had to be there, had he known."

Except for a few smaller "concert parties" in England, *Meet The Navy* stayed intact throughout the war. A few weeks after VE Day, the troupe flew across the English Channel to begin a tour of the Continent—Paris for ten days, Brussels for two weeks, Amsterdam for eight weeks, and then Oldenburg, Germany, for four weeks. For Victor Feldbrill, the most memorable experience of the European tour was the time in Amsterdam. He learned that the Amsterdam Concertgebouw, one of the world's great orchestras, was going to give a concert.

"I didn't know they had been put on the banned list by the authorities because the conductor, Willem Mengelberg, who was no longer with them, had been a Nazi sympathizer... The Dutch are not a violent people but they would have hanged that conductor. He escaped to Switzerland."

Feldbrill sneaked into a rehearsal. Suddenly, the rehearsal was stopped and somebody called him over. He thought he was going to be kicked out. But it turned out the new conductor, Eduard van Beinum, was a heavy smoker and hadn't received his ration of cigarettes. So Victor was asked if he had a cigarette for the conductor.

"I didn't smoke," admitted Feldbrill, "but you needed cigarettes to buy stuff, so I gave him the package. He was going to give it back and I said, 'No, please keep it.' He asked me to wait and he said, 'Who are you?' I said I was with the Canadian navy but I was interested in conducting, and he said I could come to rehearsals. And later he gave me scores to read. I was there for all the rehearsals, as they were preparing for the concert.

"I went to the concert, and I realized by then this was their first concert since the end of the war. It was very touching, because in the program it said, because of the recent history of the orchestra with the Nazis (through the other conductor), the orchestra would be prevented from playing the national anthem... [But when] the orchestra got on the stage, the audience, as if somebody had given them the note, all stood and sang the national anthem. I tell you, it was the most touching moment I have ever lived through."

Many years after the war, in 1956, the Amsterdam orchestra came to Toronto. "By that time, I was assistant conductor of the Toronto

Symphony and there was a big do in the City Hall for the [visiting] orchestra and we were invited, of course. I thought, 'Oh well, I'm not going to make a fuss about this.' I went past van Beinum, the conductor, [we] shook hands and he looked at me and said, 'You're the man with the cigarettes.' He had remembered!"

By September 1945, when the *Meet The Navy* tour ended, an agreement had been reached to film the show at the Elstree Studios, near London. The filming lasted through the winter.

Nobody connected with the film has much good to say about it. Ruth Phillips, who wrote a detailed history of the navy show summed it up this way: "The film catches none of the verve or essence of the original, even in the sequences taken from the stage show, and the story gluing the episodes together is hackneyed nonsense... But in 1945, even bad movies made money and royalties from showings of *Meet The Navy* benefited the Royal Canadian Navy Benevolent Fund by more than $200,000."

The most disappointed cast member of *Meet The Navy* was Blanche Lund. Two weeks before they were to go to England to make the movie, Blanche discovered she had polio; in fact, "my mother and dad got a telegram [from the hospital] saying they didn't expect me to recover," she recalls.

She was sent back to Canada on a hospital ship, the *Lady Nelson*, and could not walk until the following March. She took no part in the movie and, of course, Alan Lund danced by himself, except for one spot, where another woman (Billie Mae Dinsmore) danced briefly with him.

"I think what upset me most about not doing the picture was when I saw the gown that she wore. It was so much nicer than the one I'd had during the navy show and I thought, I missed that lovely gown," Blanche Lund says.

"We had a cottage up on Lake Simcoe after the war and we heard *Meet The Navy* was playing at the drive-in at Beaverton, so we said, 'Let's go over and see it.' Marge and Sid Smith, our friends (also from the cast of *Meet The Navy*) had a cottage behind us, so the four of us went over.

"At the end of the movie, when they put the big lights on, there was one other car and ourselves there. When it started there must have been about 300 cars, and when the movie finished there was one other car. I said to Alan, 'Honey, you see that other car? We should go over and talk to them, I'm sure it must be somebody from the navy show.'"

But her memories are mostly good ones. "It was an exciting time. You were young and you sort of had the feeling that nothing was going to happen to you. I think at that point of your life you just feel that this is going to go on forever, and you're never going to grow old. Things are not going to change. I think it was the most carefree time of my life, and one of the happiest."

When *The Canadian Army Show* decided to break up into smaller units for overseas performances, it meant more opportunities for talented soldiers and CWACs.

Trombonist Murray Ginsberg was called up when he was twenty. After some generally uninspiring military experiences—marching, drilling, learning to take a Bren gun apart blindfolded—he joined the pit band of *The Canadian Army Show*. After the national tour, Murray ended up in a band, known, with typical military flair, as *Unit A*. The leader was a violinist called Bill Charles. The pianist was Denny Vaughan, who later became a television star in Canada.

Ginsberg remembers being stationed in Dover at one point. *Unit A* was in one hut, an RCAF band called "The Blackouts" was in another, and an army military band (the Lincoln and Welland regimental band) was in another. The musicians often got together at night if they weren't working. "It was June, you know, in the south of England. Beautiful. And you could look out from Dover out to the Channel. One guy runs in [to our hut] and says, 'Hey, you gotta see this,' and we went out. The entire Channel, from left to right, from north to south, was loaded with ships. We wondered what on earth this was. It was the invasion starting, that long-expected day, a highly dramatic moment I'll never forget as long as I live."

Another of the *Army Show* units was a band led by Bob Farnon, who had been music director of the touring show in Canada. He formed a new twenty-piece band in London as well as a bigger concert band, with strings. Farnon and his musicians did five broadcasts a week, which were beamed over the Armed Forces Network to Canadians and Americans alike.

Fred Davis was a featured trumpeter in that band. He had been a freelance musician in Toronto when he and a friend, drummer Frank Wiertz, ran into another musician friend, Jack Kane, who was a member of a regimental band of the Signal Corps, stationed at Kingston. Kane raved about what a great outfit it was, so Davis and Wiertz promptly signed on. Says Fred Davis, succinctly: "We hated it.

"I had never played a trumpet (while) walking or marching. We were only in a few days when we had a Victory Loan parade or something in Kingston. With the big boots and the cobblestone streets and the uneven bricks, [I didn't know] how to keep that horn from bashing my mouth to pieces," Davis recalls.

In 1944, when the *Army Show* was being broken up into smaller units and Captain Bob Farnon was put in charge of the broadcast detachment of *The Canadian Army Show* in London, England, Fred applied for this unit and was assured he would be accepted. He was told his outfit in Kingston would be notified. But time dragged on and word never came. On his next leave, Fred went to Toronto and discovered that his bandmaster in Kingston had not bothered to tell him that he was to report to Toronto. Davis managed to get his gear together and he was on a train to Halifax within two days.

Besides the big concert band and the twenty-piece dance band, there was a small group with some of the same personnel called the Canadian Army Rhythm Group. "It was great," Davis recalls. "It was like having a steady job, seven days a week, and we did some moonlighting on the side.

"There was this civilian (a little short black cockney Englishman)... He sounded like Stanley Holloway but he looked like he just stepped out of Birdland. His name was Cab Quay, and he tried to sing like Cab Calloway. He was a real entrepreneur. He booked the rhythm group, half-Dixie, half-jazz, on civilian things whenever we had a night off. He'd get petrol from somewhere and a van, and we'd go out. He got so ambitious that he started to put up billboards in London.

"Now, we had to clear it in advance, because if we had a broadcast we'd have to leave him up in the air. Anyway, he was a real promoter, he had big three-foot billboards put up around London. We played a lot of town halls, the Reading Town Hall, the Marylebone Town Hall, this kind of thing. Well, he made the mistake of putting billboards up on the Strand, which is where the high-ranking Canadian brass walked down to Canada House at Trafalgar Square. And they're saying, 'What's this, a Canadian Army band?' Because we're charging (actually, we're not, he is, but he's paying us, you know). That was the end of it."

Some of Farnon's musicians earned a little extra money, during off-duty time by playing at various clubs. One time, they were playing at some fancy London hotel, and their pianist was sick, so they asked Farnon if he would fill in. "Bob Farnon was a captain, and all the musicians were other ranks." Officers rarely participated in these extra gigs. However, Farnon agreed to fill in for the ailing pianist on this occasion.

"Because he didn't want to look like an officer, he wore his worst battledress jacket. And he sort of darkened down the pips, so he wouldn't look like a captain sitting there on the bandstand. He didn't care, but he figured somebody else might.

"This jerk came over, some Canadian captain... Some officers treated the lesser ranks like dirt. There were some Canadian officers that were, like, snap your fingers, come here, boy... This jerk came over and very rudely didn't ask for a request. His girlfriend was in ear shot, [so he] demanded that we play something, some particular tune, but he was so obnoxious, the way he did it.

"Farnon leaned the dirty pips right in this guy's face and said, 'Why don't you fuck off?'"

Davis also remembers a gig in Norwich, at a U.S. air force base. "Part of the deal was to play for a hospital. We'd never played to a hospital audience before... We thought there could be a terrible feeling of resentment coming from this audience. They wheeled in some terrible cases, guys in traction, amputees, the wheelchairs, the quadriplegics. This was a Canadian hospital. And I'm thinking, 'They're gonna think these guys have got it lucky. They're in London and they're playing their instruments. And we're out losing lives and parts of our bodies.' Well, it was the best audience we ever played to."

On one concert party, Fred Davis got his first taste of performing—without his trumpet. "We had script-writers with us. A guy who later did walk-ons on the old Red Skelton show was our sergeant; he was British, had a very plummy accent, which I used to imitate behind his back. He caught me one day and wrote me into a comedy script as a Colonel Blimp character.

"I'd never been in front of a microphone before, other than with a trumpet in my hand. I didn't mind doing the accent but I was playing in front of a British audience, that's what worried me. But I got through it and that may have been where the microphone bug was born, the fact that I was able to talk to an audience."

Another *Army Show*, with the inspired name *B Unit*, featured four women, members of the Canadian Women's Army Corps. They were "Sunny" Wilson of Moncton, Alfreda Philip of Winnipeg, Mary Moynihan of Regina, and Ethel Hendry of Windsor. (Alfreda's husband, Major R. W. Philip of the Winnipeg Grenadiers, was a prisoner of war in Hong Kong.) The four played eight months in England and four months in Italy, returned to Canada for a furlough, then played some bases in the Maritimes and went off to England again.

As Margaret E. Ness wrote in *Saturday Night*, "Perhaps the most thrilling theatrical show they did was the one they gave the night before Florence fell to the Allies. In the audience were British officers and their Gurkha and Sikh troops, and the Canadian Armoured Brigade. The 'theatre' was the market-square at the side of a bridge and on the hills across the valley they could see the Allied guns. They could even see houses on the outskirts of Florence.

"A message from the British gunners is delivered. What time does the show go on? They would like to lay down a barrage but don't want to interfere with the show. A reply goes back.

"And so from eight to ten o'clock the Canadian Army Show entertains war-weary fighting men. And at ten o'clock sharp the guns open up with four Canadian girls watching the fall of Florence."

And then there was the unit called *The Tin Hats*. There had been a revue of the same name in Montreal before the war, in which John Pratt, Bob Goodier, and Lionel Murton appeared, but the Canadian Army's *Tin Hats* was a different group. Their history has been largely ignored—including the fact that the group was once on a ship that was torpedoed in the English Channel, causing the death of five musicians and the wounding of several other members of the cast.

The big *Canadian Army Show* and *Meet The Navy* both had mixed male and female casts, all members of the Canadian forces. Some army shows had all-male casts, one or two had all-female casts. But *The Tin Hats* was the only army show in the Second World War that included female impersonators. These were not of that broadly comical variety—men who stuffed grapefruit inside tight sweaters, smeared on lipstick and rouge, and tottered around on high-heeled shoes—that could be seen, now and then, at service club "follies." These were honest-to-goodness female impersonators, on-stage transvestites, if you will.

The cast changed from time to time, but the three best-known female impersonators were Sergeant Johnny Heawood, Corporal Bill Dunstan, and Private Jack Phillips.

"While I sat there rocking with laughter at the gags," reported Sergeant Ruth Carmichael for *The Maple Leaf,* "swooning to the baritone voice of Frank Elliot and the tenor of Norm Harper, and trying to convince myself that Jack Phillips, Bill Dunstan, and Johnny Heawood were guys not gals, I began to wonder just what makes a show without gams and G-strings click so well with the troops."

Bill Kuinka was a member of *The Tin Hats'* band. He'd been born near Prince Rupert, B.C., and had lived in Vancouver and Timmins ("because I had heard that the streets were paved with gold"). At one point he played string bass with Oscar Peterson. He was called up in 1942, by which time he was married, and fully expected to "go and fight the war." But when he identified himself as a musician, he was assigned to a small musical group at the North Bay camp.

When *The Tin Hats* played there, Bill's reputation gained him a spot in their band. He played bass and was also featured as a soloist on mandolin. By 1943, he was officially a member of *The Tin Hats.*

He remembers the three female impersonators, "presenting their own interpretations of female singers, actors, and dancers. I don't remember them trying to impersonate identifiable, specific people. But they were very convincing. In fact, there were boys lining up to date them. They believed that they were real girls. It was incredible; and every night, every time they performed, I couldn't believe how well they made themselves up."

Bill says there were no conflicts whatsoever between the female impersonators and the rest of the troupe. "What happened was that the impersonators kept to themselves and we did whatever we did," he recalls. "And occasionally, after a performance, there would be a social event, everybody included, but that's the way it was. We all got along well. Everybody respected each other for what they did."

It was Bill Kuinka's wartime experience that made him decide to pursue a postwar career in music. He used his veteran's credits to study at the Royal Conservatory of Music in Toronto and spent some twenty years with the Toronto Symphony and the CBC Symphony.

The RCAF, of course, had its own entertainment units. The man largely responsible for this was an English actor named Robert Coote, best remembered as the original Colonel Pickering in the Broadway production of *My Fair Lady*. Coote was in Hollywood when the Second World War started, working in films, usually cast as a pompous British type. In 1942, he came to Canada and joined the RCAF.

Too old to be a pilot, Coote became a Link trainer instructor at BCATP stations in Regina, Edmonton, and Calgary. Coote was annoyed at the lack of entertainment for airmen and wrote to the RCAF brass in Ottawa. As a result, he was transferred to Ottawa and placed in charge of organizing air force shows. His first effort, called *Blackouts*, was so successful that it led later to a second RCAF show called *All Clear*.

The company of *Blackouts* consisted of twenty airmen and nine WDs (RCAF Women's Division). One of the musicians in the show was bass player Sam Levine, who had worked with band leaders Trump Davidson and Cliff McKay before he joined the air force in 1942.

Levine wanted to be a musician in the RCAF, so he wrote to the commanding officer of the air force's music section. "I got a letter from him saying you cannot become a member of any band in the RCAF if you don't play a brass instrument," he remembers. "I joined up anyhow to be a radar mechanic and I was trained for that."

But early in 1943, he was transferred to Rockcliffe airfield, near Ottawa, and classified as an "Entertainer B." (He's still not sure what that meant.) He and a group of performers were in "this huge hut" one day, "and this very good-looking, tall, British-looking officer came in. He was Robert Coote, wearing the prescribed battledress and a yellow scarf right down to his ankles. You'd think he'd just fought the Battle of Britain. He looked us all over and he said, 'Ladies and gentlemen, we are going to do a show.'"

Levine remembers Coote as "the only guy around there that really knew show business." Somewhat ruefully, he adds: "Show business and the military don't mix at all." Some of the musicians provided the show's material. Levine wrote the show's title song, which served as its opening and closing number, called "You've Been Darn Swell." Some of the musicians also did comedy bits on the stage, and this involved getting in and out of the pit in a hurry.

"I was involved in a spoof we did on a radio soap opera, and I was the announcer (on stage) saying, 'Judy married Rudy and Rudy married so-and-so,' stuff like that. Then I was gone and back into the pit to play some other stuff."

Blackouts was first performed at a big bond rally in Ottawa. There were a couple of visiting Hollywood names present, to draw a crowd. "The people didn't come to see us, they came to see Roland Young or Jimmy Cagney. That was standard stuff in those days. And then they put us on and we ripped the house down."

The next day, the *Blackouts* company left Ottawa and began a tour of air bases across Canada. "You'd be amazed," he says, "[at] the number of little airfields that were dotting the prairies."

Aircraftman Second Class Terry Dowding, one of the cast members, kept a log of the show's travels. Between April 8 and September 6, 1943, they played sixty-seven performances, travelling by train across Canada. Then, after a leave, the company boarded the *Mauritania* late in November, bound for England. They arrived in Liverpool on December 1, 1943. Between then and February 27, 1945, they played 250 performances in England, Scotland, and Northern Ireland. On March 5, 1945, they began a tour of continental Europe—Belgium, France, Holland, and Germany. The tour lasted until July 21 and consisted of seventy performances, again with much travel in between.

Levine has a vivid recollection of D-Day. At the time, he and his colleagues were stationed on the southeast coast of England, near Dover, entertaining troops in the whole area.

"These were bases where we would go out every night to different parts of the coast and play for guys who were getting ready for the invasion. You could tell the invasion was coming… On D-Day we stood on the cliffs of Dover and watched the armadas going out and planes above us," he remembers.

Levine and another bass player, Murray Lauder, watched this dramatic event unfolding, and to mark the event they got their instruments and began playing bass duets—simply exercises out of a standard bass viol book. "That's the way we did our bit for democracy," he later joked.

After VE Day, the *Blackouts* group returned to England, then put together a newer show—"a little revue," as Sam Levine calls it—and continued to entertain until September 9, their last performance at the Regent Theatre in London.

Of thirty-two items listed on the program, Fran Dowie was involved in eleven. "He was the son of a man who was known as Rubberface in *The Dumbells* in the First World War," says Levine. He did comedy bits, a magic act, a bit of fiddling and "in one routine, Dowie would come on dressed in a kilt, like a Scotsman...and sing 'If You Knew Susie,' with a Scots accent. Our audiences loved it."

Dowie was also a talented cartoonist. The *Blackouts* company was in Paris on VE Day, on leave. Sam Levine and Fran Dowie were not far from the Arc de Triomphe, surrounded by jubilant crowds celebrating the great day. Dowie made some quick sketches and later created a panoramic cartoon of the Parisian scene on that memorable day. In it, you can see Union Jacks and Stars and Stripes and French tri-colors; kissing, dancing, drinking, brawling, picture-taking, and just a short distance away from the famous arch, the *Blackouts* truck, with the whole cast aboard.

While the show was in Europe, Fran Dowie married Edna Bond, a featured singer in the cast. She had to be sent home because she was pregnant. A dancer named Dick Hunter married another of the women from the show and she went home because she was pregnant, too. "Others didn't wait for the formality of marriage," says Levine. "It was real rough on our social life. There were several married men in the show but no married women. And for them it was awfully hard. You know, one of the things about everybody that went overseas, you didn't know whether you would come back. It wasn't so much that you feared that a bomb would bring it all to an end, it wasn't so much that, but there didn't seem to be any movement at all, any indication that it would ever be over. When VE Day came, it was like a bomb."

Sam Levine didn't get home until late in 1945. "I enrolled back at the Conservatory. I had made up my mind that the jazz game would be a short, happy life, and I wanted more, a more stable life." He eventually joined the Toronto Symphony and stayed with it until he was sixty-five years old.

Robert Coote also created an air force performing unit called *The W. Debs* (referring to the Women's Division of the RCAF) which consisted of eleven WDs and two male pianists. "The program was a variety of skits, songs, and dances," recalls Hazel MacDonald, one of the cast. "The show went overseas in 1944. It was designed to travel in one bus and one truck for props, etc. We could perform anywhere. And we did."

Equally mobile was a show called *Swingtime*, which consisted of four musicians (accordion, bass, guitar, and trumpet), an MC/comedian, a singer, a magician, and a tap-dancer who doubled as drummer.

The trumpeter was Winnipeg-born Paul Grosney, who was, despite his youth, an experienced musician. In January 1943, at the age of eighteen, he went to New York to study. Because the U.S. draft had decimated the ranks of the big bands, Grosney was able to work with the likes of Red Norvo and Charlie Barnet. Then his call-up came and he returned to Canada and joined the RCAF. Grosney was sent with a small group to play for Allied servicemen "all the way up the Alaska highway, all the way up to Nome." Later, the *Swingtime* unit was formed to go to England.

"The air force had something that the navy and the army never had," Grosney says, with a touch of pride. "Three dance bands. One was led by Bob McMullin [who grew up near Lethbridge], one by Pat Riccio [of Toronto], and one by Lance Harrison [of Vancouver]. They were big, fifteen-piece bands, and they all served overseas at different times."

But *Swingtime* was more a variety show because "when we put on a stage performance, it was a two-hour show," Grosney remembers. "The comedian would do twenty-five minutes, the magician would do twenty minutes. I had a thing where I did impressions of other trumpet players. I did Bunny Berigan, and then Henry Busse, then Louis Armstrong—I even sang eight bars of 'Louis,' if I'd sung the ninth bar everybody would have left—and Harry James and Clyde McCoy."

The mobility of the *Swingtime* unit was an important factor in its usefulness. Len Moss, for instance, was a pianist, but with this unit he played accordion—he took it wherever they were to play. In fact, in the summer of 1943, Len, (singer) Dave Davies, and (guitarist) Jimmy Riccio appeared one night at an Allied staging camp in Alaska. Just as the *Swingtime* trio finished its performance, a soldier rushed in and hustled them off to a waiting transport aircraft; ice in the river next to the base was breaking up and threatening to flood the airfield.

"One of the funny things that used to happen was that every American soldier that I met used to say, 'I've played for Tommy Dorsey,' because they wanted to play with the band. We used to fluff them off," continues Grosney.

"One day a guy comes up and says, 'You know, I haven't played for a long time, but I would like to sit in and play drums. Do you mind?' And I said, 'Did you play for Tommy Dorsey?' He says, 'No, Benny Goodman.' I said, 'What's your name?' He says, 'Buddy Schutz.' [Schutz had played with Goodman back in 1938–39.] And this guy...played his ass off."

Swingtime didn't use microphones, so they weren't inhibited by the occasional lack of electric power. In a way, this led to one of Paul Grosney's most memorable experiences.

Someone decided to send a small, mobile group of musicians to Belsen, site of one of Germany's notorious concentration camps, in northern Germany. "Basically, we were there to entertain Canadians, air force, army, navy, whatever," Grosney explains. "But we played for everybody, Americans and everybody... And it was just a matter of, well, there's a group here that can play.

"They [had] a lot of people there, thousands and thousands, and they were all in those striped things. We went in there and we had to play two songs here and move about twenty feet and play two songs there. We had to do the moving, because [the audience] didn't have the strength to move. And there was no sort of stage, where you say, 'Okay, everybody come to the show,' because nobody could come."

Being Jewish, Grosney was familiar with some Jewish folk music. One of the tunes he played, he remembers, was "Who'll Buy My Bublitchki?" which had been a hit recording for trumpeter Ziggy Elman a few years before. "I played some other Jewish stuff I had learned from playing weddings. And to see them trying to smile, it was painful, it was really something."

There was yet another RCAF entertainment unit during the Second World War called *The Tarmacs*, which had a cast of seven. The driving force behind the group was Teddy Cohen, a comedian from Winnipeg. There was drummer George Proulx from Quebec City; dancer Mickey Mincoff from Montreal; singer Howard Kapinsky from Ottawa; pianist Al Swayze from Regina; Elmer Leadbetter, a guitarist and country singer from Sydney, Nova Scotia; and Lorne Wickie of Stratford, Ontario, a female impersonator.

Wickie joined the Highland Light Infantry on June 10, 1940, "the day Italy entered the war, I remember." He had hoped to join the RCAF, but his education credentials were not acceptable. After some early training in Stratford, he was sent to Quebec City.

"I didn't like the army that much, you know, so what I did, I made out I couldn't eat army food. I figured I'll get out of this bloody thing, see? So they put me in the hospital, pumped my stomach out, did all that, and I got a discharge. I was about twenty years old."

By then, 1941, the RCAF had relaxed its educational requirements, and Wickie was able to join, but he couldn't get an aircrew assignment because of a faulty eye. He went overseas with an RCAF squadron, doing clerical work. When he was posted to London, he met Teddy Cohen and some of the others who soon formed *The Tarmacs*. "They remustered us all from whatever trade we were, and we were made entertainers."

Wickie had met Ross Hamilton in the army; Hamilton had been a member of *The Dumbells* in the First World War and one of two female impersonators in that show. Meeting Hamilton was "what started me in female impersonation.

"I did Gypsy Rose Lee. I did a striptease [in *The Tarmacs* show]," explained Wickie, "and I used tennis balls for tits... And I used to take them out and bounce them at the end of my act... People were taken in when they first saw me. And what a big shock when the tennis balls came bouncing out."

In his act, Lorne sang a song written by Teddy Cohen. He still remembers the lyrics.

I'm Gypsy Rose Lee, I'm Queen of them all,
I strip for a living, but that isn't all,
Now, my body is lovely, I don't want to boast,
I'm the pride of the nation, I'm the national toast.
So gals, have your husbands keep their eyes off me,
Cause I do strange movements with my anatomy.
I lean and I bend, I twist and I sway,
But if you want it, you gotta buy it,
Cause I ain't givin' nothin' away.

The Tarmacs played a lot of RCAF bases, plus a few army and navy installations. "After D-Day, we were the first air force show to go on the Continent," recalls Wickie. "We landed in Normandy, worked our way through Caen, doing shows. There was still fighting going on. I remember a German plane came over and strafed us one night, and we flew out of the hut and all I had on was a tin helmet. I was naked. I thought, I'm getting the hell out of here, I'm not gonna bother to dress."

Wickie says he got along fine in the RCAF and encountered no discrimination or unpleasantness. "At a dance, I danced with an air commodore once after the show. Oh, he knew, yeah, he knew. He says, 'Come on, I'll give you a twirl.'"

Lorne returned to Canada after the war, but didn't stay. His father had died during the war and his mother had remarried. He didn't get along with his stepfather, so he went back to England. He joined an all-male show called *This Was The Army*, made up of ex-servicemen. The show toured England and audiences "loved it because they'd never seen a striptease in England. At the Windmill [the famous London burlesque theatre that stayed open throughout the war], all the girls were allowed to do was pose. If they sneezed and their tits jumped, they got fined."

Air force audiences along Canada's west coast were treated to yet another RCAF entertainment group, called *The Joe Boys*, consisting of fourteen airmen. No WDs. The troupe included a ventriloquist named Freddie Lambert and comedian Bruce "Pinky" Pendlebury, who remembers that "most of our trips were to isolated [RCAF and U.S.]

listening posts on the Pacific coast, Marble Island, Cape Scott, and Langara Island." (At 75, Pendlebury says, "I'm still able to do a little show business when needed... When I was in the show I was a comedian. Now I'm a humorist. Same material, just a little slower.")

Some uniformed personnel, particularly those in very small or remote military installations, never got to see *The Canadian Army Show* or *Meet The Navy* or *The Tin Hats* or *The Tarmacs* or any of the other shows concocted for their benefit. In such cases, the armed service people simply put together their own entertainment, for the benefit of their fellow soldiers, sailors, airmen, or station crews. Most BCATP stations across Canada staged Christmas shows, concert parties, benefits, and even a few plays. The civilian staff of No. 7 Air Observer School at Portage la Prairie, Manitoba, staged the revue *Flying High* in April 1944 to raise funds for the Air Cadets; it was so successful that the production made an appearance in town and sold all 500 seats at one dollar a ticket.

At Central Flying School in Trenton, Ontario, the instructor ranks included enough ex-professional musicians to make up a sophisticated fourteen-piece band. It included sax-player Bill Hill (a graduate of the Boston Conservatory of Music), Ross Treumner (whose Blue Baron band had played across southern Ontario in the 1930s), trombone player Bill McCauley, and Buff Estes, former alto-sax player in Benny Goodman's 1940 band.

But ingenuity was as vital an ingredient as talent. WD Elaine Leiterman joined the RCAF in 1943; she spent much of her time in the service working as a radio-telegraph operator at a remote base near Pennfield Ridge in southern New Brunswick. None of the big air force shows played at No. 2 Air Navigation School. But they coped.

"The local people used to come and put on a show, and everybody said, 'Oh, no. Couldn't stand it.' So we decided to put on our own show. I had learned to jitterbug with a young black boy from New Brunswick, and I did the whole thing—up, down, around, and through—everything... Well, when [the brass] saw it [in rehearsal] they said, 'You can't do it.'

"I said, 'Why not?'

"They said, 'Because you're white and he's black.'

"So, I said, 'Okay, no problem.' We bought some lampblack, and covered me entirely in lampblack. They allowed it then...

"The audience loved the number because it had such vitality. The only [problem] was trying to get the black stuff off. I had to spend an hour in the shower, had to use grease paint to get it off."

The life of the travelling entertainer was not for everyone. Frank Shuster remembers a sound engineer we'll call Sandy (not his real name) in *The Canadian Army Show*. "He was always an unhappy kind of guy," Shuster says.

"When the big show was broken up into smaller units to go overseas, Sandy was part of the unit featuring Wayne and Shuster, and still unhappy, as usual. He could never see the bright side of anything, despite everyone else's efforts to keep his spirits up.

"We had fun. You had to have fun. Anything that happened that was good, you'd say to Sandy, 'What do you think, isn't this great?' And he'd say, 'Aw, you can shove it up your ass.' That was his line. Now, you gotta remember, this line runs for four years. So, he's with our little unit, about sixteen people, and you try to find good things [about the life], you know, this isn't so bad. 'You can shove it up your ass.'

"One day, we had a day off. We went to Brussels. We had gone through Normandy, and we were in Belgium and they gave us a day off and they said it's only twenty miles from Brussels, that's Little Paris. We said, 'Hey, Sandy, we got a day off, we're going to Brussels.' He says, 'You can shove it up your ass.'

"Now 1945, January, we're coming home. We're on a boat from New Zealand. We were in a convoy of fifty ships. This is when the U-boat thing was at its height. The war isn't over yet, but our unit had been six months on the Continent and the girls are all sick and nobody was feeling all that great, so they said, 'Okay, send them back...' Eighteen days it took. We zigged and zagged because of the U-boats. One day it was sunny. [The next] day [it was like] winter. We didn't know where the hell we were going. It was the longest trip.

"All of a sudden, in the evening, we're arriving in Halifax and it's lit up. We hadn't seen lights for almost two years. And who speaks up but Sandy. He says, 'Hey, guys, look, Halifax!' And, in unison, we all said: 'Aw, shove it up your ass!'"

9

The Fall of the Cards

Fate—or destiny or kismet or chance or fortune or luck, or whatever you prefer to call it—is not known for dealing impartially with all mortals. This is just as true in peacetime as in wartime, but in wartime the stakes are higher.

When the war broke out, writer Ron Poulton was reporting for the Moose Jaw *Times-Herald*. It was his first professional newspaper job and it paid "the grand sum of $10 a week." However, he enlisted with a machine gun regiment known as the Saskatoon Light Infantry (a phrase Poulton suggested was an outdated holdover from the First World War). His training began at a camp near Dundurn, Saskatchewan. But because of the "phony war" (in early 1940) there was no immediate need for reinforcements from his regiment, so Poulton and the SLI were forced to endure bitter winter conditions in tents out on the frozen prairie. Then, one day, a couple of recruiting officers arrived at Dundurn.

"One was from the Royal Rifles," Poulton recalls, "and the other was from Lord Strathcona's Horse. They both gave the little spiel about what an honour it would be for us to belong to these outfits. I looked at the captain [the recruiting officer of the Straths] who had high tank boots, black beret, and looked simply lovely. So I said to two or three fellows in the line with me, 'I think we'd better go to him.'

"The Royal Rifles ended up in Hong Kong just before Christmas [when the Japanese overran the colony]. Some of my friends got battered with rifle butts...while we were over in England chasing fish-and-chips and girls..."

Sub-Lieutenant Cliff Perry, RN, also seemed to lead a charmed life. His officer's rank afforded him the assistance of a young British seaman—a sort of servant who brought him tea each morning, attended to his laundry, and polished his boots.

"When he cleaned my boots," Perry remembers, "he used to put them on his feet to clean them... It was the easier way of doing it. So he learned that they fit him...

"My 'servant' was due for a weekend leave in London. He said, 'Sir, could I borrow your boots for my leave?' And I said, 'You want to impress your girlfriend, don't you?' and he said, 'Yes, sir. I could never afford a pair of boots like this.' I said, 'Okay, but try not to get drunk and stumble on the pavement and scuff them up too badly.' He laughed and said, 'Okay.'

"He never came back. He was killed by a buzz bomb."

During the invasion of Normandy, Perry served on a motor torpedo boat off the French coast. His was one of a flotilla of five that crossed the English Channel every night to protect Allied convoys and attack any German shipping they encountered. In return, the flotilla endured attacks by aircraft, torpedo bombers, and U-boats.

"Ours was the only ship in a flotilla of five that started before D-Day and survived," notes Perry. "Every one of those four other ships was either damaged by torpedoes or mines—in most cases—or other enemy action, and had to be replaced. One of them was replaced twice. We were a charmed ship and we stayed there through the whole thing right up to the end. The only ship that did in that flotilla."

Peter Hobley, who came to Canada in 1954, saw death come—and go. Hobley served in British Intelligence during the war, working as an instructor with a War Office school just south of London. The building housing the school was a large residence, with no external markings indicating its wartime purpose. Hobley's office was on the third floor of the residence in what had once been servants' quarters.

"This was a Saturday afternoon. We used to take turns for security purposes—somebody had to be in the place during the weekends. My office overlooked a beautiful garden with two rows of poplar trees, and in between them was a tennis court... I had just finished what I was doing and I stood up and walked across to the window and looked out.

(I'd got something wrong with my ears at the time and I had cotton wool in them, so I didn't hear any sirens.)

"I looked straight down at this end of this double row of poplar trees beyond the tennis court...and level with my eyes was a V1 [coming right at me]. I thought, 'Holy Toledo, this is it!' There was nothing I could do. I just stood there and waited for it, because it was going to fly straight in the window. Fortunately it was summer time and it was quite hot and there must have been enough thermals generated by the trees—and at the last moment, it just lifted up, went up over the top of the roof...

"There was a residential road on the other side and a house on the opposite side of that road. It landed right on that house. No part of the place was left standing any higher than a foot off the ground. There was a family killed there; they were all in the house."

Sometimes a spell of good luck ran out. Late in the war, a famed British Mosquito combat aircraft, nicknamed "F for Freddie," visited Canada to help publicize the eighth Victory Loan campaign. Although it was built in Britain by de Havilland and flew with the RAF, F for Freddie was part Canadian: its tough plywood fuselage was the product of the spruce forests of British Columbia. The fighter-bomber had completed 211 operational flights over Germany without mishap. After its distinguished combat record, F for Freddie began a flight to Canada via Iceland and Greenland, during which it established a speed record for non-stop flight from Greenland to Montreal, covering the 2,000-mile distance in a little more than five hours.

After thrilling Montreal and Toronto spectators with air shows aimed at boosting bond sales, F for Freddie headed for Calgary, with Flight Lieutenant Maurice Briggs, pilot, Flying Officer John Baker, navigator, and Edward Jack, a Canadian flight engineer, aboard.

In Calgary, on May 9, the day after VE Day, Edward Jack tuned up the aircraft. He checked it out again the following morning, a few minutes before take-off on May 10. The pilot, Briggs, asked Jack if he was going on the exhibition flight over Calgary. Jack said he was feeling tired and decided not to go.

The aircraft took off shortly after 4 p.m., circled the municipal airfield twice, went into a power dive, pulled out, and was travelling southeast across the airfield (about fifty feet above the ground) when it struck a weather observation tower and crashed a quarter of a mile away in a heap of twisted, flaming wreckage. Briggs and Baker were both killed.

Royal Canadian Artilleryman Cliff Florence recalls a brush with fate on his way overseas. In the fall of 1942, his Elgin Regiment of the RCA boarded the New Zealand troopship *Awatea* bound for Britain. Accompanying his regiment were 900 graduates of the Canadian-based British Commonwealth Air Training Plan, en route to operational postings in Britain. They were about 200 miles out to sea "when suddenly we were awakened by an earthshaking jolt and crashing noises.

"All of us at once thought we had been torpedoed and made haste to the upper decks, only to discover we had hit an American destroyer (U.S.S. *Ingraham*) which had been criss-crossing our ship in convoy. Why it happened we will never know. We were in time to see the destroyer light up and sink in a matter of minutes—most of the crew were lost.

"Our ship had an eight-foot hole in the bow, and we had to unload all our fresh water to get seaworthy. We had to turn around and return to Halifax for repairs. The trip back was slow and at times nervewracking. We were all alone out there. The rest of the convoy had continued on their way—we were sitting ducks.

"We made it back to Halifax safe and sound, and after getting survivors' leave, we shipped out again and arrived in England seven weeks after the incident—aboard the same ship, the *Awatea*." (Incidentally, the *Awatea* was the same ship that carried Canadian troops to Hong Kong in 1941.)

Serviceman Harvey Willis didn't know about his brush with fate until a day after the fact. Like Cliff Florence, Willis also served with the Royal Canadian Artillery; his battery had come ashore in Italy. During that campaign Willis's battery command post was hit. Signallers were lying on the ground with arm, leg, and head wounds. Gun Sergeant Willis was ordered to go to the assistance of the signalmen.

"I pulled out of my gun position, and left my gun in charge of the bombardier," Willis remembers. "I had a pack on my back. I could hear an 88 coming, so I hit the ground and got up when that barrage was over and ran again and then fell down on the next barrage. I got over to the Battery Command Post...and helped these guys...with their broken arms or legs...

"It was only the next day that I found out that that backpack had saved my life. There was a hunk of shrapnel in that pack."

Bert Thistle's close call occurred on his second day ashore in Normandy. Thistle had joined up in St. John's and become a member of the Sherbrooke Fusiliers before he was eighteen years old. Just before D-Day, the Fusiliers were transformed from an infantry regiment into an armoured one, so when Thistle went ashore on D-Day, it was as a wireless operator in a tank.

Eleven days later, his family back in Newfoundland received a telegram informing them that their son was missing in action. Thistle had been taken prisoner on June 7. The tank on which he was a crew member had been disabled by German 88 fire. The tank commander gave the order to bail out. Three of the tank troopers stayed together. The driver went back to the tank to see if all the others had got out safely. The driver also survived, Thistle learned later, but it took him two weeks to get back to the regiment. Thistle later heard that "his nerves went on him."

Bert Thistle, his commander, and a third member of the tank crew were captured that evening by members of the 12th SS Brigade, led by the notorious Colonel Kurt Meyer, who was later convicted of having Allied prisoners shot. Two other Canadian tank troopers from his squadron were captured at the same time. The SS men took various personal possessions from the prisoners (including a watch Bert's father had given him) and marched them up to the Abbey of Ardenne, a cluster of medieval buildings that Meyer used as his headquarters. Eighteen Canadian prisoners were killed there after surrendering to the Germans. Bert Thistle and his comrades were slated to be Meyer's next victims.

"I didn't see all eighteen of them. I saw a few guys from the North Novas," Thistle remembers. "We saw them right in front of this barn on the ground, four or five of them. One guy was in a boxcar, like a horse standing up, and with his guts hanging out, but still alive.

"Anyway, they took us into this barn, five of us, and they lined us up. We were next. Had a sniper on us. And you shook hands, you know...when in came an officer, some high-ranking officer (not Meyer) and stopped him [the sniper]... I'll never get over it or forget it. It was just a split second, that another five would be added to the eighteen." At least, Thistle and his fellow Canadians were live POWs.

Another close encounter story comes from the other side of the globe. In May 1945, Montreal infantryman Captain M.V.D. Beattie took part in an assault landing in Burma with an English infantry regiment. On Ramree, an island in the Bay of Bengal, a mortar bomb dug into the ground right in front of him but failed to explode. Later, when Beattie took out a patrol, he came across three Japanese just ten feet away behind a bush. Gunfire was exchanged.

Pinned down on open terrain, Beattie threw himself to the ground during a burst of fire and remained motionless. A group of Japanese soldiers came towards him down the hillside.

"I couldn't understand what they were saying," explained Beattie, "but they were apparently debating whether or not I was dead." He waited until the Japanese were almost up to him, then fired at them and rushed away into the undergrowth. Two days after the war in Europe ended, Beattie was reported as safe and free.

Gordon Emerson Clarke was one of the few Canadians who recognized the threat of Hitler early on. "In 1937, Hitler invaded Austria, and I said to myself, I have to learn something about the army. One of these days we are going to have to fight that son of a bitch Hitler, and I want to know something about the army."

Clarke and a buddy enlisted in Peterborough, Ontario. After considerable training and a stint as an artillery instructor, he became frustrated with what he considered time-wasting. In 1940, he transferred to the Stormont, Dundas, and Glengarry Highlanders and was commissioned two years later, in England. On D-Day, he landed with the "Glens" at Juno Beach.

"We did have a couple of casualties on the beach," recalls Clarke. "The landing craft hit some mines and I remember a couple of our contingent were wounded from the shrapnel. [But there was] no small-arms fire at that time because the Queen's Own had beaten back the beach defences. Thank God for that.

"I've always been lucky that I was always in a back-up position, but that's no fault of mine, just the fall of the cards... We have no say in that, whatever the orders come down, you go where you are supposed to go..."

On D-Day+6, as the Glens were digging in at Vieux Cairon, Clarke was walking through a slit trench when mortar shrapnel caught him in the left thigh. Since there were not yet any forward operational first-aid posts, Clarke was evacuated to England.

While he was recuperating, the buzz-bombs were flying over London. One hit a house in which one of the officers, Ted Murfit, was staying. "He was back from the front and he was killed along with his wife and children. So who is to say where was safe? In those days you might as well be at the front as in London, because nobody knew. Who knows where the fall of the cards will be?"

On his first day back in France in action, Clarke was hit again in the back and legs by grenade shrapnel and evacuated to a hospital in Bayeux. Another time, Clarke rashly walked into a German trap, was beaten mercilessly, clubbed, and kicked. When he was captured, he tried to bluff his way out, claiming his men were all around, but the Germans were not fooled. He was bandaged up and put on a half-track with some wounded Germans. The vehicle had a big red cross on it. On the road to St. Lambert, the driver smashed into a building. In the confusion that followed, Clarke managed to escape. When he got back to his battalion, his comrades were amazed to see him—they thought he was dead. "I said, 'Well, the fall of the cards again...'"

On April 27, 1945, when the Glens crossed the Ems River, near Leer, Germany, "a hail of enemy machine gun fire was raking our position. The Hitler Youth holding the dike were fighting valiantly and it took a Ronson flame thrower to dislodge some of these fanatic soldiers from their position. Suddenly a bullet found its mark and I was knocked to the ground. It had passed through my right leg. With the dike secured, I was evacuated eventually to England."

Major Clarke had already been awarded a Distinguished Service Order and was present, in July, at the investiture at Buckingham Palace. He regards the decoration with a mixture of pride and embarrassment, partly because he thinks either nobody should get a medal or everyone should, and partly because of his philosophical belief that everything is prey to "the fall of the cards."

*

The loss of a loved one must have seemed doubly tragic when the death occurred close to the end of the war. Yet Canadian newspapers, in the first two weeks of May 1945, seemed to be filled with just such stories.

On May 8, *The Vancouver Sun* reported that the day before, Mrs. May Else of Duncan had received word that her husband, Captain James Else, had been killed in action.

The Halifax Herald reported on May 10 the death of RCAF Corporal Harold Kenney, who had been promoted only a month before being fatally wounded.

On the same day, *The Gazette* in Montreal carried the news that the parents of Lieutenant Walter A. Westwood of the Black Watch had just been notified of their son's death in action.

The news that Regimental Sergeant Major A. G. Murray of the Algonquin Regiment had been killed in action on May 2 was reported (on May 11) in *The Niagara Falls Review*.

George A. Chapman of Toronto had been an RCAF navigator overseas since 1943. The mission of his Halifax bomber was to drop supplies to Polish resistance fighters. Chapman was reported missing in August 1944, but it was not until June of the following year that he was officially confirmed as dead.

Immediately after the war, the Canadian Bank of Commerce distributed to its staff a privately published book that paid tribute to the many bank employees who had served in the Canadian forces. Of the 1,523 men and 158 women who enlisted, 133 were killed—23 of them in the closing weeks of the war.

Lieutenant-Colonel Donald Alexander Mackenzie of Kincardine, Ontario, had been awarded the Distinguished Service Order for his leadership of the 48th Highlanders in the Italian campaign. He was killed in action near Wilp, Holland, on April 12, 1945.

Sergeant Edward Hodgins Brundrit of Winnipeg served with the Royal Canadian Dragoons in the Sicilian and Italian campaigns and was still with the regiment when it reached the North Sea on April 15, 1945. He was killed in action in north Germany on May 4.

Death at the hands of the enemy in war is an expected danger. Death by accident, however, seems to be a particularly unkind twist of fate. On April 25, 1945, in one of the last large-scale Allied bombing attacks of the war, 192 RCAF aircraft joined a stream of 482 Halifaxes, Lancasters, and Mosquitoes (with Spitfire escort) en route to Wangerooge Island off the north coast of Germany. Their objective was to knock out two coastal batteries that still controlled the approaches to the ports at Bremerhaven and Wilhelmshaven. It was an afternoon raid. The weather was clear and the bombing appeared to inflict severe damage to the area around gun emplacements. The bombers encountered some anti-aircraft flak and a Halifax bomber manned by a Free French crew went down.

However, the day's largest losses were the result of a tragic flying accident. At one point during the mission, one of the bombers got caught in the slipstream of another; the second aircraft plowed into a third and, in a moment, six bombers—two Lancasters and four Halifaxes—had collided with one another and were plummeting into the North Sea. Reports said there were as many as nine parachutes sighted. Nonetheless, all twenty-eight Canadians—four full crews— died in the mid-air collision.

In the chaos of war, some accidental deaths remain mysterious. The story of Carman Cecil McKague is recalled by his cousin, Berenice McKague. Carman was one of three brothers, all of whom were in the service and waiting to come home in December 1945. He would have been twenty-one on December 11, and was on leave in London.

"Carman and one of his buddies were staying at a YMCA... About 10 p.m. [on December 7] the bobby on the beat said goodnight to the two Canadians as they returned to their hostel. As he was passing the building again at approximately 3 a.m., he was surprised to find Carman's body face down with the steel pickets of the wrought-iron fence right through his body.

"No evidence of foul play was ever discovered. The cause had to be deduced. Carman had evidently reverted to a troubling habit of his childhood—sleep-walking. He had simply opened the French doors to the window ledge above the street and walked right through them—to his death on the steel spears below. For him, Victory was a culmination, rather than a new beginning."

Death is also a heartbreaking waste. Ernest Otto Pawl joined the RCAF in his native Alberta in 1941. As the war in Europe was about to end, Pawl, who spoke German and Polish fluently, was seconded by the British government to serve as an interpreter with the British Occupational Forces of the Rhine and was among the first to liberate surviving inmates at the Bergen-Belsen concentration camp. Pawl worked with many children, helping to prepare them for the new life that awaited them in homes in Canada and the United States. Tragically, many of these same children, who had miraculously survived so much horror, died when their ship hit a mine in the North Sea.

Although Canada's role in the last stages of the Pacific war was limited, it, too, provided a share of last-minute tragedies. Lieutenant Robert "Hammy" Gray of Nelson, B.C., a Canadian serving with the Royal Navy's Fleet Air Arm, led a series of actions against Japanese airfields and shipping. On August 9, 1945, Gray led a force attacking ships around Honshu, Japan. Even though his aircraft was hit, he went down after an enemy destroyer. Gray was killed—five days before VJ Day. His Victoria Cross was the last to be awarded to a Canadian in the Second World War.

The fall of the cards caught one minesweeper by surprise. Early on the morning of April 16, 1945, the Royal Canadian Navy's Bangor-class minesweeper *Esquimalt* made her way through the approaches to Halifax harbour. The war was nearing its end. Attacks from U-boat wolf packs were past and the seas seemed less dangerous. However, *Esquimalt* and her seventy-one-man crew were still on anti-submarine patrol. Orders that morning called for the *Esquimalt* to meet her sister ship *Sarnia* (on patrol in another sector) by 7 o'clock.

Waters were calm. The night watch was moonless. The ship's writer, Petty Officer Terry Manuel, who had been posted to the stern watch since 0400 hours, remembers that although the night was clear, "there was mist on the water, so fellow watchkeepers could not be seen or heard even a few yards away from each other."

At about 0515 hours, Manuel was startled by a shrill whistle from the nearby voice-pipe. He confirmed its call and was ordered to an alert on the quarterdeck below. At the starboard depth-charge thrower he unlashed cables, set the arming dial to the appropriate depth setting, removed the safety-catch, and signalled "ready" to the bridge. The alert continued for nearly an hour, but they passed the East Halifax Light Ship—an ocean marker—and nothing happened.

At 0600 hours, Manuel's watch ended. Donald White took over his position and Manuel went below. He stopped a moment at the galley stove, poured himself a cup of coffee, and made his way to his sleeping quarters—a row of foam-padded box lockers below decks. At 0610 hours the alert was called off.

With clear skies and relatively calm seas so close to the Nova Scotia coastline, *Esquimalt's* crew had reportedly switched off her antiquated radar system; it would never have been able to detect a U-boat periscope or snorkel anyway. Nor was the minesweeper stringing a "CAT"—a noisemaker towed behind the ship to attract Gnat torpedoes (built to home in on a ship's propellers). *Esquimalt* wasn't even cutting a traditional zigzag pattern through the water. Instead, her crew was relying on asdic—the navy's conventional sound-transmitting device for detecting mines or submarines.

At 0620, close to Sambro Light Vessel, *Esquimalt* ran smack into the sights of U-190, lying in the shallow waters of the Grand Banks. The U-boat captain took one look through his periscope at the escort ship coming right at him and fired off a Gnat torpedo. Seconds later, it scored a direct hit. *Esquimalt's* asdic operator had heard nothing. There wasn't even enough time to transmit an SOS or fire off a flare.

The ship's captain—Lieutenant Robert MacMillan—was a seasoned navy man; in fact, he had earned a DSC and had survived a torpedoing in the Mediterranean earlier in the war. Within seconds MacMillan knew *Esquimalt* was doomed and gave the order to abandon ship.

"I heard a muffled thud and then a shattering explosion," remembers Manuel. "It threw me over the mess table, rolling uncontrollably with tumbling equipment and debris. The lights dimmed, flickered, and went out. It was now pitch-black within. And the angle of the deck was increasing steadily as *Esquimalt* continued its unstoppable roll onto its side."

The U-boat's torpedo had penetrated the minesweeper's starboard side, right below the depth-charge thrower, where Manuel had been on watch a few minutes earlier. It exploded in the cabin of Lieutenant John Smart, who had just turned in from his night watch on the bridge. He was killed immediately.

Below decks, somebody struck a wooden match illuminating the dust-filled chaos. Shipwright Ralph Pool lay in a heap against a bulkhead as Manuel, Carl Jacques, and Norman Shave tried to open the emergency hatch. The wheel wouldn't budge. As the ship's metal whined and crashed about him, Manuel shouted he was getting out another way. "Nobody followed," he recalls. "The air was unbreathable and the rising smell of fear permeated the confined space."

In the dark and quickly rising flood of Atlantic water and engine oil, Manuel scrambled along a companionway in search of an outer hatchway and the forward deck, where he eventually spotted "a thin glint of daylight through the mass of wreckage above." He shouted out his discovery and soon had company—crew-mate Carl Jacques and the ship's mascot, a cat named Hershme, who landed on Manuel's head and promptly dug its claws into his scalp.

"A powerful wave of water then swallowed me and pummelled me against an inner steel wall. Back and forth I was flung. And I sensed the ship rolling under me. As quickly as it happened, suddenly, there was utter tranquillity. I had been flung through the hatchway and was now well under water. As I rose I could see faint light above…"

But even on the surface, Terry Manuel was in a precarious position. He could not swim. For a few seconds he latched onto the fast-sinking wreckage in the water, then a floating lifejacket with "1st Lt." stencilled on it (John Smart's preserver). Finally, Carl Jacques, who had been washed out of the hold the same way Manuel had, swam to him and pulled him to the float.

On the bridge, Able Seaman Joseph Wilson stayed at his watch post after the torpedo struck. When the captain gave the order to abandon ship he struggled up to the boat-deck, climbed onto the funnel of the then capsized vessel, and leapt overboard.

Only two of the six Carley floats (life-rafts) got off the sweeper. "I got to the Carley float," Wilson later recalled, "but was in it only a couple of seconds when the mast of the sinking ship caught it and turned it over. The six of us in the float were thrown into the water. I came under the float and thought I had hit the bottom of the ship." Seven of the thirteen men on his float subsequently died of exposure.

Captain MacMillan finally left the ship as it rolled in its death throes; he scrambled across the hull of the upturned ship and waded off into the water. Within just four minutes of the torpedo strike, HMCS *Esquimalt* had sunk, taking Manuel's bunk-mates Norman Shave and Ralph Pool and twenty-six others to their deaths.

Still, the sun was rising. And despite some remaining patches of mist, conditions remained clear. Seas were calm. Sambro Light Vessel was nearly in sight. The *Sarnia* was due to rendezvous. Rescue shouldn't be far off. However, the battle of *Esquimalt's* surviving forty-four crew members was not over.

Leading Seaman Herbert Knight found himself on a float overcrowded with sixteen other men. A strong swimmer, he plunged into the icy water and swam to the other float and then pushed the second float back to the first so the two could be lashed together. Only then did he allow himself to be pulled onto the less crowded float. An hour later, he died of exposure.

As substantial as the Carley floats were in the water, they offered little protection from the elements. Survivors outside the floats clung to ropes that scalloped the sides, while inside men stood on netting up to their chests in water. One by one *Esquimalt's* survivors succumbed to the cold air and freezing water. On the rafts, Carl Jacques, who had pulled Terry Manuel and others into the Carley floats, soon died. Donald White, who had sustained internal injuries as well as broken legs and arms in the torpedo blast, also died of his wounds. Sub-lieutenant Mike Kazakoff tied a white shirt to a paddle and waved it constantly all day. The cook, Jim McIntyre, "promised us the best of T-bone steaks, should we make it," remembers Manuel. "Jim clung to the side of the raft for about a half an hour, said goodbye, then drifted off to his death."

Air crews flying over the floats thought that the drifting crewmen were fishermen and didn't even circle. And at one point, two other Allied minesweepers approached, but no one spotted the frantic waving and shouting of *Esquimalt's* desperate crew. Hours passed and hope faded. For Huntley Fanning, who had been promoted to chief electrical artificer the night before the torpedoing, the end came in delirium.

"As he lay with his head bundled against (my) shoulder," Able Seaman Frank Smith later reported, "and with his body numbed beyond all further suffering, (Huntley) spoke to his fiancée back in his

Nova Scotia home town... He was to have married (her) on his next leave.

"'It looks as if we are not going to make it. I guess we won't be able to get married this time,' the dying sailor whispered. A few brief moments of silence followed as (we) gazed into one another's eyes. Then a 'So long, fellows. Keep plugging.' And his body stilled into death."

Seven hours after the sinking, *Sarnia* came across the Carley floats and twenty-six survivors. On board was Liam Dwyer, a four-and-a-half-year veteran of the RCN. He recalls picking up the freezing and frozen *Esquimalt* crewmen and taking "those that were alive below decks to be treated by the sick bay attendant and crew. The dead ones were wrapped in blankets and laid on the boat-deck.

"Our messman, Gordie Marsh, was trying to get the clothes off the captain [MacMillan] who was shaking so much Marsh could not hold him. I sat on him and we got his clothes off and wrapped him in blankets. He was gnashing his teeth together so hard, I thought he would break them into a thousand pieces. I got a napkin from the table, tied it around his mouth like a gag. This helped, but the survivors were also retching from the fuel oil they had swallowed. We had to watch that they did not choke."

One of the *Esquimalt* crew, Leading Seaman Duncan MacDonald of Dartmouth, N.S., was first listed as missing but later turned up. "Missing? I'm very much here," he said. His feet were frozen by long immersion in the icy Atlantic after the minesweeper went down. With other crew members, MacDonald spent several hours in a Carley float, his feet dangling over the side.

"My feet are still a little sore," he said, "but they weren't frozen as badly as some of the fellows, who kept them out of the water. I remembered I had read somewhere to keep your feet under in such cases, and that's what I did."

Sarnia steamed at full speed to Halifax. The gates and the submarine nets were swung open. On her way through, the minesweeper stopped to pick up doctors and nurses. By this time, all ships had been cleared from *Sarnia*'s berth. Dwyer remembers a sea of white-coated medical personnel at the dock as well as the civilians lining Barrington Street overlooking the dockyard.

"Our captain put his cap and greatcoat on the surviving captain [MacMillan]," explained Dwyer. "And he walked down the gangplank unassisted. When he was helped into the ambulance the crowd clapped and cheered. The young officer [Kazakoff] was carried ashore on a stretcher. The dead were loaded into waiting ambulances last, to be taken to their loved ones."

The news of the sinking was not announced for three weeks, after VE Day.

A subsequent board of inquiry seemed unable to answer the questions surrounding the loss of *Esquimalt*, such as: Why wasn't the sweeper zigzagging? Why was she on patrol alone? What happened to the planned rendezvous with *Sarnia* at 0700? And why weren't her CAT or her radar operating? In the end, Naval Service Headquarters decided the findings of the board were "inconclusive."

Unfortunately, the board did not interview J. Ross Young, who could have shed some light on the incident. At the time, Young was a petty officer radio artificer in the RCN. He was stationed at the central maintenance depot of the Halifax shipyards. A day before the sinking, he remembers *Esquimalt* sending a radio message that her radar system had broken down, and that the ship was returning to port for repairs. Young was assigned to take out a boat, meet the ship at the harbour gates, and carry out the repairs.

"The crew was obviously scared," explained Young, "and kept pleading that I advise it couldn't be repaired so they could return to base; whereas the officer kept pressing as to how long it would take to repair. It was obvious that the captain wanted to head back out to sea." He had his way. Young managed the repairs. "*Esquimalt* went back to sea the following morning—the day she was torpedoed."

There was an unusual sequel to the *Esquimalt* story. The German U-boat (U 190) that sank the Canadian minesweeper was captured a week after VE day. It was commissioned in the RCN for "testing and evaluation." Two years later, it was "decommissioned" and was subsequently sunk by Canadian naval aircraft near the position where she had sunk HMCS *Esquimalt*.

Sometimes the fall of the cards leads to extraordinary circumstances. George Aley was an RCAF bomb-aimer/front-gunner during the war.

Of the five and a half years he served, two and a half were spent on loan to the RAF Bomber Command. He was the only Canadian on the seven-man crew of an RAF Lancaster.

On the night of January 5–6, 1944, their target was military installations at the Baltic port of Stettin, not too far from Berlin. It turned out to be a terrible night: sixteen of the planes were shot down—fourteen Lancasters and two Halifaxes. Aley's plane had successfully bombed the target and set course for home when it was attacked from behind by a Messerschmitt 210, a twin-engined night fighter. Although the Lancaster was in serious trouble and rapidly losing altitude, two of its gunners managed to hit the pursuing German fighter.

The enemy plane went down in flames, but the Lanc was not out of trouble yet. After a hair-raising trip across the North Sea, the pilot managed to crash-land on a grass-covered air strip just inside the coast of Norfolk. All seven of the crew "walked away in one piece," Aley says.

Over the years, Aley kept in touch with some of his old RAF buddies, including Dickie Dyer, the navigator. Dyer had remained in the RAF as a career officer for twenty-five years. In 1965, Dyer was attached for a time to NATO (North Atlantic Treaty Organization) and attended a meeting in Italy.

"My friend Dickie struck up an acquaintance with one of the West German representatives, a chap about his own age," Aley relates. "During the course of their conversation, it transpired that this German chap had served in the Luftwaffe during the war...as a night fighter pilot in the general area north of Berlin... Dickie asked the German chap if he had ever been shot down. His reply: 'Only once, it was by the crew of a Lancaster bomber northeast of Berlin on the night of January 5–6, 1944.'"

The two men compared their flight-log books. "The entries coincided exactly with respect to time and location of the attack," says Aley. "Here then, some twenty years later, was the very pilot who had so badly shot up our aircraft and whose aircraft we had subsequently shot down! He had been able to bail out...landed in a farmer's field...and returned to his duties as a Luftwaffe pilot... His name: Hans Mundt... Truth can indeed be stranger than fiction."

Maybe Major Gordon Clarke had it figured right: who knows where the fall of the cards will be?

10

"KAPUT!"

As German troops retreated before the might of Allied forces in the spring of 1945, it became increasingly evident that the war in Europe would soon be over. A key clue was the suicide of Adolf Hitler.

Margaret Los was one of the first in Canada to get the news of the death of Hitler. In 1945 she had been a Wren for nearly three years. She was a high-frequency direction-finding wireless operator, eavesdropping on German submarine traffic all over the Atlantic from her listening post at Moncton. Even though the German "wolf packs" had officially thrown in the towel in the war in the Atlantic in 1943, individual U-boats still prowled the sea lanes between North America and Europe—until May 4, 1945.

"In those days," she explained, "the submarines had to come up every twelve hours to pump out the stale air and recharge their batteries. With German efficiency, when they were on the surface, providing no Allied shipping was around, they'd send a message home. We monitored them...

"They made two mistakes. They didn't know or didn't believe that our electronic equipment was good enough to pick them up in the middle of the Atlantic. And they hadn't known we'd broken their code."

Los and her colleagues didn't have to break Admiral Karl Doenitz's code on May 4, because "he sent it out in plain German, informing all ships that their dear Führer had died a hero's death...committed suicide. We sent a copy of what we'd picked up to the British Admiralty.

"And we all said, 'Well, Hitler's dead, what now?'"

Four days later, when VE Day came, Los was again on duty when she heard "the transmissions to the submarines telling them to go to the nearest port" to surrender. But her radio shift ended at midnight on May 8, so she missed all the celebrations going on in downtown Moncton.

The same day that Margaret Los heard Admiral Doenitz announce Hitler's death, David Francis, a twenty-three-year-old captain in the 2nd Medium Artillery Regiment of the 1st Canadian Army, was stationed in the village of Otterlo, in Holland. Francis had been overseas for three years. He'd fought his way up the boot of Italy with the Eighth Army, and now, in the Dutch countryside, was trying "to avoid last-minute casualties." On May 4 Francis found himself at a party "arranged for the men by our quartermaster, Captain Mike McHarg.

"The local citizenry were also invited," recalled Francis. "At the height of the party—up to then a pretty tame affair—news came over the radio of the surrender of the German forces in Holland and certain other parts of northwestern Europe.

"The loud resulting cheers were suddenly hushed as all the Dutch people present stood and, with tears streaming down their cheeks, sang their national anthem, and sang it again, and yet again. For the next several minutes the best efforts of the MC to get on with the program were drowned out as these normally undemonstrative Dutch people gave vent to their pent-up emotions as the realization sank in that they were free at last of the Nazi yoke."

William Brydon, who had been evacuated to Canada from England and had returned home late in 1944, was helping his sister, who worked in the Land Army, on a farm. Bill, then about thirteen, was responsible for taking food out to the German prisoners of war who were working on the farms. "They ate in their quarters," he remembers. "They were crying. They had just heard Hitler had been killed and, well, to them, it was like the Messiah had gone."

Some who heard the news were not in a position to do much celebrating. Wallace Bambrough, who had joined the Royal Canadian Engineers in 1940 and helped fight all the way into Germany, remembers that he was angry "because we were right up, past Wilhelmshaven, and we celebrated with two bottles of beer, and I thought to myself I bet they are having a hell of a time in London and Toronto and here we are with two bottles of Labatt's."

Beer wasn't a prerequisite for celebration at Walton Hospital in Liverpool, England. Emma McCann was a student nurse at Walton Hospital when the war in Europe ended. She remembers someone running into the ward, yelling: "The war is over!"

"The hospital grounds were full of patients rejoicing—hospital gowns, bare bottoms and all—and nurses trying to get them back to bed where they belonged. A couple of days later we started receiving convoys of POWs from Bergen-Belsen. These men were in very poor condition from abuse and starvation."

At a hospital in northern Belgium, Canadian Army Nurse Madge McKillop was also attending to the medical needs of POWs—from both sides. Word of official victory in Europe was expected daily at her hospital, but "it was still exciting and almost unbelievable that the war with Germany was indeed at long last over. We first heard the news on the radio and later in the day listened to broadcasts by King George VI and Winston Churchill.

"I don't think most of the patients believed it until a piper marched through the building playing the bagpipes. As well, *The Maple Leaf*, the Canadian Army paper, had only one word on its front page: KAPUT. I think many of the older [German] patients were relieved, but one young soldier, about fifteen and a real little Hitler Youth, was stunned and bewildered to think that his idol, Adolf Hitler, had committed suicide!

"At the end of the day shift, all of us who were off duty gathered to celebrate the marvellous news. We started out with a church service of thanksgiving, remembrance, and a reminder of those still fighting in the Far East. Then we had a party—singing, dancing, and drinking champagne."

It was a long way from Normandy to VE Day. But Joe Oggy made it all the way, from a first-wave landing at Juno Beach on June 6, to guard duty in a farmhouse in Emden, Germany, the following May 8. It was late that night, Oggy recalls, and "I'm with the Signals and he's got this radio going. I'm cooking up some German sausage, frying the grease out of it. Someone said, 'The war's over, the war's over!' and I'm hollering, 'Stand to!' I figured this could be a ploy. I woke everybody up, yelling 'Stand to! Get up into position,' at this farmhouse. Apparently the war *was* over..."

George Findlay was still awaiting a posting when he got the news. Findlay's trip to England aboard the *Mauritania* in January 1945 "taught me all I needed to know about seasickness." He can even remember crawling on his hands and knees to get a seasick pill "which I couldn't keep down." On arrival in England "as infantry reinforcement material," Findlay was put through various courses of training, most of them pointless.

"On this one day," he recalls, "our platoon was to be transferred to another camp, so we were marched out that morning onto the parade square with full kit, to await the lorries to take us to our new posting. A sergeant came out on the parade square, smartly saluted the lieutenant in charge, spoke to him, and then they both walked off the parade square. Being good soldiers, we stood there for about an hour. Finally someone broke ranks and went back to the orderly room to see what had happened...

"You guessed it—it was VE Day and just about everyone had taken off. We finally rounded up lorries to take us to our new posting but when we got there everyone including the cooks had been paid ten shillings and given leave. Being broke and hungry, some of us had a tough time scrounging enough for a beer, let alone getting to town early enough to get one."

Walter Wright celebrated in Belfast. The Winnipeg-born wireless air gunner had finished a tour with the RAF on heavy bombers, and had been transferred to an operational training unit that prepared other aircrew for combat missions. Just before VE Day one of the crews from Wright's station went on a cross-country flight to practise navigation. The trip took them over Ireland, where they had engine trouble and were forced to land. There were no parts available there to fix the aircraft, so Wright volunteered as wireless air gunner on a crew to fly parts to the downed plane in Ireland.

"When we got there," he remembers, "the other crew took our aircraft and flew back to home base. We had to wait until the other aeroplane was repaired. We learned that it would take more than a day, so we took a bus and went to see the sights in Belfast...and enjoy a few drinks. We did not buy many, as the local people kept us supplied."

The next day, Wright and his crew went back to the airfield, only to be told their aircraft wouldn't be ready for another day or two. So back to Belfast they went.

"Meanwhile, VE Day was announced, so all flying was cancelled for forty-eight hours to give everyone a rest and time to celebrate. We were stuck there. We thought the pubs would be a good place to celebrate, but quickly found out they, too, were shut down. We went back to our second-storey room overlooking the main street and watched wall-to-wall people go crazy."

Many communities lit bonfires on VE night to celebrate the end of wartime blackouts. One Canadian airman and his British bride saw them on their honeymoon. RCAF pilot Edgar Brown had been stationed in northern Scotland; his fiancée, who was with the National Fire Service, was stationed at the opposite end of the country in Southampton.

"We'd planned to get married on May 5, 1945," explains Brown, "in her home town of Stockport, England. I had a few more flying hours to put in before I could leave my base and on account of bad weather we were grounded. On May 1, I still had not completed my flying hours and sent a telegram to my fiancée (who was now at her home) letting her know that I might be a little late in getting there.

"The telegram was sent to Southport, not Stockport. My fiancée, of course, never received it, which left her wondering if I had stood her up. I finally arrived at her home May 3 much to her relief. We were married on May 5 and proceeded to Llandudno, North Wales, for our honeymoon.

"On May 8, as we were walking along a road in Conwy, Wales, a little old lady came running from her house shouting, 'The war is over, the war is over!'

"That night, as far as you could see along the coast, there were bonfires burning and the Welsh people, many of them in Welsh dress, were singing and dancing around them. We, of course, enjoyed partying till the early hours of the morning."

Everywhere people celebrated with fires and lights. For the last year of the war, D. Crawford Smyth had been a technical officer working in a ground control interceptor station at RAF Langtoft, north of London. Their radar station helped organize hundreds of USAAF bombers over central England for daylight raids over Europe. Word of VE Day reached him at the same time as his brother Bert, an RCAF wireless air gunner recently posted overseas from Coastal Command.

"VE Day was the big one we looked for," remembers Smyth. "Our station WAAFs were billeted at Maxey House in Market Deeping, and that night we had one big bonfire. We burned all of the blackout shutters."

Harry Bowes of Stouffville, Ontario, who had completed a tour of operations with the RAF in April 1945, was among a group of Canadians going by train to Liverpool to catch a ship back to Canada. "We suddenly saw bonfires being lit at dusk on May 7. It didn't take long to realize that the war was over. Since the ingredients for a good celebration were not available to us, we did the next best thing. After six years of blackouts, we celebrated by turning on all the lights and raising all the blinds."

Along with the lights, it seemed important to make as much noise as possible. R. J. Hanlon (who came to Canada after the war) grew up on a small farm in Sussex. His father was in the Canadian Army and his mother worked in a plant that built Halifax bombers. Hanlon remembers the "blow-out in London," but more vividly "the bells and the lights...down in our little backwater...

"On VE Day itself the church bells all started to ring in all the villages in our area. Up till then we had not heard them, as they were supposed to signal an invasion, but with the end of the war everybody just cut loose. That night was different.

"The lights came on! Everyone turned on all their lights and opened their windows and doors, all the street lights came on and all went outdoors just to stare. No more blackouts! It was amazing.

"Right around that time the radio announcer said that Vera Lynn was going to sing 'When The Lights Come On Again' and I think every radio for miles around was turned to full volume. That's all you could hear. Since then, any time I hear that song all I can see is hundreds of people standing in the brightly lit High Street singing along with Vera."

Carman Eldridge had served on several ships of the Royal Canadian

Navy between 1941 and the end of the war. His final wartime posting as acting petty officer was to the corvette *North Bay*. Just before VE Day, his ship put out to sea.

"Sailing up the River Foyle to Londonderry, we saw many...German subs tied to buoys along the river. It was unbelievable...

"We did not get a chance to [go on] leave, as a convoy had already been formed to sail west, and our orders were to accompany it. On our first day, when darkness fell, we were treated to a spectacle that, after six years of blackouts, was phenomenal. All the ships in the convoy turned on their lights. A floating city sailed victoriously westward under the twinkling stars. We could only rub our eyes in disbelief and satisfaction."

Under normal circumstances, most of the communication that radio operator Elaine Leiterman heard on her headset at Pennfield Ridge, New Brunswick, consisted of chatter between Coastal Command aircraft, or between training aircraft and her home station. She was most often on duty in a "homer," homing in on RCAF aircraft. But on VE Day, "It was so quiet. I was surprised, because we heard [all kinds of] things in our station. We heard Russian pilots and people ferrying airplanes across to England. We heard all kinds of things that had nothing to do with us and we were always told [to say] that they had to use the proper jargon. They'd often say, 'Can we have a date?' and stuff like that... And I had to say, 'Please stick to the proper procedure. Wilco, over and out.'

"Anyway, it was so quiet, everything felt strange... We didn't get newspapers there, we were far from Saint John, and even radio was local stuff, full of Don Messer and the Islanders, and stuff from Bangor, Maine. Rumours were what everybody lived on, and there were rumours going around. Then I thought to myself, this strange silence, this has something to do [with it]. This must be it, it must have happened."

When Corporal Leiterman left the radio silo and went off duty, the world had changed. Word of VE Day had reached Pennfield Ridge, and everybody was rejoicing. Back at her barracks, she changed into her civilian clothes, which for her was a big plaid shirt. Then word arrived that the CO had ordered everybody to the parade ground on the double. There was WD Elaine Leiterman—a plaid shirt in a sea of blue.

"Welcome everybody," said the CO. "We have good news." And then he added, "I see you down there, Corporal Leiterman in your plaid shirt!"

After that, all she remembers was that "they closed the station down. Nobody could go anywhere. They thought people might get out of hand in Saint John, or something like that. We had a big dance and somebody poured a whole bottle of beer on my head."

Corporal Ron Poulton was in Brussels on VE Day, as correspondent for *The Maple Leaf.* "I got drunk. I got flaming drunk. I couldn't see the keyboard on my typewriter, but I wrote this article. It didn't appear to be too bad on the day when I saw it. Maybe somebody doctored it a little, I don't know.

"Two days later I was in London. London was still celebrating. Crowds were still in Piccadilly. The first thing you want, of course, when you land is a drink and I couldn't get a drink. Just to get through the damn door was a feat. If you didn't have a glass you couldn't get a drink, but you couldn't get a glass, this was the kicker. And the beer went around...and I never did get a drink. I got a glass, but it was empty by the time it had passed over the heads of the people."

In another part of Piccadilly, Winnipeg-born trumpeter Paul Grosney was celebrating without beer. Since the fall of 1943, Grosney had been touring with an RCAF entertainment unit *Swingtime.* He had played for troops across Canada and behind the lines in Holland and in Germany. On VE Day he was back in England in Piccadilly Circus, "where the pubs were full, but I'm not that much of a drinker.

"So Bob Burn (he's a fine saxophone player from Perth, Ontario), he and I went into a Lyon's Corner House and had tea and scones. He was a tea granny. He hated tea made in urns; he had to have the kettle and the whole thing. The place wasn't crowded. Everybody was on the streets and everybody wanted booze, you see. Except that we couldn't care less."

Trumpeter Fred Davis from the Canadian Army Band also went to Piccadilly Circus to celebrate. In fact, whenever he sees the black-and-white newsreel film footage of the VE Day crowds in London, he says, "I'm there among the throngs.

"The Londoners! There's never been a New Year's Eve like that, the euphoria, and everybody was your friend and every woman that walked by kissed you, this kind of thing. And none of the rowdyism that you have today. Nobody was trying to overturn a bus—everybody was your friend."

Not far away, another Canadian, Brian Jones, was in London on leave from the 65th Canadian Motor Torpedo Boat Flotilla, which was based in Ostend, Belgium, at the war's end. He and a couple of his mates were staying at the Duchy Hotel near Marble Arch when VE Day festivities spilled into Hyde Park.

"[We] went into the park and were promptly dragged into a gigantic circle of armed forces men and women—there must have been two or three hundred who had formed a giant double circle going round and round. After a while we tried to slink off, but...they dragged us back in and continued round and round, singing all the bawdy songs that have ever been written. I recall ending up the evening at a pub nearby...singing and rejoicing that we were at last going home.

"I remember performing a mock marriage ceremony with a soldier and a CWAC. Somebody had given me a copy of the things to say so it seemed to be OK, except the bride and groom and I staggered around and eventually we all fell over."

A victory drink was also the order of the day for RCAF pilot Ted Woolley and his fiancée Wynne, an English WAAF. Woolley had just been returned to England after three and a half years in a German POW camp. Both were on leave in London on VE Day. They too remember that "the line-ups at the pubs were enormous, but eventually we got inside the Brasserie Universal. The next hurdle was to obtain a glass from somebody who was leaving. Then, if not already sold out, eureka! A victory drink. Their policy was only one to a customer, so there was no danger of getting tipsy."

Soon they found themselves in Trafalgar Square, "where Lord Nelson, atop his column, was surely sharing the victory. A group of sailors astride the lions were singing 'Rule Britannia.' People were hanging out of hotel windows cheering the crowds below, others were climbing lampposts for a better view. Song and dance were a great part of the scene. Sing-alongs broke out spontaneously as various groups all sang different songs at the same time—a cacophony of noise—but who cared!"

Otto Sulek was a long way from Trafalgar Square when the surrender was signed at Rheims. Born in Czechoslovakia and a resident of Saskatchewan when war broke out, Sulek had enlisted in the RCAF in 1943 and was posted to No. 429 (Bison) Squadron in Britain. On a mine-laying mission near Flensburg in January 1945, mid-upper gunner Sulek and his fellow Halifax crew-mates were hit and forced to bail out over Denmark. After some three months as a POW, he and numerous other Canadian and Allied airmen were liberated by American troops late in April and taken to a former Luftwaffe airfield in Bavaria, to await flights to Brussels and points west.

"During the morning [of May 8]," recalls Sulek, "a small number of ex-POWs went to wash in a small stream which ran alongside the airfield, when suddenly, from a small wooded area across from the stream, shots rang out. Result: one dead, three wounded. An American patrol raced to the woods, there was some shooting, the Yanks returned with two SS men—dead.

"Just after the noon hour, word spread that the war was over, which some of the older [longer-serving] POWs would not believe, as they had heard this before. But confirmation came shortly after. Since there were no aircraft expected to come in, off we went into town... The town was shut tight... All we did was walk around and as there were a large number of those 'slave labourers' walking around, there was a lot of greetings, which no one understood, and if there were girls, a lot of hugging.

"By evening we drifted back to our airfield for some food, and to our dirty barracks and into our dirty sleeping straw sacks—in our dirty clothes, the same [ones] I had on when I bailed out... This was VE Day.

"Next day, there were Dakota aircraft of the USAAF and I managed to get on one of these, to Brussels. Here we got some toiletries, had a long-needed hot shower, but [got] back into the same dirty clothes. Next day it was back to Britain—at Bournemouth, the Canadian Reception Centre—hot bath and clean clothes. Couldn't sleep for excitement."

In the last week of March 1945, an RCAF pilot with the City of Ottawa Squadron took off in his Typhoon fighter aircraft for a mission over northern Holland. Montreal-born Flying Officer John Flintoft encountered heavy anti-aircraft fire and was forced to crash-land his "Tiffie" behind German lines. Like hundreds of other Allied aircrew who parachuted into German-occupied territory, and who became the celebrated "evaders"—eluding German troops, connecting with various underground operations, and making their way back to Britain— Flintoft managed to dodge ground forces for six full weeks and turned up safe and sound on May 7, the day before the official end of the war.

Ed Baker from Ontario was still in action on VE Day. He had joined the Royal Canadian Artillery in 1941, spent some time in advanced training in England, came back to Canada in 1943 as an instructor, and went back overseas in 1944. This time, he was a gun position officer with the 7th Medium Regiment, RCA, in Holland, in range of German guns at Emden.

"Sadly, one of our positions received a direct hit by shelling from these guns on April 28, 1945, and we suffered casualties, three killed. All of that while hearing over the BBC that London, and the world, were preparing for the Victory Parade.

"I was in my troop command post on the morning of May 6 when the signal sergeant, Oliver, rushed in and said he had just heard a radio report that 'the war is over.' I suggested to him that he had sneaked into the rum ration, but the news, happily, was true. The order 'cease firing' came through, qualified by 'unless fired on.' Then, later, the welcome order, 'empty guns.'"

Norm Davidson was relieved by the news—he had had enough excitement for one war. He had gone overseas as a trooper in the B.C. Dragoons, trained at Sandhurst throughout 1944, received his commission, and was sent into action with the B.C. Regiment early in 1945. Davidson had stayed with the Allied push into Europe (losing two tanks along the way). On May 5, 1945, he wrote to his wife Jane back home in British Columbia.

"My Darling—Can you believe it? Word that the Germans had quit came just in the nick of time. We were attacking a strongpoint, shooting our infantry in at the time. I had already lost my tank, knocked out by an anti-tank gun; the crew all got out. I had taken my corporal's tank over and we were just waiting for an obstacle to be cleared so we could get forward, and we knew there were three 88-mm anti-tank guns someplace just behind the obstacle, but we had to push on.

"I wasn't feeling very happy about the situation, in fact I had pretty well made up my mind that I had had it. And then the order came to cease fire and withdraw to the village a short way back. We sure got out of there in a hurry. The Lord was really looking after me, darling, or I wouldn't be here now.

"I am horribly tired. We had been going steadily for some time now, night and day, getting shelled, mortared and sniped at steadily and it is a hell of a strain on a man. I didn't feel too badly until I heard the news and then I just let myself go and now the reaction has set in and I am really dead beat."

On May 8, Private Stan Anderson was on his way home as a "U.4." (upper-body fourth level) wounded infantryman. One of nine children from a farm north of Regina, Saskatchewan, Anderson had joined up in 1943 and had come ashore in France with the Calgary Highlanders in July 1944 (a month after D-Day). In late July, in the battle around Caen and the Falaise Gap, a German 88-mm shell landed behind his platoon. Shrapnel penetrated Anderson's helmet, fractured his skull, passed through his spine, and riddled his shoulder-blade. Anderson didn't regain consciousness for a week, when the Red Cross transported him back to the coast and loaded him on to a duck boat.

"This took me perhaps a mile out from shore to where the water was deep enough for a much larger Red Cross boat," explained Anderson. "Loading us onto this larger boat was done by four men. One held each end of our stretcher and waited until a wave raised the smaller boat up far enough to make it possible to swing us over to where two men on the larger boat could catch the handles of the stretcher. I was then put into a bed on the larger boat. There were railings on the bed to keep me from rolling out."

Ten months later, after long stays in British convalescent hospitals and rehab centres, Anderson was well enough (and there was space enough aboard a troopship) to sail for Canada. He had been several days at sea. He had joined a foursome playing bridge (even though "none of us knew how to keep score") when the ship's PA system came alive with the news that the war in Europe was over. Anderson and his shipmates feared it all might be a rumour or a sick joke...but "when we were issued two bottles of beer each, we had to believe it must be true.

"This was not quite the end for us yet, however. I don't know if the German U-boats had not been informed, or if they just did not want to surrender. At any rate, there were still some underwater explosions felt aboard ship for a few days.

"It was a storm at sea that was perhaps as bad, though. The seas were mountainous... When a big wave struck us broadside, tilting the boat over so far that the dishes came crashing down on the tables, many of the troops below deck thought we had been torpedoed and stampeded for the stairways to the upper decks. The big wave slammed the ladders against the side of the boat so hard the railing was broken.

"When we got to Halifax we found that telephone lines had been torn down and communications were in a mess throughout the Maritimes. We were happy to be back in Canada, and would not trade Canada for any other country."

Another native of Saskatchewan, Murray Westgate, was also at sea on May 8, 1945. He had spent much of his Royal Canadian Navy time on different warships escorting convoys from St. John's to Londonderry. On VE Day his ship was 300 miles north of the Azores where the seas happened to be flat calm. When his ship got the surrender signals at sea—not in code but in plain language—it set course south back to St. John's.

"The signals came out, 'Splice the main brace.' That was when everybody had a drink of rum. It was a beautiful day and the signals told all German submarines to surface immediately, fly a black flag, I think it was... Ships that surrendered on the eastern side of the Atlantic went into Londonderry...

"When we next got to Londonderry, all these U-boats [were there]. I said, 'We gotta get aboard one and see what we've been up against for these last three or four years.'... We went aboard. It was just incredible that they were able to survive. They were so small and so cramped...the wireless office was no bigger than a phone booth. I picked up one of the charts and brought it home."

The crew aboard the River Class frigate HMCS *Ribble* got word of the German capitulation while in the English Channel on U-boat patrol. RCN asdic operator Bill Coutts remembers that *Ribble* was ordered to sea for twenty-four hours to allow all Royal Navy vessels into port for ships' companies to celebrate the occasion. Only then were they allowed "to enter the port of Portland, U.K., that evening, when we received the order from His Majesty King George VI to 'Splice the main brace'—an extra tot of rum to all hands.

"Since we had endured several storms at sea (especially in the Irish Sea, which matches the Bay of Fundy for rough weather), there were not enough cups on board for every officer and rating to contain his 'tot.' I remember receiving my tot in a saucepan from the ship's galley.

"The following day we were given leave to celebrate VE Day in the city of Brighton at the bar of Tommy Farr, the professional heavy-weight boxer."

When word of the cessation of hostilities in Europe reached HMCS *Fredericton*, the corvette and its crew couldn't have been closer to the middle of the Atlantic nor further from a way of celebrating VE Day. Like many of her sister ships, *Fredericton* had been escorting merchant ship convoys on the Newfoundland-to-Londonderry run for much of the war. Crewman Bill Beales was looking forward to the end.

He remembers the cheering on board at the announcement, and the captain ordering a double tot of rum for all hands, but to add to the pleasure of the moment, says Beales, "when some icebergs came into sight, the convoy ships were allowed to waste a few rounds of shells aimed at these bergs. The results looked rather feeble as a few chips of ice were blown off these icy mountains."

The day before VE Day, Lance-Corporal W. R. Moore learned that after five years and four months overseas he was eligible for leave. During that time, he had served with the 11th Army Field Regiment Signal Section in Italy and southern France, as well as in Belgium. On May 8, Moore took a boat from Ostend to cross the Channel to Britain. He was sitting on deck near the crew's quarters. "The radio was playing and all of a sudden the program was interrupted. Churchill came on to announce the end of the war. I cannot remember what he said, but that was the gist of it.

"We landed...some hours later. What was first-class traffic a day or two before suddenly became about fiftieth class as we were shunted around London for about five hours before we reached Witley camp. All along the right of way, people came to cheer us as the train shunted through. Wine and beer was handed to us as we passed through the stations. People were all over the streets. We had a swastika flag hanging on the side of the coaches.

"When I arrived at Witley, I got a seventy-two-hour embarkation pass and went to meet my wife, who lived in Waldingham, Surrey. I had left her a year and a half before—exactly one week after we were married."

When Winston Churchill's "Victory in Europe" speech was broadcast on radio, Bill Warshick was in Emden, Germany. As a signalman attached to the 3rd Canadian Division, Warshick had experienced the Allied invasion from its dash up the Normandy beaches to its march across Germany nearly a year later. But instead of marching orders on May 8, Warshick was ordered into a local church where a radio amplifier had been set up to broadcast Churchill's words of congratulations. "That was all. No extra rum ration... Nowhere to buy a drink. No other source of liquid refreshment—and NO FRATERNIZING!"

For the cast of *Meet The Navy*, May 8 was supposed to be business as usual—the same musical numbers, the same jokes, the same wardrobe, and much the same kind of audience—except that "everybody went wild," remembers Bob Goodier. "We were all playing jokes on each other, and we still kept the show going. I mean, we realized that we had the audience to entertain, but they didn't know some of the jokes that were going on backstage... We were wearing each other's costumes and doing all kinds of crazy things... We had a couple of barrels of beer backstage that Oscar Natzke went to get from a local brewery...and we were helping ourselves through the show... So the show we put on that time was quite something."

Many others celebrated with impromptu performances. John Mair, a signaller for an artillery battery, came ashore at Normandy on D-Day with the Winnipeg Rifles and was still on active duty in Europe by May 8, 1945. That day Mair and other members of his 14th Field Battery were sheltered in a barn, when news of the German surrender arrived, along with a bottle of wine and some bottles of beer for a small celebration.

"One of our chaps got out a 'liberated' violin and bow and began to saw away. After a while, I asked to be allowed to play it and, after warning me not to touch the hair, he gave it to me to try. For some time, I was able to play as many requests as I was asked. I believe it was then and that quickly that I experienced the letdown that we all had at some time.

"At any rate, the sergeants organized their mess, where they had available a piano. Another of our signallers, who played the piano, and I were asked to entertain. That pianist was Ralph Cooper, who, after his return, played at the old Metropole [in Toronto]." After his own return, Mair studied viola and pursued a successful career in music.

Musician Ed Hall began celebrating VE Day earlier than most. He had gone to England in March 1942, posted to a Canadian Artillery Reinforcement Unit, but was transferred that fall to the band of the Royal Canadian Artillery. The band toured England, playing for army parades, dances, and shows, and later was sent on a tour of Italy, France, Belgium, Holland, and Germany.

"On May 4, 1945, at 8 p.m. we began playing for a sedate officers' dance at the Park Plaza Hotel [so named by the Canadian Army] in Apeldoorn, Holland. About 9 p.m. came the media-leaked news that the official surrender of the German forces in Holland would take place next day.

"Well! Jubilation exploded. Only time I was ever hugged by an officer. And booze—I didn't think there was that much in Europe. In a short time, a sober soul was not to be seen—officers, musicians, civilian waiters, and kitchen staff, especially the civilians, were as happily sloshed as they ever had been or would be. For the life of me, I can't remember the civilian lady guests who must have been there. [Two musicians] engaged in a wrestling match in the middle of the dance floor. Back in the kitchen the staff were passing around some black, evil-looking liquid. After gulping it down, one was required to smash the glass against the wall.

"Somehow, we got through the evening, playing such big band charts as 'In the Mood,' 'Strictly Instrumental,' 'Cow-Cow Boogie,' and 'Begin The Beguine.'" Finally, the band members loaded up their truck and headed off to their tents in the woods in the Dutch national park, De Hoge Veluwe, a few miles out of Apeldoorn, where they were encamped with the 5th Medium Regiment, RCA. "Most of the guys crashed in their bedrolls in the tents but four of us gathered around a dying campfire to savour the wonderful news of peace."

On VE Day, the place to be was in or near populated areas. And from D-Day on, Muriel Green had been in some of the busiest places in England. She was a WAAF ambulance driver, stationed at RAF Yatesbury. Her daily orders included driving wounded soldiers, sailors, and airmen to various hospitals in southern England. She was sometimes on the road nineteen hours a day. However, on VE Day, her ambulance shift finished in time for her to get home for the evening; still, she missed "the local train that stopped at the whistle stops.

"I didn't know whether to walk the four miles (home) or wait for the milk train. As there was no one around, I decided to walk. During my walk I had to pass a cemetery. A wind came up and blew some papers around and frightened the life out of me... During that walk I never saw a soul..."

Many of those who were children on VE Day remember their feelings when they heard the news. Six years after the Second World War ended, Marcel Braitstein left his native Belgium, travelled to Canada, and became a landed immigrant. Nearly six of Braitstein's boyhood years had been spent under Nazi occupation in the small Belgian town of Charleroi. He attributes his survival to the efforts of his aunt—a member of the resistance—who provided young Marcel with false identification, hiding places, and ration cards for food. Braitstein's parents had been arrested "for the crime of being Jewish."

Marcel was eleven years old at the time of the liberation. Shortly afterwards he moved to Brussels; it was there he heard the news of the German surrender. L'ALLEMAGNE CAPITULE SANS CONDITIONS! read the headline in the newspaper. Marcel hopped for joy. His aunt wept "tears of relief as well as of sadness.

"Her husband, my uncle, was also in the Resistance, and he had been arrested shortly before liberation. His whereabouts were unknown then, although she found out shortly thereafter that he had been executed by the Germans as a political prisoner.

"As for my parents, the Red Cross informed us a few months later, after having checked the well-kept German records, that my parents had been shipped to Auschwitz where they disappeared with millions of others in the night and fog...

"The end of the Second World War for me was the day that Germany capitulated. Since that day, there have been in the world, and there are still at this very moment, unbelievable horrors taking place. Due to my own experiences, I cannot help but empathize with the children, the refugees, the absurdity of it all, so that in a sense I wonder sometimes if it ever really ended."

Another postwar emigrant to Canada was Eileen MacLennan. She had been born and raised in India and under normal circumstances would have been sent to boarding school in England, "but in 1939 no one in their right minds would have deliberately sent kids to beleaguered, battered Britain. We had therefore six blissful years of life in India. On VE Day, I, most inappropriately, had German measles."

Some people celebrated in unusual ways. Private Sam Shantz of the Armoured Corps was sent overseas between Christmas 1944 and New Year's 1945. Two months later, he joined the Essex Scottish Regiment of the 2nd Division in Germany. He was wounded on March 13 and taken to the Canadian General Hospital in Bruges. After seven weeks he was discharged from hospital and was awaiting a posting to England when he and other Canadian soldiers were asked if they wished to tour Vimy Ridge—where the Canadian Army had won its greatest victory of the First World War.

"We were just leaving for the tour when they announced that the war was over—it was May 8.

"While travelling through several small Belgian towns we were invited to join the various Victory Parades, but we declined the offers because we wanted to have more time at Vimy. We toured three different cemeteries, the Memorial, and the trenches and the long tunnel systems that had been preserved.

"At 3 p.m. we were invited by the curator to listen to Churchill's victory speech in his home. The curator told us he was a Canadian who had been liberated recently and [had] returned to his home (which was considered Canadian territory). He brought in three bottles of liquor and after we had our first drink we were surprised to learn that it was Seagram's V.O., which he had hidden before he was captured. Of course, this was the highlight of our trip, to be able to drink Canadian rye on Canadian soil on VE Day!"

Donald Tracy was a twenty-three-year-old signalman with the Royal Canadian Corps of Signals. Just before May 8, Tracy and two other signalmen crossed the border into Germany. They were at Oldenburg providing communications from the 11th Field Company, Royal Canadian Engineers, to headquarters and to other signal trucks in other field companies, when they heard the news that the war in Europe was over. The three signalmen took out a small Nazi flag, put it on the floor of their truck, and took great pleasure in tramping on it each time they entered or left the truck.

By the summer of 1945, Tracy was back in England waiting his turn to be repatriated and "acquiring one of my better tans," but he knew he had really arrived home "when, on the train from Halifax to Toronto, I heard the long drawn-out 'whoo-o-o' of the steam whistle, as compared to the 'toot-toot' of the English locomotive."

In the first week of May 1945, Ernie Long of the 15th Canadian Field Ambulance in the 4th Canadian Armoured Division was scheduled to go back to England for one week's leave. Several nights before VE Day, Long's ambulance crew was holed up in a schoolhouse in the German resort village of Bad Schwischenan. They had eaten supper. Some were reading, others writing letters, when the radio operator came in with a message he'd just received:

"Cease fire 0800 hours tomorrow, May 5," was all it said.

"We sat there in stunned silence," recalls Long, "looking at each other until one of us said what we were all thinking—'The war is over, and I'm still alive!'... No cheers. No shouts. Just a shocked realization that we had made it through the war.

"After a year of action in a front-line medical unit, seeing men die almost every day, we had steeled ourselves to the realization that any day our number could be up...but we had made it!"

The following day, Long's ambulance unit moved to another small town near Oldenburg. As in Bad Schwischenan, they found a school that would be appropriate for a medical station. However, Long's crew discovered that the school was filled with German civilians who were "camping out" as refugees. A senior Canadian officer told the refugees that he needed the building and that they would have to move out.

A very large woman stepped forward, set her feet apart, crossed her arms and informed the officer: "You cannot order us out, the war is over."

"Yes, the war is over," agreed the officer. "And guess who won?... Everybody out." Whereupon the refugees packed and left.

On May 8, Long took a train to Calais to board a ferry to England to begin his leave. When he got to Calais, he was greeted by a small hut that "looked like a toll booth," with a sign outside saying "London Hotel Reservations" and a couple of soldiers operating a reservation system out of the little booth. They told him London was packed because of the VE Day celebrations and advised him to make hotel arrangements before getting on the ferry. He paid for a room at the Canadian Legion Hotel and left.

"When I arrived at the hotel with my reservation slip," said Long, "they laughed... They had never heard of the 'reservation service' in Calais. That was my first experience with scam artists."

Victory in Europe was especially sweet for RCAF Spitfire pilot Livingston "Cap" Foster (named "Cap" after his godfather, Captain Livingston, a First World War veteran). Flying in Fighter Command fulfilled two of Foster's life-long dreams: first to become a military pilot (something he had wanted since his first airplane ride with a barn-stormer in 1934) and second to avenge his father's mistreatment at the hands of German captors during the First World War. Foster's father was a Mohawk—a full-blooded descendant of Chief Joseph Brant—and Foster claimed that his father's native features had provoked the abuse he had received in a POW camp.

By the time the German surrender was signed on May 8, 1945, Cap Foster had flown more than 200 sorties over Europe, two full tours of duty, and had been awarded a Distinguished Flying Cross. But for Pilot Officer Foster, the icing on the cake was one of his last sorties in a fighter aircraft just after VE Day.

At the former fighter base in Lubeck, Germany, "I got the Luftwaffe base commander to service a Focke Wulf 190 fighter," recalls Foster. "My checkout on the fighter consisted of finding out where the lever was to get the wheels up and what the landing speed was. I had them paint British roundels on the plane so I could fly it back to my base...

Then I took the aircraft up and gave the Germans a display of aerobatics they would never forget."

W. J. Swanson, a Canadian pilot who served in the RAF, experienced the end of the war in Europe from the strategic mid-Atlantic station at Reykjavik, Iceland. Swanson had been posted there in October 1944 to join a meteorological flight that was soon to be raised to squadron status as No. 251 Squadron of RAF Coastal Command. There were several other Canadians in the squadron—three or four wireless air gunners and two navigators.

The Allied military personnel stationed in Iceland after 1939 were Johnnys-come-lately and relations between them and the Icelanders were strained throughout the war. Before the war, the German Army had established a base in Reykjavik with a number of military engineering personnel and they, according to Swanson, "went out of their way to create a good relationship with the local residents. Among other things, they constructed a number of buildings in the city and they constructed the aqueduct which still brings hot water from the geysers to the town to provide heating for the city of Reykjavik."

When the war began, Iceland, being halfway along the main North Atlantic sea lane, became of great strategic importance. "The British sent an expedition to seize and hold the island and the German troops based there were taken prisoner. The British were involved in a war and had no time to start constructing buildings for the Icelanders," Swanson continues. "Very few Icelanders spoke English and I believe it would be safe to say that none of the British troops spoke Icelandic. The result was a cool tolerance of each group towards the other."

Soon after his arrival there, Swanson had joined a group called The Anglo-Icelandic Society, "the only organization that sponsored social meetings between the local people and military personnel."

Acting on requests from several squadron members, Swanson formed a committee and planned a dance in Reykjavik—for Wednesday, May 9, 1945. The process was slow. "We were not allowed to advertise our dance openly, but we had to let the women of Reykjavik know about it, otherwise there would be no dance. So, after renting the dance hall about the middle of April, we delegated one member of the committee to go to the hall before each dance until

May 9, and post an announcement of our upcoming dance in the ladies' washroom—and remove the announcement after each dance." Then came VE Day, with great revelry on the base. "Much liquor was consumed and many gambling games were in evidence." In the late afternoon, some of the military personnel coming back to the base from town brought rumours of fights and possible riots there. "Being very concerned about our dance scheduled for the following night, I decided to walk into town and see the situation for myself."

Swanson found the main streets in the centre part of town "jammed with people—mostly Icelandic civilians but with enough servicemen among them to make feelings run high. Most of the servicemen were quite drunk and rather belligerent. Some windows had been broken, but I didn't see anyone actually breaking them at that time. I worked my way through the mob of humanity to the middle of the block and stood there in a store entrance to watch."

Swanson remembers watching the crowd start to surge eastward along the streets. He soon realized the Icelandic police and the military police were working together to forestall any major riot. Canisters of tear-gas were being discharged and the slight breeze wafted the tear-gas slowly along the street. Swanson encountered one poor civilian who was affected by the tear-gas and was totally bewildered by it. He tried to explain to the man, who had never even heard of tear-gas before, that the police were trying to break up the crowd to prevent fights and damage to property, but the poor man could only shake his head in disbelief.

"As I made my way back towards camp I was, for a way, following a group of several well-soused, belligerent English soldiers. As they walked...they poked a foot through six or eight windows, which was all they could conveniently reach. I was tempted to try and stop them; however, they were intoxicated and in a vile mood. Some army personnel resented the air force, some ranks resented officers, and some English resented Canadians, so, being alone, I decided cowardice was more prudent than heroism. I turned at the next corner and made my way back to camp by a different route."

Nevertheless, "the squadron dance went off the following night without a hitch. And it must have been a success because, starting the following day, the men began requesting another dance... With the end of the war and the—just slightly—warmer weather of summer, feelings began to thaw somewhat and by the time I left Iceland on June 6, 1945, the tensions had eased."

Arthur "Barny" Barnard tried to spend VE Day in Canada, but it didn't work out that way. He had enlisted in the RCAF as the Blitz was intensifying over Britain in 1940, but he didn't get overseas until September 1941. After two years with the RAF and two more with the RCAF, flying Spitfires with No. 402 (RCAF) Squadron, Barnard came home to the Maritimes for a thirty-day leave in March 1945.

"As it was obvious that the European 'upheavals' were coming to an end," explained Barnard, "many of us tried to convince the RCAF administrative wallahs that it would be an unnecessary expenditure of time, effort, etc., to package us up and ship us back to the U.K. What a forlorn hope!

"So on May 1 we obediently embarked the *Volendam* in Halifax for our springtime Atlantic cruise. Seven days later in mid-ocean, VE Day was formally proclaimed. That was it! Our daily routine was otherwise uninterrupted...

"Foremost, I experienced intense relief that I was actually there to 'celebrate' the occasion... But most emotional was remembering, one by one, the many 'absent friends'—those who, I later learned, were buried or commemorated in so many distant places—England, Scotland, Wales, France, Belgium, Holland, Germany, the English Channel, Italy, Egypt, the western desert, Tunis, and even Iceland. Finally came a disturbing and numbing question—how would I cope with the transition to the unknowns of civvy life?"

In mid-September 1944, the Second World War made Ivy Wilkins a widow. That month the Allies launched "Operation Market Garden" and British Lance-Corporal Bill Wilkins was among the casualties, killed near Arnhem, Holland, during that action. At the time, their second daughter was two years old; their first had died as an infant in the London Blitz.

"It's a horrible thing to say," acknowledges Ivy (now Ivy Emery-Miller, living in Elliot Lake, Ontario), "but as long as the war was on, I could pretend he was still alive out there. Peace meant facing up to the fact that not only was he never going to come home, but I could not even let my tears flow at his grave."

Ivy said she often found release from her grief by writing poetry. On VE Day, she wrote:

I heard the sound of a barrel-organ drifting through the bomb-smashed pane; then other unfamiliar noises wakened me to dawn again—other people shouting, church bells pealing, factory whistles long and loud; opening wide the windows brought to view a happy crowd.

I called out to the newsboy, "What has happened, why the noise?" "It's peace," he said. "The war's been won. My Dad's coming home, the fighting's done."

I guess he didn't understand why I could not smile, why my eyes grew dim, as I murmured, "Thank God," and clasped hands with him. For he asked, "Why the tears now? It's over now, soon they will all be back home." "Not all," said I, as I drew the blind, for I might always be alone.

My tears were bitter as I denounced the God I had just thanked; I covered my ears up with my hands, wanting no part of rejoicing and bands. Then came a tug at the side of the bed, and a little girl clambered up and said, "Love you, Mummy, don't cry, come and see." I instantly thought how much worse it could be.

So clasping her thankfully to my breast, I asked God's forgiveness and promised my best—my best, just as they gave for you and for me, that we might have peace and liberty.

11

"It Was Like Heaven"

The sustained eruption of joy that rocked the western world in May 1945 had never been seen before. The giddy, celebratory mood flashed across the Atlantic and inundated North America.

Canadian newspapers captured the spirit of the moment.

The Ottawa Citizen spotlighted the celebrating in London: "It was the Coronation, the Jubilee, the Wembley Cup and every other gathering rolled into one."

In *The Winnipeg Tribune*, the front-page story was headlined: "Holland Goes Wild."

R. L. Sandburn, writing for the *Calgary Herald*, reported that "the last Canadian to enjoy the doubtful honor of being shot at by hostile Germans was Pte. G. S. Warrel, of Fort Wallace, N.S."

"Montreal," wrote that city's *Gazette*, "joined the rest of the Allied world in celebrating...after reading the news flash for which the world had waited since September, 1939."

VE Day came to Montreal with a bang.

Henry Gordon ran a radio repair shop downtown on Park Avenue in Montreal at the time. Gordon's war was long over. He'd signed up at an RCAF recruiting office in September 1940; the recruiters could hardly believe their ears when Gordon told them he already had his commercial radio operator's licence and could send and receive Morse code at twenty-five words a minute.

Two months later, when he graduated from training as a Wireless Electrical Mechanic, Sergeant Gordon expected to be posted to England on operations aboard Halifax bombers. Instead, the air force (desperate for good teachers) streamed Gordon as an instructor into the British Commonwealth Air Training Plan (BCATP). Within his first year in the air force, Gordon had helped establish the BCATP's No. 3 Wireless School in Winnipeg. But the stress of getting a new school off the ground and getting scores of green recruits from New Zealand and Australia through the course every few weeks took its toll. Gordon developed stomach ulcers and was honourably discharged home to Montreal.

And that's where he was on May 8, 1945, "sitting in my service repair shop on Park Avenue listening to the likes of soap operas such as 'One Man's Family,' as I worked on the sets. All of a sudden three or four of the radios on the workbench started blaring with the news of victory in Europe," and the street celebrations began.

Margaret Adcock had a ringside seat for the Montreal festivities on VE Day. At the time, she worked on the ninth floor of an office building at St. Catherine and Stanley streets. In fact, Montreal had been preparing for the celebration for nearly a week, because "the large department stores on St. Catherine Street...had boarded up their plate-glass windows. No one knew what the pent-up emotions of six years would produce, once peace came.

"On May 7, a lovely day, I went to my office... We turned on the radio to Don McNeil's much-loved 'Breakfast Club'... and somewhere between 9:30 and 10 a.m. there came the announcement that the war in Europe was over.

"We watched from our windows as St. Catherine gradually filled with people coming from stores and offices, as the news spread. As if on cue, an army jeep came from west to east carrying four khaki-clad veterans of the 1st Division. An effigy of Hitler was lashed on the front of the vehicle. They were wildly cheered. We ran adding-machine rolls out the window as streamers. We were notified that the building would close in half an hour. Who wanted to work anyway?

"Following lunch at home, I returned uptown with a friend. [Her husband was still overseas.] Traffic had been banned from St. Catherine, [and] four airmen squatted peacefully square in the inter-section of Peel and St. Catherine, playing cards!"

Gordon Black, in Montreal on VE Day, was thirteen when the war ended, and he too was drawn to the commotion at the corner of Peel and St. Catherine streets, where it was "wall-to-wall people for as far as you could see. Everyone was in high spirits. Cars and trucks that tried to inch their way through the crowds were covered, roofs, fenders, everywhere, with cheering people. Streetcars couldn't move because pranksters kept pulling the trolleys off the overhead wires. And of course girls were being kissed at every opportunity."

Churches filled that day, proving to a *Gazette* reporter that "Montrealers can pray as well as play." And there was a sobering sign hanging outside a Montreal recruiting depot. It said, "Open for business—with Japan."

However, by evening all sobriety was gone. In Montreal's theatre district mobs tossed an iron post set in cement through a Quebec Liquor Commission store window. Others looted a front-window exhibit at the Orpheum Theatre to get kindling for a bonfire in the middle of the street. And in Montreal as in other cities, trolleys took the brunt of the violent celebrations; mobs smashed the windows and doors of at least thirty trams.

Alan Skaife remembered the rocky side of VE Day in Montreal. Skaife had joined up in May 1940 with the 4th Light Anti-Aircraft Regiment. On D-Day, he was with the 9th Brigade, the Highland Light Infantry. Later, he was wounded at Nijmegen and arrived back in Montreal in March 1945.

"Downtown on St. Catherine Street was one mass of people, happy, drinking. Anything you wanted you could have," described Skaife. "I was still in uniform, of course, and a few people didn't like the fact that I was in uniform, either. I remember being pushed off the sidewalk, but that was only a couple of times, by civilians. And somebody made a pass at my sister...at the corner of Peel and St. Catherine. I belted him and he fell back and hit the streetcar, but he didn't go under it or anything."

The groundswell of emotion wasn't restricted to bustling downtown streets. In Verdun, a suburb of Montreal, the children organized a large VE Day parade. Al Jared, who was ten when the war ended, remembers that it was a spontaneous event beginning "as each street gathered its gang together with quality instruments [garbage-can lids and sticks]... Marching down the individual streets, the gangs coalesced like blood in the arteries... We clanged and banged our way down through the centre of town while parents came out on their verandahs and threw money or toilet paper...

"It was like heaven! I couldn't believe my eyes. There were pennies (which were worth something then), nickels, dimes, even a few quarters all over the road—people literally emptied their pockets on every balcony and let the money fly—it was unbelievable. The noise, the din, the chaos, the money, the toilet paper. Wow!

"To top this off, some of the kids made an effigy of Hitler and stuffed it with *The Montreal Star, Saturday Evening Post,* and *Life* magazine—whatever was available. Then it was strung from the hydro wires in that unforgettable gallows position, and set on fire while everyone yelled and screamed and cheered! The old yellow de Havilland trainers made a flypast and again everyone cheered and sang 'Rule Britannia.'"

The northern Ontario town of Cochrane celebrated VE Day with a parade. Participants and spectators came down from all the surrounding communities. Among them was young Margaret Ruttan from Nahma (just outside Cochrane). Margaret's oldest brother was in the Army Cadets at the time, "so he was in the parade. Our teacher had us each make a hat to wear in town while we were watching the parade. The town made two archways near the railroad station that people had to go under to reach the street."

In the tiny Ontario community of Powassan, just south of Lake Nipissing, teacher Joyce MacDonald recalls that suddenly all the town's church bells began ringing at once. Her school principal "sent a boy on a bike to pedal in and get the news; and everybody hung out of the school windows watching him return as fast as he could... The news was easily read on his face."

The habitual dignity of life in the national capital also cracked that day. In Ottawa, Lew Robinson worked at the Department of Northern Affairs located across from Parliament Hill. Robinson was still trying to get used to several recent upheavals in his life; he had been married only a few months when Northern Affairs offered him a job as federal geographer (only the third such appointment in Canada's history). They also hired his wife, Josephine, as his assistant.

About noon, when VE Day hysteria hit their office building on

Wellington Street, Lew and Josephine dashed outside and down the street to the National War Memorial. There Lew managed to photograph his wife just before they were both swept up in a sea of jubilant servicemen and women. By evening, 10,000 had gathered near Parliament Hill. Traffic was diverted to side streets. At the height of the party, four airmen—like the Four Horsemen of the Apocalypse—rode through downtown Ottawa on the backs of horses drawing a farm wagon at full speed.

In Quebec City a group of young people hoisted some Russian flags in honour of Canada's wartime Allies and began a march to Quebec's basilica to celebrate the cessation of hostilities in Europe. Another group took offence, stopped the parade, ripped down the Russian flags, and the fight began. There were no arrests, no casualties and no damage—save the shredded flags.

Not all flags were for waving that day. The Spanton family of Toronto lived next door to a Canadian army veteran who had already been repatriated. "Among his mementos," recalled Marion Spanton, "was a large German flag. On VE Day, [Major Tom Murphy] brought out the flag, laid it on his lawn, and all the children stood on it, while we had our pictures taken. I was nine years old... I remember feeling excited because we had defeated [Hitler], but also slightly naughty because we were standing on a flag and we had always been taught to look upon a flag with respect."

Six-year-old Gwen Farrow didn't have much to celebrate on VE Day; she had chickenpox. But her family wrapped her up in a blanket and took her out on their front lawn to see the fireworks over Toronto. She and her brother Stanley (aged eight at the time) were also given special treatment that day when "we were allowed into the front parlour—a rare occasion—to listen to the news on the radio."

One of Stanley Farrow's friends, Vern Hill, recalls being in Grade 9 that year. When word of the German surrender reached his Toronto school, his "class was in the pool, which was not connected to the public address system, so when they got out of the pool, they found the school empty as everyone had flocked outside."

Eunice Tristram was shelling peas on VE Day. She was twelve at the time and the eldest of four children living with their divorced father in the Riverdale area of Toronto. She remembers the peace just before the excitement. She was "sitting with an elderly neighbour across the street from our house. Another neighbour...was sitting a few doors up, she was bent over, knitting socks for the men in the service with sightless eyes.

"Then, the excitement of people yelling, screaming, laughing, crying, hugging, and dancing in the street..."

Things were busy in the emergency ward at Toronto's Hospital for Sick Children for nurse Peggy Tucker. Her fiancé, Arn Lonsdale, had been posted to Burma with the RCAF, so she had thrown herself into her nursing career. On VE Day, "we worked a regular shift from seven to seven and then went out and joined the crowds down on Yonge Street in our uniforms...

"Absolutely forbidden... You never wore your uniform out of the hospital, apron and bib and blue uniform and our cape and our cap... [but we] went out, down Yonge Street. The crowds were just astonishing. Finally, we decided we'd better find a way back. We were within months of graduating; we could have been kicked out on our ears...but (someone) left the cellar door open, so we snuck up to our rooms. Lucky we didn't get caught. The celebrations were still going on the next night..."

Bette Mulvihill was a sixteen-year-old attending farmerette camp in Cooksville, just outside Toronto, that first week of May. "A bunch of us [went downtown] to take part in the victory celebrations. Yonge Street was a sea of humanity. You went in whatever direction the crowd was moving because you simply couldn't go any other way. We rode on the streetcars for free all evening.

"Everyone was kissing and hugging. It didn't matter that they were total strangers. We were one huge family—filled with terrific excitement and a great relief that the war was over at last."

Seventeen-year-old Marie Jackman spent a quieter VE Day evening than most. She was ironing in the tiny apartment kitchen of her landlady; this was how she paid for bed and board. The woman—Jeanne Poile—had a young son, whom Marie also took care of, and a husband who was overseas in the military. When she heard the news she thought, "at last, this father, husband, and stranger to me, would be coming home.

"And this he did in due time before the school year ended in June.

Such an occasion it was, and the family meal put together in those lean times was something to remember. It was a very formal affair with best china and included my introduction to oysters..."

Sudbury celebrated the end of hostilities in Europe with an official ceremony, and numerous unofficial ones. Seven-year-old Claire Sandford lived in Sudbury at the time. She suffered from rheumatic fever; consequently, she was often wrapped in a comforter, placed in the sunshine and not allowed to eat anything cold. During the VE Day festivities a woman offered Claire an ice cream, but her mother stopped her. Then at the height of the celebrations, the short-sighted Sandford remembers that "two men were being strung up from the neck on hydro wires.

"I heard shouting and yelling and it became apparent that Mr. Whistle, the mayor of our town, was the head lyncher. The shouts were about Hitler and Mussolini. Later in life I figured out that it was an effigy burning."

Russell Cushman worked in the BCATP in an RAF Mosquito dispatching unit at the London, Ontario, airport. Cushman had a day off on May 8, so he took his wife to an appointment to have two impacted wisdom teeth removed.

"While she was in the dentist's office," explained Cushman, "I slipped across the corner to the barber shop with the hope that I might get a quick trim before she had fully recovered from the anaesthetic. Luck was with me, the chair was empty.

"I had just settled in, with the apron on, when a low-flying aircraft passed over with a thundering roar, followed immediately by another. It sounded like a Mosquito from the airport. The barber, listening to the radio, said, 'The Germans have surrendered.' Sure enough, details of the surrender were being announced.

"He then walked over to the mirror cabinet and took out a full, unopened bottle of Scotch. Taking off the cap, he said: 'I put this there the day war was declared and said it would stay there till we had 'em licked. Today's the day. Help yourself, boys.' And everyone in the shop drank a rousing toast to Victory.

"It was a hard decision, but I got out of the chair knowing after a few more toasts my Victory haircut might leave a bit to be desired.

Hurrying back to the dentist's office, I found my wife completely bewildered. She thought all the noise and chatter was the effect of the gas anaesthetic the dentist had used.

"By this time, bells were ringing, locomotive whistles blowing, and everyone was talking at once. When the dentist told her the war was over, she started to cry... Unfortunately, the discomfort of the extractions began to set in, spoiling any notion we may have had of joining the celebrating crowds gathering in the downtown area."

Bob Jarvis was fifteen and in Grade 11 at Ridley College in St. Catharines, Ontario. He and his friends felt that St. Catharines was too small a city in which to spend VE Day ("to celebrate you'd go into the local bakery and buy a jelly doughnut").

"Many of the boys from school were Americans and one of my best friends was an American from Buffalo," remembers Jarvis. "We were looking for something to do, something extraordinary, to celebrate the end of the war. So he suggested that we 'borrow' his Dad's car and drive to Times Square, New York...

"We got there for VE Day... Times Square was absolutely crammed with people. And the police had barricaded both ends, north and south... I guess the thing I recall specifically, other than just the noise, incredible noise, was crossing Times Square without touching the ground. This was at the north end, around 46th Street. There were cars, not bumper to bumper but side to side, and we walked over the tops of the cars to get across Times Square."

In Windsor, Ontario, on VE Day, the families of six Dieppe veterans received word that the servicemen (members of the Essex Scottish Regiment) had just been repatriated from German POW camps to England.

Meanwhile, a special CNR train pulled into Winnipeg and disembarked half its load of 285 returning veterans. Members of the Greater Winnipeg Co-ordinating Board supplied coffee and cigarettes as the din of hundreds of family, friends, and well-wishers filled the station concourse with the joyful sound of welcome. Among them was nine-year-old Glen Thompson, dressed in a highlander's kilt and sporran in honour of his father. Major Robert Thompson was among the first off the train; Thompson had seen action at Dieppe and in Normandy with the Cameron Highlanders of Canada. Father and son had not seen each other in four years.

"He's suddenly grown," was all Thompson, Sr., could say, while son Glen proudly announced to a *Winnipeg Tribune* reporter, "I'm going with him the next time."

Vancouver seemed to want to drop everything and celebrate. To mark the occasion, air raid sirens woke the city just after seven o'clock in the morning. Trading was suspended that day on the Vancouver Stock Exchange. Civic authorities announced a mass religious service that afternoon at Brockton Point and a memorial service in West Vancouver that night. The British Columbia Electric Railway removed trolleys from the streets in anticipation of the crowds, while harbour officials soon had ships and ferries in the harbour decked out in streamers and bunting. Most government offices and businesses closed—except for the Boeing plant (which was still manufacturing bomb bays for the USAAF Superfortress B-29 aircraft) and the Federal Income Tax office. (Did the tax people perhaps hope that an outpouring of pent-up emotion might spur some to deliver their back taxes?)

No matter. May 8 in Vancouver turned into a city-wide street festival. Vendors sold streamers, flags, and New Year's horns to passers-by along Hastings, Granville, Georgia, and Main streets. At first cars and trucks packed with people filled the streets; no one seemed to mind the scores of fender-benders as cars were soon gridlocked across the city. Then people poured into the roadways. Some formed conga lines and danced. Others linked arms and sang. Still others adorned themselves in striped suits and Uncle Sam hats, perhaps in tribute to American sailors in the city.

Across the country Canadians celebrated, cheered, kissed passing girls, got a little drunk, or a little drunker, burned effigies, paraded, dreamed up pranks, and generally had a well-earned hell of a time.

In some places, however, the celebrations got out of hand. There was the looting in Montreal's theatre district and the smashed windows of the Quebec Liquor Commission store there. In Sudbury, Ontario, twelve people were injured over the two-day celebrations, most of them in traffic accidents, and one young man was accidentally shot with his own rifle. There was a riot on Cape Breton Island. And at a Liquor

Commission store in Kentville, N.S., nearly a thousand rioters were persuaded to go home by First World War veteran and hockey hero Irving Bickerton; at the height of the assault on the store, Bickerton reportedly raced to the scene, stood up before the mob, and shouted: "Hold it, boys! This war is only half over. We still have Japan to lick!"

And then there was Halifax.

Haligonians disliked what nearly six years of war had brought to their city—thousands of servicemen pouring through on their way to Europe, beaches fouled by oil from a harbour filled beyond capacity, rationing, blackouts, curfews, and general overcrowding everywhere from restaurants to streetcars.

Meanwhile, service people complained that food in Halifax was bad, rents were sky-high, and services non-existent. "The average guy off a ship," explained RCN crewman Jim Hazlewood, "when he went to a store, they didn't treat him very well. Sometimes the prices were higher for navy than for anyone else."

"Navy men felt they were dreadfully exploited," agreed Thelma Ransom, a Wren in Halifax at the time. "When I was only about two and a half days in basic training, my name was on the list to go to Halifax. And the situation was so bad there, that girls in the navy were mailing their laundry home to have it done. Their facilities were strained to the nth degree."

"There was supposed to be a sign in Halifax," explained RCN sailor Roy Harbin. "It read, 'No Sailors or Dogs Allowed.' I knew there were places that you really weren't very welcome."

Perhaps it was inevitable that the frustrations of 65,000 permanent residents and as many as 55,000 transient navy and merchant seamen would end up in confrontation on the streets.

Both civic and naval authorities were aware of threats heard throughout early 1945—threats that navy men wanted to "take Halifax apart." A month before VE Day, Halifax Police Chief Judson Conrod decided that the best way to avoid trouble would be to shut down all liquor stores in the city on Victory Day. In turn the liquor commission put pressure on the navy to shut down their wet canteens when the war's end was announced. But Rear Admiral Leonard W. Murray discounted civilian warnings of potentially violent VE Day activities and declared his faith in the discipline of his 18,000-man command in Halifax.

Neither strategy worked.

At 10:30 a.m. on Monday, May 7, with the news of the imminent German capitulation in the air, whistles began blowing, people began abandoning their workplaces, and everything was locked up tight. Thousands of civilians and seamen streamed into the streets, but there was nothing to see, nothing to buy, and nothing to do. Despite the mayor's request, movie houses in Halifax and Dartmouth closed for the day. Only sixteen out of fifty-five eating places stayed open. And provincial liquor stores were closed.

That left HMCS *Stadacona*, the naval barracks with its wet canteen, as the only place where sailors could get drinks to celebrate victory. That day, 2,000 navy men drank their way through 6,000 bottles of beer, not to mention "at least one bottle of rye that every man had put aside for this day." This was before the sailors went downtown. But at closing time—9 p.m.—with no organized entertainment planned and with "open gangway" declared (allowing seamen to come and go as they pleased), Barrington Street filled with thousands of celebrants with nowhere to celebrate.

And "the boys got mad." That's the way Eve Arnoldi explains it. She had joined the Wrens in the fall of 1942 and was doing code and cipher work in Halifax when the war ended. "These boys came off ships like corvettes...very narrow, very uncomfortable, very rough. They were wet, cold...and hungry. And they can't go to the *Stadacona*, our shore ship, because they didn't have a station card for it. And they couldn't have anything to eat or drink in the city of Halifax, because they'd boarded up the restaurants... And what we got for a celebration was a church parade. Well, whoopee!"

Within fifteen minutes of *Stadacona*'s closing that night, the chief of navy shore patrol, Lieutenant Commander R.W. Wood, reported sailors surrounding a streetcar on Barrington. The seamen were shouting happily, but also putting their fists through the streetcar windows and laughing at the surprised riders inside. Wood took his thirty shore-patrol officers and dispersed the crowd. But by the time he got back to his office, he was told that 4,000 people were jamming downtown streets, ripping down flags, and "having a hell of a time."

The commotion in the heart of the city reached up Citadel Hill, where 15,000 community singers were peaceably celebrating victory over Hitler. Before long civilians were drifting down the hill to join the fun and noise-making.

The violence began to escalate. Gordon Ward, an airman with the RCAF, saw "rioters rampaging down Barrington Street, pulling the trolleys of all the streetcars off the overhead wires... The looting and pillaging continued into the night. Dozens of people were crazed with drink. And it's a solemn fact—beer was running in the gutters."

The crowd was not only ambushing streetcars, it was breaking windows, pulling down trolley poles, and even leaping into the operators' seats and crashing the streetcars into each other. Lieutenant Commander Wood and his meagre force managed to remove all trolleys from the streets, save one. That car was in the midst of a mob intent on tipping it over. And when that failed, the mob of sailors and civilians put shredded newspaper under the oil-covered trolley undercarriage and set it on fire. When city police arrived with the force's largest patrol wagon, it too was commandeered, rolled on its side, and torched. The street crowd tore the trolley to pieces, unintimidated by police or firefighters.

Meanwhile, on Sackville Street, about a hundred people arrived at the central provincial liquor store. They overwhelmed the six-man police force dispatched there to defend it, and in a good-natured but determined fashion handed out the booty. Overnight, revellers ransacked three Halifax liquor stores and dispensed 1,280 cases of beer and 27 cases of wine to fuel the all-night partying in city streets.

The next day, May 8, was VE Day.

The traditional signal—"Splice the main brace"—flew at the admiral's yardarm in the dockyard. As a gesture of gratitude to naval forces, Colonel Sidney Oland and his brewery warehouse staff handed out a free case of beer to each sailor who wished it until there was no more to give. Then the supply of liquor at HMCS *Stadacona*'s wet canteen ran out at one o'clock, and the trouble started all over again. Again it was "open gangway" and again liquor stores and restaurants remained closed.

Beatrice Geary was a Wren in Halifax at the time; she remembers they were "being protected from possible drunken sailors" crashing the Wren block.

"From our top bunks," she remembers, "we watched the shore patrol ushering sailors through *Stadacona* gates, removing bottles from the sailors' tunics, and emptying their contents at their feet... The highlight of our VE Day was when a sailor appeared from nowhere, riding a horse into the front door of our Wren block. We never did hear what happened to horse or rider."

As well as the navy barracks, Halifax had the Citadel Barracks and the Wellington Barracks, home to about 500 Canadian Women's Army Corps servicewomen. CWAC Major Grace Collyer remembers saying, "Let them all go and celebrate." She thought that everybody was having a good time downtown, but then "it all turned nasty. And I had to get the girls back as best I could."

She dispatched a jeep and a truck to go searching for 500 CWACs to coax them home. "We finally got a lot of them back... Some of them got frightened and came back on their own. Some of them—with all the looting and everything—were having a wonderful time...picking up this, that and the other thing... [but] the biggest percentage were frightened out of their wits and came home..."

Air force personnel were rounded up in similar fashion. That day, Pilot Officer Larry Foley was working in the operations room at RCAF Eastern Air Command, across from the Nova Scotian Hotel. The control room where he worked was entirely enclosed with no windows, so he had no idea what was going on outside, "until the senior air staff officer came along and without so much as a by your leave, rounded up a bunch of us and a whole fleet of trucks with service police. And we literally picked air force fellows up off the street... We rounded up all airmen and airwomen and took them out to a beautiful old golf course where the command had organized a big party."

Outside the *Stadacona* barracks on Barrington Street, several hundred sailors pelted the canteen with sticks, stones, and bottles. More trolleys were smashed. A beefed-up shore patrol (now ninety strong) waded into the crowds and dispersed the trouble-makers with axe-handles and truncheons.

A thousand men—civilians and servicemen—filled Salter and Water streets at the main gates of Keith's brewery. They pushed in the gates and forced helpless shore patrolmen back through the yard to the brewery's store of kegs and cases of beer. As the liquor was handed out, 107 Provost Corps officers and city police arrived in wagons, cars, and trucks to reinforce the shore patrol. The rioters inside dispersed, the yard was cleared, and a six-ton army truck was jammed into the gateway. Fifteen minutes later more rioters arrived, pushed the army truck (which was in gear with its brakes on) out of the way, brushed past the police, and continued looting the brewery, "liberating" nearly 120,000 quart bottles of beer.

Six blocks away—at the Garrison Grounds—Mayor Allan Butler, Rear Admiral Murray, Brigadier D. A. White, and Air Vice Marshal A. L. Morfee presided at a sedate VE Day ceremony. Nearly 20,000 people gave thanks to God for the defeat of Germany. During the ceremony, Mayor Butler received word of the assault on the brewery and pleaded with Rear Admiral Murray for action. When the ceremony concluded—about 2:30 p.m.—Murray assembled a parade of 375 navy men to act as a show of strength and discipline and, in Murray's words, to provide "a diversion by marching the navy through the city."

The effect was just the opposite. As they marched down Barrington Street the paradesmen were pushed, shoved, and intimidated. Bottles of rum, whisky, and gin were waved under their noses or poured over their heads. Between the Garrison Grounds and the *Stadacona* barracks nearly a third of the parade participants disappeared.

Despite every effort of the shore patrol, the Provost Corps, and city police, the drunken celebrants fanned out across the city—to Grafton Park, St. Paul's Cemetery, and Cornwallis Square in front of the Nova Scotian Hotel, where they could drink openly and tell the world they'd won the war. Men and women made love in public parks. Celebrants clad only in Union Jacks ran through the streets.

Throughout the afternoon and evening, the riots continued. Crowds turned on the merchants' stores in downtown Halifax. Some emerged from Birks, their arms adorned with watches. Others carried off clothing through broken Eaton's windows, or looted and burned downtown restaurants, and stripped Buckley's, Barnstead's, and Fader's drug stores of all their patent medicines. No authority—civilian or military— could stop them.

"At the end of Barrington Street," Wren Arnoldi recalls, "there were furniture shops. I saw this old pick-up truck come up and these civilians piling furniture into it. They couldn't get a big easy chair. They had a little boy with them, and they sat him in the chair and said, 'Don't you get out of that chair until we come back.' They just made the child stay there.

"One sailor was wearing about three ladies' bras and a couple of nighties all over his stuff... He was smoking a great big cigar; it had an ash on it about four inches long. He looked in this furniture store window—the only one not broken—at one of those standing ashtrays. He looked at the ash on his cigar. Then he looked at the window. And pow! He smashed the window, flicked out his ash, and walked away."

At four o'clock that afternoon Wren Rodine "Ronnie" Egan completed her clerical shift at HMCS *Stadacona*. Egan had been married the year before and lived away from the Wrens' barracks. That afternoon she and several Wren friends joined the crowds in the Halifax streets just in time to see "a group of sailors running around with mannequins in their arms. Some had them over their shoulders... Others put them down on the cobble stones and used them like toboggans to slide down the street... Oh, it was comical."

Later Egan and her colleagues found the Zellers store open and went in for some VE Day shopping. As they were leaving they met a half dozen "liquored up sailors who let on that they were going to burn down the store. Well, we confronted them and told them, 'No you aren't.' It was a little tense for a minute or two. But eventually the sailors backed down and left the store... I felt badly that they were ruining the city. Halifax had been good to the Wrens, I thought."

"I had a couple of friends who got sat upon by sailors," recalls Dave MacDonald. He was sixteen at the time and living in Halifax. "One of my friends had his nose plastered from ear to ear. But another guy, Jim (who was crippled and had a big, thick sole on his boot), was very agile on his feet...even played English rugby... He brought this boot up and under a guy's chin." That was the end of that encounter.

"There was an animal loose down there," concludes MacDonald. "A mob is an animal. It was a dreadful thing."

Not even Rear Admiral Murray himself could bring an end to the rioting. At six o'clock that evening, Murray led a convoy of nine trucks packed with shore patrol men. He used a loud-speaker to entreat his "lads" to return to their barracks and to admonish them that "the navy by its action this day has undone the good reputation in Halifax for the last six years... This is not a joke!" he concluded. It was only when more than 1,000 soldiers arrived late that evening from Debert, Nova Scotia (100 kilometres to the north), that order was restored.

It was too late. Two days of rioting had wrecked downtown Halifax. Estimates of damage ranged from three to five million dollars. The navy blamed the city. Civilians blamed the navy. Rear Admiral Murray publicly blamed civilians for the destruction, but there is no doubt that his handling of the situation was inadequate, to say the least.

A Royal Commission headed by Mr. Justice R. L. Kellock of the Supreme Court of Canada blamed the riots on the failure of the naval command to control the first disorders. There was also criticism of the "passive conduct" of the naval command.

The commission's report said that 564 businesses had been damaged by the riots, more than 2,500 windows had been smashed, and over 200 business premises looted. More than 150 had been arrested for drunkenness, while 19 airmen, 41 soldiers, 34 naval ratings, and 117 civilians were charged with a variety of disorders.

Rear Admiral Leonard Murray retired from the navy in 1946, moved to England, and became a distinguished barrister. Over the years he was given various honours and awards, including France's Croix de Guerre and America's Legion of Merit. However, the events in Halifax on May 8, 1945, were forever dubbed "Murray's Folly," tarnishing his wartime career. By rights, Murray should have been savouring victory, as his arch enemies, the German U-boat captains, surrendered in Allied ports around the Atlantic.

It was, after all, Victory-in-Europe Day.

Surrender of the 25th German Army, May 5, 1945. Lieut.-Gen. Foulkes (left) commander of the 1st Canadian Corps, accepts the surrender of Gen. Johannes Blaskowitz (second from right) commander of German forces in the Netherlands. *Alexander Stirton, National Archives of Canada PA-138588*

Hats are in the air as wireless operator Pte. Mackeays relays news of the end of hostilities to a group of Seaforth Highlanders. *Michael Dean, National Archives of Canada PA-134450*

Swastikas were for sitting on at the Toronto home of the Spanton family. Above, Jacqui Spanton, sits on a Nazi flag brought home as a war souvenir by a neighbour. *Marion Spanton*

Happy Torontonians gathered along Bay St. near City Hall to celebrate VE Day. *John & Madge Trull*

The people of Calgary poured into the city's downtown area to take part in the jubilant celebration marking war's end, VE Day. *Glenbow Archives, Calgary*

A Canadian seaman blows his own salute to VE Day on this downtown Halifax street. *Department of National Defense, Kellock Collection*

Two Canadian servicemen walk brazenly through Halifax carrying "liberated" clothes. Not all of the looters were in the armed forces. *Department of National Defense, Kellock Collection*

A downtown Halifax shoe store after looters had been through it, helping themselves to whatever might fit. *Department of National Defense, Kellock Collection*

A boy surveys the aftermath of the Halifax riots. Note that the bike looks rather big for him. *Mrs. Lillian A. Delaney*

"HERBIE"

"HE SEZ HE'LL BE IN CANADA AHEAD OF US—I WONDER HOW MANY POINTS HE'S GOT?"

The Maple Leaf

Lieut. Art Cole holds Sgt. Karen Hermeston on his shoulder on VJ Day in London. His wife in Toronto was not amused. *Art Cole*

Londoners abandoned their traditional aloofness on VJ Day. *Art Cole*

Toronto's large Chinese community converged on Elizabeth Street to express its delight on VJ Day. *Toronto* Telegram

This informal shot of Gen. H.D.G. Crerar was treasured by Willis Egan, his Army driver during part of the war. *Ronnie Egan*

Airman Donald Carty used his wit to combat racism when it confronted him during his RCAF service. *Donald Carty*

Lieut.-Gen. Guy Simonds in a pose symbolic of Canadian might. *Charles Richer, National Archives of Canada PA-141689*

"HERBIE"

Ronald Brent Bartlett Taylor, the infant, was barely aware that this was a reunion of his parents in England, 1944. *Brent B. Taylor*

"NOW THAT THE WAR IS OVER WE'LL BE SOON LEAVING FOR UNCLE HERBIE'S BIG RANCH IN TORONTO!"

The Maple Leaf

A group of war brides of Canadian servicemen and their children embark for their new homes almost a year before the war's end. *W.J. Hynes, National Archives of Canada PA-147114*

Name:	Gibson
Vorname:	William Russell
Dienstgrad:	Sgt.
Erk.-Marke:	8090 Kgf.Lg.d.Lw.3
Serv.-Nr.:	R-252323
Nationalität:	Kanada

Baracke: 62

Raum: 13

Airman Bill Gibson's identification card at Buchenwald, the Nazi concentration camp, where he was held in 1944. *Bill Gibson*

SENIOR RUGBY TEAM

In 1942, the Northern Vocational School senior football team won the Toronto city championship. Within two years, the war was to claim a terrible toll among its members. *Northern Vocational School*

12

Sweating It Out

From Amsterdam to Brussels to Paris to London, and every city, town, and village in between, and across the Atlantic, from St. John's to Victoria, on May 9, 1945, countless millions of people, who had gone all-out celebrating VE Day, experienced a hangover of epic proportions. But their rude awakening was as nothing compared to the realization by the many thousands of Canadians (and others) overseas that the war wasn't over, after all.

In every Allied capital, statesmen who'd felt called upon to make stirring speeches to mark VE Day lost no time in reminding all concerned that there was still another war over on the other side of the world that had to be fought and won. Typical was C. D. Howe, sometimes known as the "minister of just about everything," who sternly reminded Canadian war workers that although they could celebrate VE Day, they would be expected back on their jobs the next day.

"Let us mark our joy at the good news from Europe," said Howe, "by rededicating ourselves to the task of beating Japan."

Even *The Maple Leaf* sounded a sober note in its editorial on VE Day+3. "One annoying fact that must be kept in mind in the mental approach to the future is that the war is not over. The task of applying the same treatment to Japan as Germany has yet to be handled. What might be regarded as an obvious reaction to victory over Germany, a let-down in effort, must be guarded against. VJ Day is a good deal closer than it was at this time last year but the road to Tokyo is bound to have plenty of pot-holes in it."

On the same day that *The Maple Leaf* was reminding its readers of the "annoying fact" that had to be kept in mind, *The Winnipeg Tribune* carried a story headlined: "Pacific Volunteers To Get Home First."

"Defence headquarters today issued details of arrangements showing how soldiers will come marching home and how they will march off again to the Pacific.

"Here, briefly, is the general plan, similar in many respects to the British plan:

"1. First men home will be the troops who volunteer for the Pacific. They will have thirty clear days leave and then go to concentration areas for training and transport to the Pacific as the Canadian Far East Force, or C.F.E.F. Men under thirty-five will get preference for this force.

"2. Then will come the men whose priority point score—based on length and type of service and certain other factors—is high. They will have thirty days leave with pay before discharge."

The story went on for several more numbered paragraphs, but the message was clear: the carrot was the thirty-day leave, a very tempting carrot for somebody who had been overseas for two or three or four years. The stick: more war in the Far East.

The next day, *The Maple Leaf*'s editorial referred to reallocation, repatriation, and demobilization as three "husky words" describing what was going to happen next to the Canadian Army. "Obviously, the fastest way to get back to Canada is volunteer service in the Pacific."

This was to become a familiar refrain during that summer of semi-peace, but not everyone in uniform liked the tune. Certainly, the idea of going home on a thirty-day leave was tempting. But the knowledge that the leave would be followed by a trip to the Pacific and more war was disheartening for many battle-weary Canadians.

On May 21, Prime Minister King announced that 30,000 Canadian troops would be going to the Pacific theatre and that every man would receive extra pay for the job. The "Pacific bonus," according to *The Maple Leaf*'s story, would range from thirty cents a day for privates up to one dollar a day for officers of the rank of major or higher.

Some veterans of the war in Europe might have been attracted by this windfall or by the carrot of the thirty-day leave; others were not. John Macfie, who served overseas in the RAF, still has some of the letters he received during that period. Most of his friends were reluctant to volunteer for Pacific duty. One wrote, "I guess you will be volunteering for the Pacific now, eh? I'm sure not going in the infantry anyway and to all intentions right now, I'm not going at all. Wouldn't mind knocking off a few Japs, but it's all the training leading up to the fighting that gets me." Another wrote from Holland, "Just now we are...in a little town near Almelo and nothing but spit and polish as we are going to Berlin. I don't know for how long, but likely a month or two. So will be damn lucky if I get home for Xmas yet, unless I sign for Burma and I sure don't feel like sticking my neck out that far." Another said, "Quite a few are leaving now for the CFEF [Canadian Far East Force], but I'm not one of them and I don't intend to be, have seen enough rice in this area without asking for it."

The prospect of going home was uppermost in the minds of many servicemen. A Black Watch sergeant who was interviewed as he embarked for Canada told a reporter from *The Maple Leaf,* "I don't care how seasick I am this time, long as I can crawl down that gangplank at Halifax, I'll make it home on my hands and knees." The reporter also spoke to one Private Fournier, who said, "If I get a foothold on the soil of Canada, it'll take a damn good man to get me off."

On his return to Canada, Cliff Perry, who had served for five years, first in the Royal Canadian Navy and then in the Royal Navy, was sent to Ottawa. He remembers the Navy trying to persuade him to do two things:

"One was to volunteer for the Far East... And secondly to stay in and join the permanent force. But when VE Day occurred, my war was over. Mentally, I was finished and nothing would change my mind."

In contrast, aboard the corvette HMCS *Fredericton* on May 6, 1945, seaman Bill Beales recalls his captain asking for volunteers to fight the Japanese. "Most of the older married men declined the offer. But I was young and footloose, so I signed up for the Pacific war."

RCAF airman Brock Hunchberger was twenty-five years old and married with three children when he joined the RCAF during the war. He served in England right up until VE Day, then was repatriated. He remembers "when we came home, they called for volunteers for the Pacific. Some did and some didn't... I didn't."

Wallace Bambrough had joined the Royal Canadian Engineers in 1940, when he was eighteen. He went overseas that same year and was in Germany when the European war ended. He too was encouraged to sign up for the Far East, with the usual carrot of going home on leave first. But says Bambrough, "I thought one long war was enough for me, and I could wait."

Batteryman Joe Baker had served in anti-aircraft artillery in France, Belgium, and Holland, and been wounded twice, yet he volunteered to go to the Pacific. He returned from Europe on the *Queen Elizabeth*, occupying his own stateroom (he was not an officer) and believes he was given the preferred accommodation because he had volunteered.

George Hutton came home aboard the troopship *Ile de France*. Hutton, an RCAF tail gunner, had been shot down over Germany in 1944 and spent the rest of the European war as a prisoner of the Germans. "All the guys who volunteered to go to the Pacific, that never flew an operation in England," says Hutton, "they put them in the cabins. All us guys they stuck down with the army, no different. They shut the water off and you could only get water from the tap so many hours a day."

As the troops sweated it out, each day seemed to bring a new story, a new announcement from Ottawa about what was going to happen to whom and when and why.

On May 14, 1945, the fighting men's paper carried a short item under the headline: June 1 Deadline. "Canadian naval personnel have until June 1 to make up their minds whether they want to serve with the Pacific force."

On May 26, the London edition of *The Maple Leaf* ran a story about Canada's representation on the occupation force in Europe. The story included this bit of information: "Men now serving overseas who wish to join the occupational force will have the opportunity of volunteering for this duty. The balance of the force will be made up of men with lower repatriation point totals, who will be directed into the new units."

A few days later, the London edition of the army paper carried a story announcing that "provisional arrangements" had been made for the return to Canada "within the next six months" of all Canadian servicemen who had been overseas for more than four years. The story attributed the statement to Prime Minister Mackenzie King, who also indicated that "men on occupational service and certain key personnel will be excepted." The same story also revealed that Colin Gibson, Canada's air minister, had announced that 100,000 RCAF personnel would be needed for the Pacific war, European occupation, and administration in Canada, but nowhere was there to be found any reference to the Canadian Army, or how many men it would need for the Pacific.

Once the war in Europe was over, the singleness of purpose that had united the Allies began to show signs of crumbling. The weary Brits began to feel that the Canadians and Americans had outstayed their welcome.

Cliff Perry, who spent more of his service time with the Royal Navy than with the Royal Canadian Navy, was paid by Canada—and thus was paid more than a British navy man of equal status would have been paid.

"I honestly can't remember the details (of how much), but I believe it was something on the order of a third more," he says. "Which is one of the reasons the English people resented the Americans so much. The Americans flaunted that. They always had silk stockings for the girls and chocolate bars for the kids and what have you. You've heard the expression so many times—the Americans were over-paid, over-sexed, and over here. And they really were resented. The Canadians were too, to a lesser degree, but because we were Commonwealth we had enough sense, generally, to be careful about that."

Joe Baker, who spent considerable time overseas while he was in the Canadian Army, remembers a difference in attitude between the British soldiers and the Canadians. "The British army man was very Army and very much a disciplinarian. And [they felt] we didn't know how to drink. Like, he'd go in and have a pint of bitter, where the Canadian guy would knock back ten or twelve rums or whatever and then make a fool of himself. They didn't appreciate that. And [the Canadians] took all the women, you know."

Friction between the Canadians and their British hosts erupted in a riot at Aldershot. Throughout the war, Aldershot, fifty kilometres from London, had been Britain's primary military training centre, and served as "home" to thousands upon thousands of Canadian troops. The presence of soldiers was no novelty to the people of Aldershot. Men in uniform had come and gone from Aldershot since the days of the Crimean War.

Some citizens of Aldershot were hospitable in their dealings with the visiting Canadian soldiers; some were not. By the same token, some Canadians appreciated the hospitality and treated their hosts with courtesy and respect; and some did not. However, the German bombings helped the Canadians to understand what the British were going through, and prompted the visiting servicemen to be more considerate of their hosts.

When the war in Europe ended, however, the cordiality began to disintegrate. The Canadians waiting at Aldershot for shipping orders got fed up with seeing pictures in the papers (even in their own *Maple Leaf*) of American troops boarding planes to be flown home, and shots of the *Queen Mary* packed with Americans arriving in New York. When the hell would it be their turn? By early June the mood turned ugly.

On the evening of July 4, 1945, a group of Canadian soldiers gathered in the centre of the town to complain about their situation. The crowd of soldiers grew and a rumour went around that three Canadians had been arrested and locked in the local jail. The men began to move towards the jail, breaking windows as they went. According to one newspaper, one group broke all the automatic machines in an amusement arcade; another overturned several parked cars. Although reinforcements of British and Canadian military police were summoned, the soldiers returned quietly to their barracks when they found that the rumours were baseless and there were no Canadians in the jail.

David Veitch of the Royal Canadian Engineers recorded the events in his diary, which he wrote up afterwards. Veitch was a veteran of the D-Day invasion, who had volunteered for the Pacific and was waiting in Aldershot for reposting.

"4 July—Canadian troops rioted at Aldershot. I believe that the primary cause of the trouble was the troops' dissatisfaction with the speed in returning them home—many of them had been away five [or] six years from Canada and their families, and were fed up with sitting

around Aldershot [again], but this time with nothing to do... I was told
that the incident that triggered the riots was the arrest and incarcera-
tion in the local jail of one [or] two soldiers whose mates then tried to
rescue them by force. Rumour had it that the miscreants were from the
Cape Breton Highlanders of 5 Div.

"5 July—Another riot, this time with approximately 10,000 pounds
damage to the town. Major General Spry...senior Canadian commander of the repatriation depots at Aldershot, ordered all officers out in
pairs to patrol the streets. It was hoped that the presence of the officers
would quieten the troops, but it was not to be, since we were all reinforcements on our way home, and neither the troops nor the officers
knew each other. In fact, most of the paired officers had never seen
each other before.

"Dan Spry...commander of Canadian troops in Aldershot, carried
the can for this affair for the rest of his service, which I thought was
unfair since he personally could do little to speed up the passage of the
troops. However, in retrospect, I think that if more public announcement had been made about the troop schedules so that everyone could
have had a better idea of where they stood in the queue to go home,
the riots might not have happened."

The Maple Leaf reported that Major General Dan Spry had reprimanded the men for the "schoolboy" action, which would "undermine
the good reputation the Canadians had built up on the battlefield." He
acknowledged that their grievances were real: the shortage of shipping,
which was delaying repatriation, the "establishment" food rations,
which were less than they had received in the field (but still more than
civilians received), and their pay. The men had drawn pay when they
left for embarkation leave, but when sailings were delayed, their money
ran out.

The newspapers were full of expressions of outrage. Wallace
Reyburn of The Montreal Standard wrote of walking "ankle-deep
through broken glass" in Aldershot and of getting "black looks and
cold shoulders" from the townspeople. One woman said to him, "I
wish we had had the Gestapo billeted here. They wouldn't have treated
us nearly as badly." Another, "purple in the face with rage," said, "I
used to like Canada and Canadians. Now I'll never speak to another
Canadian in my life." Yet Reyburn claimed that no one criticized the

Canadians for drunkenness or looting, and no member of the public was molested in any way. One shopkeeper pointed out: "The amazing thing is that few of them were the worse for liquor and practically nothing was stolen. They only broke windows."

The Maple Leaf called the men "hoodlums," but London's *Daily Telegraph* said, "The deservedly high reputation of Canadian troops in this country will certainly not be affected by the incident...whose causes are entirely comprehensible." *The Daily Express* (Lord Beaverbrook's paper) added, "Let it never be forgotten that these Canadians who now are so anxious to get home have been in England longer than troops of any other ally... Every effort must be made to speed the departure home of Canadian soldiers... Justice would be done if repatriation was based to a much greater extent on length of service in the European theatre of operations."

Meanwhile, Canadian troops were leaving Aldershot—not for home, but to get them out of the sight of the offended townspeople. The leading "hoodlums" were dealt with severely. Six men were convicted by courts martial and given sentences ranging from sixteen months to seven years. (It later turned out that three had volunteered for the Pacific.)

It is unlikely that a single Canadian got home a day sooner as a result of the incident. But several hundred had let off some steam, at the cost of eighty-seven windows and some very ruffled British feathers.

A few months later—more than six months, in fact—little had changed for many Canadian armed services personnel.

Jack Rae's experience was typical. Rae had joined the RCAF in September 1941 and had served in ground crew, repairing and maintaining the radios in the cockpits of Spitfires, until the end of the war—and well beyond. He was in France by the middle of June 1944, and also served in Belgium and Germany. In a letter to his mother, dated January 12, 1946, he wrote, "Today we had the minister for air, Col. Gibson, and the deputy minister and the air officer commanding RCAF overseas, Air Marshal Johnson, here to speak to us. Col. Gibson spoke for about ten minutes and then he let the boys ask questions and they really let him have it. It was surprising the way in which the boys greeted his answers with loud laughs...

"The boys gave him quite a blast about the way the papers back home tell the people we'll all be home for Christmas, then Jan. 16, then March 31. Now he comes along and tells us it will be June 30 to Sept. 30 and by the time that date rolls along it will be postponed later still. He said that this was definitely the final date and he admitted that the publicity had fallen down on the job.

"Another fellow asked him what [had] happened to the fellows who volunteered for the occupation force and were sent home for 30 days leave. He said that these were in the same category as the volunteers for the Interim Air Force and were not returned because we were coming home so soon. Another fellow, a pilot, wanted to know why so many pilots were discharged without having been overseas after they completed their training while other pilots who had been overseas a considerable time still have no chance of getting home.

"They really had him tied up in knots trying to answer some of the questions and I could go on filling another page with the questions they asked him but I won't get home any sooner. So I guess I was right when I wrote you last June and said I would be home a year from then.

"So I'll see you in July or August. So long for now. Jack."

Rae spent some leave in Dublin. On February 7, 1946, he was still in England. That day's letter to his mother said, "Just now our squadron in England is on strike and it's going to last until Ottawa gives us a good idea as to when we are getting home. None of the ground crew here volunteered for the Occupation but they are trying to make us stay. The strike is well organized and is spreading to other Canadian stations; it's really good to see the fellows sticking together, everybody keeps away from work and at nights go out as usual. The officers are gassing aeroplanes, and washing their own dishes, and shoveling coal. Yesterday Ottawa was supposed to have sent a reply, but the fellows aren't satisfied with it so the strike stays on..."

Well before that letter reached Jack's parents, the Canadian newspapers had picked up the story of the airmen's strike. Also, the strike had spread from Oldham, Hampshire, to Down Ampney, and there was talk of similar strike action at Topcliffe, Yorkshire, and at Leeming airfield, also in Yorkshire. About 1,500 RCAF personnel participated.

On February 8, *The Toronto Telegram* reported that at Down Ampney striking ground crews booed a headquarters officer who threatened them with charges of mutiny and possible stoppage of food. The *Telegram*'s editorial the next day viewed the whole business with distaste: "Because a strike opposes duty, discipline, order, service, those who take part in it reduced themselves to the level of a mob with the difference that they lay themselves open to the charge of mutiny."

But, being a good Tory paper, the *Telegram* couldn't pass up a chance to knock the King government. "The government at Ottawa may now be questioned as to why conditions are such that the men were driven to strike. Why is it necessary, in the first place, to maintain large RCAF establishments in the United Kingdom? Why, if it is necessary, are replacements not more effectively despatched? Why is it that 500 replacements now being despatched were not sent before the strike took place? Why did Air Minister Gibson say that four-fifths of the RCAF occupation force were volunteers, a statement that he has now retracted? What is the repatriation situation?"

The *Telegram*, while disapproving the strike action, had—in the same editorial—conceded that the complaints of the airmen were valid. However, by that time the strike was over, the airmen having given in to the government's ultimatum about charges of mutiny.

Once again, the "perpetrators" were punished, although they were given somewhat less harsh terms—no doubt because a strike, however distasteful to those in authority, is not as blasphemous a sin as window-smashing.

"The tail can't wag the dog, anywhere, at any time, and the airmen realize this fact," scolded the editorial in the London edition of *The Maple Leaf* (not the one edited by Major Doug MacFarlane). At no point did this newspaper of the fighting forces express any sympathy with the grievances—let alone the action—of the striking airmen.

Particularly depressing is the realization that these two incidents of upheaval among the ranks were separated in time by seven months.

Oh, what a lovely postwar!

13

Dancing in the Streets

VJ Day was notably different from VE Day. In Europe, the relent-less push forward of the Allies had made it fairly clear that the col-lapse of Hitler's Germany was imminent. Every day's news brought the end closer and closer, so that people both overseas and at home were preparing for VE Day by the end of April.

In the Far East, the Allies were whittling away at the gains the Japanese had made in the earlier years of the war, and the retaking of various Pacific islands was heartening, but most people still believed that the war in the Pacific would not be won without a landing in Japan itself. That had been the strategy in Europe, and that was the thinking about Japan.

Then, on August 6, 1945, the Enola Gay, a B-29 bomber named for its pilot's mother, dropped the atom bomb on Hiroshima. Three days later, on August 9, a second bomb was dropped on Nagasaki, causing similar death and destruction. American President Harry Truman threatened the destruction of Japan if that country did not surrender.

On August 14, the Japanese emperor threw in the towel, accepting the demand for unconditional surrender, and the war was over. VJ Day was celebrated on August 15, 1945. However, people began to cele-brate several days before.

Once again, the newspapers of the world—including Canada's—dredged up all the available superlatives to describe the unbridled joy that swept up everyone.

The Windsor Star captured a poignant moment in this brief story of VJ Day:

"With his right leg off and using crutches, Lance Corporal Norman Delina wasn't going to miss all the fun. He lost his leg on May 1, in Germany. He wandered downtown smiling at the crowds that were passing by.

"'This is the greatest sight I've ever seen,' he said. A small boy handed him a flag and the lance corporal smiled and waved it merrily. A pretty girl, overcome with emotion at the sight of the wounded veteran, threw her arms around his neck and kissed him."

Regina's *Leader-Post* offered up a montage of VJ Day moments. "Two young fellows pushed their way through the crowds. Said one of them: 'I am going right home to put my uniform on. This is sure a day for a uniform if there ever was one.

"A sailor grabbed a girl who was only too willing to celebrate the victory with a good-natured kiss. That gave him and two civilian friends the idea and they tramped on down the main streets collecting from every girl they saw.

"'It's wonderful, only I'm so sleepy I can't get excited.' This was the comment of a nurse-in-training at the Grey Nuns hospital on night duty when she was awakened and informed of the news.

"On the streets people stood and talked everywhere, in the middle of the street, in the doorways of stores and on the edge of the curb. Little children jumped up and down, hardly old enough to know what they were excited about, only knowing that excitement was in the air."

The Toronto Star's London correspondent, Ross Harkness, reported on the mood in the English capital:

"There is unanimous agreement VE Day was tame as a tea party compared to VJ Day.

"Today (August 17) London is without beer, without ice cream, without pop, without fireworks and without pep. For five nights in a row the people have been what the English call 'mafficking' until there doesn't seem to be another 'maffick' left in them. [Mafficking is a term that was coined to describe the extravagant celebrations in London after the relief of Mafeking during the Boer War, in 1900.]

"A woman who so forgot her age and sex climbed a lamp post the better to see the King and Queen at Buckingham Palace, got so excited when the princesses came out about 11 o'clock and joined the crowd that she fell off and had to be carried away on a stretcher."

During the VJ Day celebrations in London, the King and Queen, the two princesses, and Winston Churchill rode through the streets in open carriages. Among the thousands of well-wishers craning their necks for a better view was Calgary Highlander Private R. C. McKenzie. On Easter Sunday that spring, McKenzie had been wounded and evacuated to the Canadian hospital at Bruges, Belgium. By VJ Day, he was on leave in London, and waiting for a ship home. He and two Highlander buddies managed to scrounge a few boxes to stand on for a better view as the dignitaries passed.

"It was a very emotional event," said McKenzie, "with the throngs of people waving and cheering as the royal family went by, and the beautiful carriage horses tossing their heads.

"The pubs in London were crammed with people all that day. There seemed to be enough beer for everyone, but most of the pubs didn't have enough glasses for all the celebrators. We finally bought three mugs, solving that problem.

"In the evening, we found ourselves with three young ladies and ended up with them on Leicester Square and Piccadilly. I can remember us in a large group with our arms linked together singing and dancing to 'Knees Up, Mother Brown.'

"The celebrating crowds were enormous. I can clearly recall a beautiful showgirl dancing in the raw on top of a theatre canopy. All the searchlights that had been playing over the crowds were concentrated on her—the best and biggest audience she ever had! Probably the best performance she ever gave, too.

"We were jammed in so tightly by people, we could hardly move and my lady friend's ankles were actually bleeding from being kicked and trampled on, but we carried on till the wee hours."

The jubilation was global. Canadian merchant seaman Dave Broadfoot was serving on a ship that had just put into Sydney, Australia, when the Japanese surrendered. He recalls vividly the reaction of people "just dancing in the streets. I've never seen such pure joy. There was no vandalism of any kind, and yet there were thousands and thousands of people in the streets."

RCAF Flight Lieutenant E.F. Horton flew the last trip of his tour of operations in a B-24 out of Minneriya, Ceylon. The mission took nineteen and a half hours as he and his crew dropped six Gurkha paratroopers and six canisters of ammunition and radios at Rawang, Malaya.

"It had been a long and successful flying tour," recalled Horton, "so when we were invited to spend our post-tour leave at a tea planter's home in the hills of central Ceylon we jumped at the chance... We were there when VJ Day came along on August 15, 1945.

"Well, we were instant heroes and were treated to a real feast of curried lamb and all the trimmings. I still treasure the picture of myself and my second pilot, Chas Dunn, standing with the tea planter and all his Ceylonese workers in front of his tea factory."

Albert Drager, who emigrated to Canada after the war, was a Dutch prisoner of war in Japan on VJ Day. He spent the last year of the war in captivity, forced to work in a Japanese coal-mine. On August 15, 1945, as he and his fellow prisoners stood on the parade ground, waiting to be marched off to the mine, the Japanese commandant handed the prisoners' commander a piece of paper which was read aloud. The details were skimpy, but the message was clear:

"It is stated that the war is over completely today and the agreement of peace is now being negotiated, so you must be patient until the day comes when you can go home," the statement began. Towards the end, there was this stern warning: "To make noise, singing or whistling is forbidden. Always keep quiet and wait for the day comes when you can go back home. It must be remembered that the Nippon soldiers are fair and dependable protectors of you all."

It was late September before Drager and his fellow captives were on their way home.

Word that the war had ended reached outposts and individuals in unique ways. Monica Czanyo was eleven years old then. At the time she, her parents, and younger brother and sister were "spending the usual one-month vacation at Bathsheba in Barbados. As there were no phones in the 'pay houses' of those days, we got the news that the war in the Far East was over from one of our fellow-vacationers who had been into Bridgetown. Although the war had hardly touched the Caribbean, I remember everyone's profound relief that six years of war were over."

On the other hand, some received VJ Day news early. In Vancouver, Betty McLean heard "the prime minister's premature speech about the war's end. King had prepared it (in advance) but the media aired it too soon...

"The first I knew that an armistice had been signed was the racket on Richards Street. Streetcars were clanging their bells, cars honking their horns, and people leaning out of car windows, shouting and waving. Heather was playing out on the street—now three and a half years old. She came running to me, wondering about all the racket. I told her it was because the war was over and now all the servicemen and women could come home. Putting it in simple terms for her understanding, I said, 'Yes, the war's all over and now your Daddy can come home and stay home... I doubt I'd ever used the word 'war' to her before that day.

"The impact of the bomb bothered me. I didn't see that as a glorious victory but as one more horrific event of a nasty, nasty war..."

Clyde Gilmour was also in Vancouver for VJ Day. "What a riot that was on the streets of Vancouver. God, it was fantastic. The only time I have ever myself seen glorious sexy scenes on the street, luscious gals kissing guys, rubbing their boobs up against strangers. And dates being made, phone calls lined up, and guys grabbing a girl and putting her into a car, but nobody thought of any molesting or harassing.

"It was VJ Day, you know. And of course the mood was that nobody ever thought possibly there could be any other war. There'd be permanent peace and that would be it. And we had a lot of stuff about how well they were going to look after the veterans, everything would be fine, you could go to university and everything."

The Chinese community in Vancouver was especially elated. According to *The Vancouver Sun*, the celebrations started a day early. "Vancouver staged a preview night of what the city can expect to see when VJ Day really comes, and in Chinatown the delirium hit the roof.

"The Chinese celebration banged out the moment the erroneous report announced that Japan had accepted the Allies' surrender terms, and continued for hours after, as the Chinese colony refused to permit its spirits to be dampened by a few heroic citizens who strove to tell them it wasn't so.

"Thousands of Chinese jammed into two blocks on East Pender

between Carroll and Main, dancing and shouting to an overture of crackling firecrackers.

"A few seconds after the first report, a bumper crop of flags of the United Nations blossomed out in shop windows, on building roofs and on autos in the street.

"Chinese youths stood on upper-floor balconies, tossing lighted firecrackers to the street below.

"A group of Chinese children perched themselves on one balcony and beat steadily on cymbals and a drum for at least an hour.

"A solid line of cars drove through Chinatown for two hours, each driver pushing his horn down and holding it there."

The story in Windsor, Ontario, was much the same, according to that city's *Daily Star*: "Windsor's Chinatown went out on a bender.

"It was like Mickey Mouse on a binge... It was like a Chinese gong, pounding at your temple. It was a snake dance looping around your brain... It was that squeaky, sing-song record, making you forget that you were the imperturbable Occidental as the Chinese girls flung their arms high in Pitt Street.

"It was, in short, Windsor's Chinese marking the end of eight nightmarish years of war with Japan."

Montreal's Chinatown was no less exuberant, according to *The Gazette*: "In Chinatown last night the dragon danced—really danced.

"The dragon, always symbolic of Chinese success, victory and happiness, had danced once a year in Chinatown—on the occasion of the Chinese New Year's celebration—even during the past 15 years that China had been fighting a desperate fight of resistance against the hated Japs.

"The dragon's appearance last night was not officially scheduled, but the dragon did appear and the dragon did dance after the surrender of the Japs was officially announced. Amidst exploding, soaring, colorful fireworks, clashing cymbals, tom-toms, and Chinese fiddles and other instruments competing with the blare of modern juke boxes, the dragon made an impromptu appearance.

"Weaving its way through the largest crowd of Chinese and all other races ever gathered in Chinatown at one time, the dragon not only danced the usual formal steps witnessed at the New Year's celebrations, but waltzed, fox-trotted and offered a good demonstration of jitterbug and rhumba stepping."

Herbert Whittaker, then a young theatre and movie critic for *The Gazette*, recalls being dispatched to Chinatown in Montreal that night "to accompany our photographer who was going down to take pictures of how this event was celebrated there. And I followed him along, catching the bulbs that he ejected from his camera... In following him I found myself walking on—as you know all news photographers are absolutely fearless—walking right on to the stage where they were doing the Peking Opera in stylization, full make-up and everything. It was out in the street, the stage being set out. The audience found two new characters in a traditional Chinese opera: a photographer and a stupid-looking reporter who was waving his arms...to receive the bulbs."

At the time of VJ Day, Marguerite Vorvid was eleven years old. She lived with her family above her father's shop in downtown Whitby, Ontario. From her vantage point, she recalls "the exuberation and excitement of that day. Along Brock and Dundas Streets...people were on the roofs of the two- and three-storey buildings, unfurling rolls of toilet paper which drifted down to the street and road below. I suppose that was the 1945 version of tickertape. The sidewalks and roads were a tide of moving, laughing, talking, singing people. Wandering through the crowds were people ringing cowbells, blowing whistles, and banging on pans. In my years in Whitby, I have seen street dances, fairs, parades, and runners carrying the Olympic torch on the way to the Calgary games, but never have I witnessed such a tumultuous, noisy, elated throng in the downtown area."

Getting caught up in that throng wasn't difficult. Madge McKillop had served in Europe as a Canadian Army nurse, but on VJ Day she was back home in Moose Jaw, Saskatchewan. She had volunteered for the Far East, but her posting had not come through. So, on August 14, Madge, her mother, her sister, and her three-and-a-half-year-old daughter "went to Regina to see a display of RCAF aircraft. We were particularly interested in a Lancaster bomber from what had been my young brother's squadron before he was killed.

"When we returned to the centre of the city to get the train home to Moose Jaw, people were pouring out of stores and offices, singing, dancing, and announcing that the war with Japan was over. Two young sailors whom I had never seen before in my life stopped on the street to give me a big hug and say, 'It's all over, sister.' When we returned to Moose Jaw, the scene was similar, with the streets jammed with happy people. Unbelievably, it was indeed at long last all over."

One of Canada's most popular band leaders, Mart Kenney, recalls that he and his Western Gentlemen were playing at the Cameo Pavilion in Fenelon Falls, Ontario, on VJ Day. "The people at the dance were obviously buoyed up by the news, but the atmosphere was one of happy relief rather than wild celebration.

"There was only one disorderly incident, which came toward the end of the evening. A burly fellow began elbowing his way through the crowd, using some pretty foul language in a very loud voice. I told him to cut it out, there were ladies present, and for some reason this infuriated him. He took a flying leap at me, miscalculated by a few inches and fell down on his knees in front of the stand."

The announcement of victory over the Japanese found RCAF Squadron Leader John Turnbull in mid-Atlantic. Following thirty-four operations in Bomber Command, Turnbull had been posted to instruct on heavy bombers when VE Day occurred, and was en route home to Canada to join Tiger Force against the Japanese.

"We had sailed on the *Duchess of Richmond*," recalls Turnbull. "Those were long lazy days as *Kitty* was read by almost everyone aboard...or was it *Lady Chatterley's Lover*? And the pages of those naughty books were well thumb-marked by the time our lazy days were interrupted by news of the atomic bombs and Japan's surrender.

"All 25,000 tons of the *Duchess* rock 'n' rolled, it seemed, although the sea was calm... Later, as we hastened up the St. Lawrence, the *Duchess* rubbed a sand-bar. It was said in the captain's defence that he had not been home for five years...reason enough to be in a hurry."

A few days later, Turnbull was "home, in the village of my youth, Govan, Saskatchewan, where the drayman refused pay for hauling my shipped trunk...the post office manager (badly gassed in WWI) insisted I use his electric razor until my reddened neck became accustomed to local hard water again...a visit to the school where nature study things made in Grade 8 remained on display...the district's big 'Welcome

Home' evening of misty-eyed entertainment and the presentation to each of its 'boys and girls' of a chest of Rogers silverware (which is still in service in our home today)...and mother, being mother, cooked a special dinner for her baby son's first Sunday home."

Another RCAF airman, Robert Warner, was serving at an RAF radar school at Yatesbury, England, on VJ Day. All those wishing some extra spending money received a special issue of pay before noon that day and then Warner and friends headed for the local pubs, which "had been setting aside extra supplies of ale for the celebration that would occur with the end of the war.

"There were music and street dances for those celebrating. This was in contrast to the quiet celebration in the small country pub near Yatesbury for VE Day."

Joyce Harper was able to celebrate with her husband, a Canadian soldier who was on a forty-eight-hour pass and had joined Joyce and her parents in the south of England. When they heard the news on radio, "My husband said we have to do something special. First thing, he grabbed an old school bell from the hall and then ran outside, me behind him, and jumped up on the wall in front of the house and started ringing the bell like crazy. Well, windows and doors opened and it was, 'What's going on?' He yelled back, 'The war's over,' and it seemed like we were the only ones who knew, so there was a lot of whooping and laughing. It was something everyone had waited for for so long.

"So then we decided to start a fire on the large traffic island at the end of the road, that was something that was taboo for so long. We gathered all the grass clippings we could find, including our neighbour's, who was a friend whose husband was a prisoner of war in Italy. We tramped down the road with our arms full and started a fire in the middle of the island. It wasn't long [before] we were joined by people from all over the area. They came dragging everything they could find to keep the fire going...

"We had a marvellous time, hugging everyone...singing, crying... It was so great. It seemed to be our way of showing how happy and thankful we were less than an hour after it was announced that peace was declared. The next night, the neighbourhood celebrated at the local pub."

On VJ Day, Lieutenant Arthur Cole was in London, serving with the Canadian Army's Film and Photo unit. He and two other photographers—Lieutenant Harold Robinson and CWAC Sergeant Karen Hermeston—were assigned to cover the activities around Buckingham Palace and St. Paul's Cathedral involving the royal family. After that they were instructed to go to Piccadilly Circus to take pictures of the tumultuous celebrations going on there.

"At the end of this rather long day, which ended in Piccadilly Circus," Cole remembered, "the three of us, Robinson and this little girl who weighed about ninety pounds and I, discovered I had half a dozen (shots) left on a roll of film, so I said to Robbie, 'Take a picture of Hermie.' (That was Sergeant Hermeston's nickname.) So I hoisted her up on my shoulder and she had her cap in her hand and she's waving it over my shoulder right in front of the big mob in Piccadilly Circus.

"When I got back to Pall Mall, which was where we were headquartered—we never developed our own stuff—there was a dark-room staff, but I went to tell the guy the last six pictures in this roll were not to be given to the photo lab, they're personal pictures.

"And, of course, that was the best picture of the whole works, and he sends it out not only to *The Maple Leaf* but to Canada and it was on the front page of *The Globe and Mail* the next morning. People were calling Elva [my wife] to say they had seen a picture of me before she did. So she got it and she was a little miffed, I think. One of my hands, you couldn't see. I was holding Hermie around the legs. I wasn't really touching her, but you couldn't see my other hand."

Elva Cole's sense of humour was up to the occasion, as Art later realized.

"Later that year, as a Christmas present, she sent me a picture of herself sitting on Santa Claus's knee at Eaton's. He was a little surprised when she came up after a bunch of kids and she said, 'Would you mind putting your one hand down behind me (as though) you might be holding my leg?' He said, 'Okay.' And her caption on the picture was, 'Guess where his right hand was?'"

Don Carty was stationed at an RCAF holding station at Debert, N.S., on VJ Day: "They assembled us and we went to the mess hall and the officers were pouring beer for all the men... About three hours into it, you saw the men shampooing the hair of the officers [with beer] who were so soused they didn't know whether they were coming or going..."

Brian H. Jones had served with the 65th Canadian Motor Torpedo Boat Flotilla, based in Ostend, Belgium, but was back in Halifax when the Pacific war ended. "I recall on VJ Day anybody who could walk was given an MP armband and trucked to downtown Halifax to patrol the streets in case of any riots similar to what had happened on VE Day. It was very quiet, no real trouble. When we finally left Halifax in trucks to go down to the train station, the women stood on the sidewalk and spat at us as we went by. The navy had a great reputation in Halifax!"

On the west coast, there were minor disturbances reported in Victoria and Vernon. In Vernon, two soldiers were arrested by military authorities for breaking a window in a liquor store during a premature VJ Day celebration. And in Victoria, a crowd of several thousand civilians and sailors was dispersed by police, helmeted marines, and the navy shore patrol after they converged on a downtown liquor store and hurled rocks through the front windows.

Not so lucky was the city of Sudbury, Ontario, where the city's newspaper reported, on August 15: "VJ Celebrations Darkest Record in History of Sudbury."

"The most disastrous night in the history of Sudbury marked the end of World War II.

"Sudbury's riot was the only one in Canada to mark VJ Day. This morning, it was estimated that at least $40,000 damage was done, and the figure may exceed this as the result of looting of supplies at the city's liquor, beer and wine stores and shattered plate glass windows said to number 40. One police officer...is in hospital, two other police were slightly injured, and 28 men are under arrest."

The Sudbury Daily Star ran an editorial headlined: "Sudbury Shamed."

"Today Sudbury should hang its head in shame as the result of last night's demonstrations of mob rule, during which almost half a hundred of the city's plate glass windows were broken, the stock of the liquor, wine and beer stores looted and scores of other depredations recorded in a mass display of violence never before witnessed in the history of the city... As many of the instigators as possible should be rounded up and punished to remove, to some degree, the smirch on the name of Sudbury."

The same day's paper carried a short story about a baby born on VJ Day to a Sudbury couple, Mr. and Mrs. G. A. Poulin, at 5:30 on the morning of the day of celebration. The story added: "*The Sudbury Star* was unable to contact the father, who is an attendant in a Sudbury service station, but learned from the young mother that they plan on calling the baby girl Victoria Jacqueline to co-incide with VJ Day. Both mother and baby are doing well."

14

A Clash of Brass

Henry Duncan Graham Crerar, of Hamilton, Ontario, was the first Canadian to be promoted to the rank of full general at the front. In the drive for the Rhine, late in the war in Europe, Crerar deployed the largest force ever commanded by a Canadian—more than 450,000 men.

In the late summer of 1945, General Crerar was about to return to Canada and would be succeeded by General Guy Granville Simonds, another outstanding military leader.

Shortly before Crerar's departure for home, a lunch was planned in his honour for assorted army brass. Among those present was Major J. Douglas MacFarlane, MBE, the managing editor of *The Maple Leaf.*

"He and I had become quite good friends and he invited me to the lunch," MacFarlane recalled. "And I was there when he said to [General] Simonds, 'This MacFarlane has done a marvellous job with this paper and one thing I'm advising you is to leave him alone.'

"Simonds said, 'I have no intention of interfering.'"

It turned out to be a commitment General Simonds could not bring himself to keep. Not long after Simonds succeeded Crerar, the new commander phoned Major MacFarlane to complain that the editor was not using "proper army language" in *The Maple Leaf.*

MacFarlane brushed off this seemingly insignificant rebuke. He was, after all, running a newspaper for ordinary soldiers, not for stiff-upper-lip brass hats. He had never made a secret of the fact that his obligation, as he saw it, was to the fighting men of the army, the thousands upon thousands who had worked and fought so hard to defeat Hitler's forces.

Simonds's complaint was a warning shot. A bigger battle was brewing. When the war in Europe ended, a point system was devised for the repatriation of members of the armed forces serving overseas. There were to be points for length of service, points for serving overseas, points for being in a certain campaign, and so on. Thus, those with the highest number of points would be sent home before those who had served less time overseas or had seen less combat. That seemed eminently logical, certainly to the high-point men.

On May 11, a Canadian Press story from Ottawa announced extensive details of the repatriation plans. "One of the highlights of the program is the provision for returning regiments to parade down their own main streets. Units to return as entities will be mainly armored regiments, infantry battalions, artillery batteries, engineer companies and larger units having military affiliation or territorial identity.

"A reposting system will be introduced to bring the units back as territorial entities. General Crerar gives this part of the program high importance and adds 'the trouble of reposting will be very much worth while.'"

One of the "troubles" with such a reposting system was the fact that many of these infantry, armoured, artillery, and engineer units had suffered considerable casualties during the fighting and were likely to be under-strengthened. If such units were to be brought home to march triumphantly down hometown streets, their ranks would have to be filled with other soldiers—whatever their combat experience or qualifications for repatriation. But no mention was made of this potential bug in the proposed reposting system.

The press, especially *The Maple Leaf,* continued to report on the various zigs and zags the repatriation "policy" took. High-point men were assured they would be going home; then there was talk of sending "units" home that "might" include lower- or medium-point men.

The Maple Leaf also heard from its uniformed readers. Many of their letters were printed during the spring and summer of 1945. As usual, most of the writers had a bone to pick.

"It doesn't seem just to have the chap who lived in slit trenches and dodged 88's receive the same number of points as the soldier in a base area or in a hazardless zone." (Signed: Sid Gray.)

"Why shouldn't us fellows who have been serving over here in the thick of the battle be allowed to count more points? After all, we didn't have the comforts they had back in England and Canada. Our leaves didn't amount to much, either." (Signed: Pte. L. T. Myrkam.)

"In a copy of *The Maple Leaf* issued 20th July I read a part stating that the pledge was still being kept concerning first in, first out policy. I myself cannot see where it has been kept as I have been in the army since June 17, 1940, and came overseas Dec. 1940. I have been told that I have a total of 200 repat points. If so could you please tell me why so many boys have already left on repat with as low points as 174 and 171." (Signed: A.O.K.)

"I'm one of those 238 or 241 point guys, it just depends on the math you use. Anyway, I arrived in Scotland on the 17th of December, 1939. I'm 39 years of age, so I'm not exactly a youngster. Yet no matter how I try, no matter who I ask, I'm no closer to knowing when I go home than when I arrived in Scotland." (Signed: Disgusted.)

On August 28, 1945, J.D.M. wrote an editorial about Canada's 1st Division heading for home. "The First is truly the veteran division," he wrote, "the first to come overseas, the first to see sustained battle action and, rightly, the first to head for Halifax." But as the summer dragged on and VJ Day came and went, it became increasingly apparent, at least to the impatient combat soldiers, that the "first in, first out" policy was being fiddled with.

One Canadian infantryman who had gone in on D-Day remembered that there was talk, in the late summer of 1945, about NRMA men going home. (Late in the war, Canadians who had been conscripted under the National Resources Mobilization Act were sent overseas. Some of these men saw combat in the late stages of the war; others got no farther than England.) "There was the usual slamming of those guys," he recalled. "You know, they were calling them rotten bastards... Mind you, there were guys there in the occupation who had way more service than I had and they were still there. There were guys who'd been in since 1939 and 1940, and [were] still waiting, and then when they'd hear about these guys who had been over a couple of months...well, you know, it was frustrating."

MacFarlane began to hear rumblings to the effect that the point system was being bypassed in the selection of those men who would go home first. "There was talk in the forces about these guys that just got overseas from Canada going back home. One of our [*Maple Leaf*] guys [Corporal Ron Poulton] was going to the repat depot at Aldershot and I told him to investigate and find out what the hell was going on. He went to Aldershot and this guy gave him all sorts of evidence of what was happening. The records were available to him, but he said, 'Don't ever let on where you got this.' So [Poulton] sent all this material to me. And I wrote a front-page editorial."

The editorial ran the full length of the front page of *The Maple Leaf* on September 19, 1945. It was headed: "On This Repat Question The Maple Leaf Reveals..."

What followed was the information sent to MacFarlane by his "informant," citing chapter and verse instances of NRMA men who had seen no action being lumped in with battle veterans in homeward-bound units.

"Something which bears an investigation and a good answer is how these men got posted to a First Division unit for return to Canada when they hadn't even left the U.K. on VE Day. If this practice is being carried out by the reinforcement depots, which everything would lead me to suspect, then it's not good enough. There are a lot of fellows...with high points who rate ahead of the NRMA men...who could be posted to units for return to Canada, not even taking into consideration the high-point men from other active units who might like to have a look at Canada."

Poulton had the numbers to back up the argument. He had asked to see the documents of some of the NRMA men "to get a picture of their points and service." Of four cases chosen at random, none had seen active service. This was proved by their serial numbers, which revealed when they had left Canada.

At the end of this detailed report, MacFarlane added his own stringent comments:

"*The Maple Leaf* was established in Naples, in Italy, back in January 1944, for Canadian forces IN ACTION. *The Maple Leaf* has always done everything in its power to help the fighting men get a break. It's not stopping now.

"This sort of business isn't funny. The men who volunteered to come overseas, who either went into action as volunteers or did their best as volunteers to see that the fighting men were equipped with the necessaries, deserve better treatment. This is an appeal on behalf of the volunteers who made this Canadian Army an army of which to be proud. All that is wanted is justice."

As usual, the editorial was signed: "J.D.M."

The next day, J.D.M. was still seething and wrote another editorial, which minced even fewer words. It was headed: "To Continue..."

Referring to the NRMA men (and prudently avoiding use of the pejorative term "zombies") he wrote: "These men were called up as far back as 1942. So they didn't go active. So maybe that's their business. Some blame the system, some the men. Some don't blame anybody. Some, on the other hand, think everything worked out just dandy. Some on the other hand, wrist and elbow still think Canadian men should never have gone overseas at all. It's a matter of opinion.

"But whatever the opinion, these men didn't come overseas until early 1945. And they didn't come to Europe until after VE Day, after the shooting had stopped. And they came in garrison battalions. Those garrison battalions, if memory serves correctly, were slated for the occupation force.

"And what happens? Some of the men in them, who have just come overseas, who have never fired a round anywhere but on the ranges, are steered into a First Canadian Infantry Division unit draft for HOME!"

When an editorial writer uses capital letters *and* an exclamation point, you know he is angry.

MacFarlane built up a full head of steam in his closing paragraph:

"It may be said that it's the system, that's the way it's laid down, and that's the way it's got to be: that the men in charge of repat overseas are hamstrung, are doing their best in the face of policy. That is probably the real answer. But policy has been changed before and can be again.

"This situation cannot be corrected too soon. J.D.M."

The next day, Friday, September 21, all was silent.

The Saturday *Maple Leaf* was the first issue in almost two years to appear without any editorial, but there was a cryptic letter from Major MacFarlane (printed in the "letters to the editor" column) in which he said this would be the last writing he would be doing for the paper and gave thanks for the appreciation of his efforts to produce a paper "for the soldiers."

The same day's paper carried a lengthy statement from Major General Chris Vokes, commander of the Canadian Army Occupation Force, saying he had been asked by "the Editor of *The Maple Leaf* to clear the air on certain misunderstandings evidenced by the number of complaints he has received in letters to the Editor of *The Maple Leaf.*" These had to do mostly with regulations concerning leaves for members of the Occupation Force.

General Vokes went on for some space answering the various questions and complaints and ended up pointing out that there was "no necessity to start a controversy in *The Maple Leaf* about any remarks I have made in this memorandum. If there is anything you don't like, arrange a personal interview with me...

"FINALLY: Stop bellyaching and set about this occupation task in a soldierly manner which will resound to the everlasting credit of the great Dominion to which we belong."

Flags flying, *The Maple Leaf* seemed suddenly to have switched from a tone of sympathetic understanding of soldiers' concerns to one of impatience with any whisper of complaint.

In Monday's paper, the name of J. D. MacFarlane, managing editor, had vanished from the masthead of *The Maple Leaf.* Indeed, no managing editor was listed.

There was, however, an editorial, signed "C.W.G." That was Lieutenant-Colonel C. W. Gilchrist, listed on the masthead as editor-in-chief.

"It was the aim of *The Maple Leaf* to do all in its power to help maintain a team spirit within the Canadian Army, whether in or out of battle.

"Whether it has succeeded or not you will be the best judges.

"But *The Maple Leaf* has no place in its editorial column for anything detrimental to morale.

"Neither will it be used to represent a one-sided case.

"It cannot, for instance, attempt to discuss either the merits or demerits of the repatriation scheme."

Prominently displayed on *The Maple Leaf*'s front page in that same edition was a story headlined: "And This Is the Other Side of the

Picture," which contained an official statement from Lieutenant-General G. G. Simonds. The man who had told General Crerar he had "no intention of interfering" with MacFarlane's running of the paper now argued that J.D.M.'s two editorials "presented a biased point of view and were unjust." Curiously, he next said: "I am not challenging the facts as presented and have no desire to suppress them."

The general considered the editorials "unfortunate" because they implied that "*The Maple Leaf* has unearthed something that the authorities are trying to conceal." He then launched into a staunch defence of the policy of repatriating NRMA men along with high-point volunteers when it was necessary to fill up a unit heading home.

"Some with very high scores, others with medium-group scores, must subordinate their own personal wishes to return home to their duty to the group as a whole," Simonds maintained.

There was yet another story on an inside page, with the headline: "Editor Dismissed; Commander Gives Reasons for Order." In this story, yet another statement by Lieutenant-General G. G. Simonds, he outlined his reasons for firing MacFarlane. While stating that "freedom of the press is a vital principle which we are all concerned to uphold," he argued that *The Maple Leaf* differed from "the ordinary newspaper in that it holds a monopoly—it is the only daily newspaper regularly presenting its news and views to the whole Canadian Army Overseas."

Simonds said that he had met with Major MacFarlane and given him "the other side of the picture...and told him that he was under an obligation to present those aspects, as well as his own personal views, in an editorial in *The Maple Leaf*. This he refused to do and he further stated that he refused to adhere to the principle that a balanced expression of opinion as opposed to his own personal opinion should govern the editorial policy of *The Maple Leaf*. Under these conditions I considered I had no alternative but to order his removal as editor."

Doug MacFarlane remembers it a bit differently. The managing editor, after listening to the general's arguments, offered to give General Simonds as much space in the paper as he wanted to present "the other side of the picture." But he flatly refused to do what the general demanded—namely, to write and sign an editorial endorsing the general's position.

Of the staff's loyalty to MacFarlane in this moment of crisis, there can be no doubt. Corporal George Kidd, a sub-editor, recalled it this way: "The repat issue still sticks out in my mind. Doug MacFarlane handed me an editorial with orders to put it on page one. Obviously this was unusual as we had never put an editorial on the first page. The next day Doug was immediately called to report to headquarters. As he was leaving he handed me another editorial and told me to put it in the same place... To me Doug MacFarlane was the most brilliant newspaper man that I ever met."

Sergeant Ross Parry adds, "When Doug was sent home over the Zombie issue the entire staff refused to write any material, in protest. After a few days we began to recant as it was made clear that we were in the army, hence this action would be considered insubordination.

"In fact, we were all penalized by having our return home delayed. I was sent to cover the occupation in Germany as my reward. When I returned to Amsterdam in December 1945, I was finally informed that I was going home."

At first, there was some talk of the staff going on strike to express their support for MacFarlane, but the major told them: "You can't strike, you're in the army."

One man went further. "Ed Ingraham, who was my assistant, quit at the same time as I was canned," MacFarlane recalled. "I said, 'Ed, you can't quit.' He said, 'I have enough points, the hell I can't quit.' And by God he manoeuvred it, somehow."

Thus, with bangs as well as whimpers, ended Major J. D. MacFarlane's year-and-a-half tenure as managing editor of *The Maple Leaf.* For the next few weeks, the name of MacFarlane did not appear in the pages of *The Maple Leaf.* Then, on October 15, there was a short and generally colourless story headlined: "Maple Leaf Staff Honors MacFarlane."

"On the eve of his departure for home, Major J. D. MacFarlane, MBE, former managing editor of *The Maple Leaf,* was guest of honor at a gathering of members of the editorial, mechanical and circulation staffs.

"In a brief word of 'thank you,' Major MacFarlane expressed his appreciation for the work of the staff and his regret at leaving the newspaper he began editing in war-pocked Naples in January 1944.

"Lt. Col. C. W. Gilchrist spoke on behalf of the staff and complimented Major MacFarlane on his work with the paper. He expressed regret that 'Doug' was leaving and wished him success.

"Captain Doug Smith, business and circulation manager, made a presentation on behalf of all members of the staff. He spoke of Major MacFarlane's long association with *The Maple Leaf* and wished him the best upon his return to civvy life."

Glaringly absent from the story, in violation of fundamental journalistic principles, was any reference to *why* MacFarlane was leaving.

Even before MacFarlane attended that sad little farewell party, *Time* magazine was on the case. "For nearly two years, the Canadian Army's daily newspaper *Maple Leaf* has marched nervously between editorial freedom and brass-hat control. In Amsterdam, Holland, its No. 1 editor, big, hard-driving Major Douglas MacFarlane, decided he had had enough... He laid down a two-day editorial barrage on Canada's repatriation policy... Charged MacFarlane: the 'zombies' who had refused to volunteer for combat duty were going home ahead of soldiers who had imposed no conditions on their service... Next day he printed a second blast: Ottawa had changed its policy before, could change it again.

"The crackdown came like an echo. Canada's commander in the Netherlands, Lieut. General Guy Granville Simonds, called in MacFarlane, read the riot act for 'biased and most unfair comment.' Then the General suggested that the Major write a third editorial giving the other (i.e., Government) side of the picture. MacFarlane refused, was fired pronto... Doug MacFarlane...had at least solved his own repat problem (the Army would pack him off without delay)."

Breezy, irreverent, adjective-happy *Time* didn't quite get it right. MacFarlane never once used the word "zombies" in his editorials. And the sarcastic comment about solving his own repat problems was gratuitous.

Press reaction back in Canada was swift and mostly in support of MacFarlane. *The Globe and Mail* in Toronto ran a lead editorial headed: "Firing Editor Helps Nothing." But that was probably predictable, given that the newspaper had long since established its enmity to Mackenzie King's government and would not pass up a chance to embarrass it.

In Montreal, the Honourable Douglas C. Abbott, who had just

become defence minister in August, said he had no statement to make about the removal of Major MacFarlane, and then proceeded to make one, defending General Simonds's action and pointing out that the repatriation policy now in use "was determined over there by Gen. Crerar and his officers—it was not made in Canada, although we approved it."

When Doug MacFarlane got home, later in October, the press swarmed about him, asking for statements about his side of the argument. "It was difficult for me," MacFarlane recalled later, "in that I was sort of bombarded with press attention and I had to convince them, and I did it very bluntly. I said, 'I've said all I'm going to say and I'm done with it as far as I'm concerned.'"

MacFarlane promptly resigned his commission, and a few weeks later, was working as city editor for *The Globe and Mail*. Later, he shifted to *The Toronto Telegram* (when George McCullagh, owner of *The Globe and Mail*, bought the *Telegram*) and remained there for a quarter of a century, rising to become editor-in-chief and a director of that paper.

If there was a lesson to be learned from MacFarlane's bold actions in *l'affaire repat*, it was pointed out by Major Bill Austin, second-in-command to Colonel R. S. Malone, who was in charge of setting up *The Maple Leaf*. Austin, who dealt with many war correspondents during the European war, explained wartime censorship of the press. "The way it worked was simple. There was agreement with the (newspaper) publishers who then got the agreement of their managing editors that if the military said 'No' or if the government said 'No, don't print anything about that...' (or 'You can print up to this, including this and this and this...') then that's what you did. And if you tried to get funny, you could be in deep trouble, you could lose your job. Because the publishers wouldn't take any nonsense."

Long after the war, Doug MacFarlane talked about the repatriation policy. "They wanted to fill up units with people to go home. They wanted to parade, let's say, 'The Toronto Stars,' just as an example, as a battalion. There probably were half enough troops left overseas for 'The Toronto Stars' to put on a decent show, so they'd fill up the ranks with anyone. The policy was to bring men home by units, so they could be paraded back home. Points were a factor, but not the only factor. Initially, points were the only factor. And to fill up the units they'd use anybody handy."

MacFarlane had lost his long-waged battle on behalf of what he considered his constituency—the volunteer fighting soldiers.

When Defence Minister Ralston had appointed Colonel R. S. (Dick) Malone to set up *The Maple Leaf* in Italy, the latter had accepted, but with conditions: there was to be complete editorial freedom with no obligations to any "brass" and no directions from military or governmental sources. In return, it was agreed (between Ralston and Malone) that the newspaper would not express opinions on domestic (Canadian) issues or comment on internal military problems that might have a negative impact on morale.

If MacFarlane, or any other editor, criticized in print, say, some military strategy during the war, that certainly would have been a flagrant abuse of the agreement between the army and the editors of *The Maple Leaf*. But when it came to criticizing the repatriation policy—after the war was over, mind you—it remains a debatable point as to whether the criticism or the policy did more to undermine the morale of the soldiers.

Long after this corrosive clash of wills between the major and the general, Bill Austin, Colonel Malone's second-in-command when *The Maple Leaf* was established, was asked about the incident.

He replied, "He got bloody bad advice—I mean Simonds did."

15

The Darkest Page

For most servicemen and women, the war ended when they returned to Canada. Adjusting to life back in Civvy Street wasn't easy, but there was usually help from the government and there were often memories of camaraderie, adventure, or achievement that made them feel that their efforts had been worth it.

There were a few, however, whose experiences were so terrifying that they could never completely put the war behind them. Sometimes their sufferings were compounded by the lack of official recognition of their difficulties. Many of those who were taken prisoner after the fall of Hong Kong encountered this problem. So did a group of RCAF airmen whose extraordinary story is less well known.

Sergeant Air Gunner Bill Gibson was in this group. He was eighteen when he joined a Lancaster bomber crew, and he saw his first action three days after D-Day. On its ninth bombing mission, the Lancaster was hit and the crew bailed out. Gibson came down on a French farmhouse. He and the pilot ran all night and managed to elude the prowling German troops. Finally they lay down to sleep near what they later learned was a German aerodrome. They met a French farmer, who hid them. Later, they were moved by the French Underground to the house of an old couple who were caretakers of a little church.

"They kept chickens and tame rabbits for food, and each morning for breakfast they would give us café au lait..." According to Gibson, the pilot became increasingly paranoid, convinced the French were trying to poison them. "He wouldn't drink coffee, he wouldn't eat chicken or rabbit, he just started causing trouble," Gibson says. "Now, he was a flying officer at that time and I was still a flight sergeant. He was saying, 'They are trying to poison us, don't drink anything.' And I said, 'Don't be so damn foolish, they are trying to save our lives.'"

A couple of days later, the Underground brought in the crew's wireless operator. Then a fourth Canadian, Leo Grenin, turned up. The pilot started to blame the (still missing) mid-upper gunner for the plane's fate, "which was ludicrous because you can only look one way and this was a head-on attack. He [the pilot] saw it before any of us did." When Gibson argued with his pilot, the latter threatened him with a court martial.

The Canadians were moved from place to place and were told they were going to be taken by car to Paris, then down through France and Spain to Gibraltar, and finally back to England.

"We were in civilian clothes. I had the funniest pair of shoes I ever saw in my life, and a brown suit and a beret. I was a real Frenchman," says Gibson.

If they had been smarter, he says now, they would have realized there was something fishy going on. Where would French civilians get gasoline for cars? Everything was controlled by the Germans. Why were they routed through Paris, a German occupation stronghold? However, they went to Paris, where they were put into a room in a hotel, where "these two guys kept visiting us." There were other Allied airmen in the hotel as well.

One day, the airmen were told that at 4:45 that afternoon they would be picked up and sent on their way to Spain. "Well, sure enough, at 4:45 [there's] a knock on the door. We went out of the hotel, out the side door, and into these two big cars. It was authentic-looking and there was still no suspicion in our minds. I was in the front seat with my pilot, and in the back seat was the second man and my navigator and wireless operator."

As the car was driven past the Arc de Triomphe, Gibson looked out the windshield ahead and saw "two swastika flags over an archway. It still didn't register on me, I didn't know what in the hell was going on. But I felt something in my ribs and looked down. It was a .45 automatic. [The driver] said in German, 'Police. You're our prisoners,' and with that he turned into this archway and...we were taken into Gestapo headquarters."

After some fruitless interrogation ("the only words we could understand were gangsters, terrorists, and saboteurs") and a bit of roughing up, they were driven to a big prison (Fresnes) near Paris, where Gibson was held in solitary confinement for thirty-two days.

On August 19, they were taken out of their cells and put aboard trains—"forty and eights," they were called, meaning each freight car was meant to hold forty men or eight horses. There were ninety-five in Gibson's car. Most of them were French Underground fighters or political prisoners of various nationalities.

But the ordeal was only beginning. The train was bound for the infamous Nazi concentration camp, Buchenwald.

Ed Carter-Edwards has good reason to believe Bill Gibson's story. His own experience was strikingly similar. He had joined the RCAF in Hamilton in 1941 when he was eighteen and had become a wireless air gunner. The Halifax bomber on which he served successfully completed twenty-one missions. On its twenty-second mission, it was hit by flak. The port wing was "just a mass of flames." Everybody bailed out before the plane crashed and exploded.

Running to elude prowling German troops, he met his bomb-aimer, Tommy Farr. The two men buried their parachutes and went on into the bush. But soon Carter-Edwards lost sight of Farr. He came to a fork in the road and stopped. Which way had Tommy gone? Ed decided to go to the right. He later learned that Farr had gone left and was liberated by the Americans after hiding out for three months.

"That one turn in the fork of the road," Ed says, "changed my whole life."

After two days and nights of running and hiding, he was taken in, hidden in a barn, fed and given civilian clothes. He kept his identification tags. Soon, he was moved to another house for a week or so. A man and woman arrived from Paris and, after being satisfied that he was really a Canadian airman, provided him with a fake passport (he became Edouard Cartier, a jeweler's helper), and accompanied him to Paris by train.

There he was moved from one small hotel to another by the French Underground. But, as in Bill Gibson's case, a collaborator had infiltrated the Underground group and Carter-Edwards, too, was turned over to the Gestapo and sent first to Fresnes prison, where he was interrogated and beaten, and eventually put on a train, which delivered him a week later to Buchenwald.

Both Gibson and Carter-Edwards—who had never met before their stay in Buchenwald—tell a chilling story about an incident on that horrific journey. The prisoners, about eighty or ninety of them in Carter-Edwards's car, were warned not to go near the windows. "We had stopped. This young French kid put his hand on the window to look out, and a German guard going by saw it and shot him through the hand," Carter-Edwards recalls.

A German guard opened the car door and asked who was shot. Thinking he was being helpful to the victim, one of the Canadian prisoners pointed out the lad who had been wounded.

"They took this young kid out, made him walk down the railway tracks, and one of the German guards shot him several times in the back. Killed him," says Carter-Edwards. "They forced a couple of our fellows to dig a shallow grave there and bury him."

Bill Gibson was in the same car of the same train and he, too, remembers the incident.

A third Canadian aboard that train was David High, of Edmonton, who had enlisted in the RCAF in 1940 and become a wireless air gunner. His Lancaster bomber was shot down over the outskirts of Paris in mid-June 1944. High soon made contact with the Underground and helped with various acts of sabotage—blowing up bridges and railway tracks. But a collaborator reported them to the Germans and High was arrested, beaten, and eventually sent to Buchenwald.

After the war, David High told his story to the War Claims Commission. His report makes chilling reading.

"Upon discovery that four from my car were missing, a couple of hundred shots from a machine gun were fired into this car. I was one of those assigned to the task of putting the corpses of those killed into gunny sacks and of digging the shallow graves where they were buried. Afterwards, I was beaten with a rubber hose by a member of the Gestapo. I was struck mostly on the head, shoulders and arms and was able to move about only with difficulty for three or four days. I was black and blue for weeks...

"They continued to regard me as a civilian in Buchenwald camp until I was removed by the SS guards and sent to Stalag Luft III. While at Buchenwald, I was given very little food. The daily ration consisted of one litre of soup made from water and about one tablespoonful of cabbage (there was no fat whatsoever in this soup) and one slice of black bread. I lost considerable weight. When I was shot down I weighed 163 and when I reached England, my weight was 119.

"There were many occasions when mental cruelty was applied. For instance, upon our refusal to work in the munitions factory, we were given the same meagre rations and treatment handed out to the Jews in this camp. On at least two occasions, I was compelled, with my companions, to witness mass hangings. For refusal to fill out a form which would have disclosed the type of aircraft I had flown and other military information, I was placed with ten companions in a sort of corral surrounded by a number of vicious dogs and kept there for several days. We were told that we were to be shot."

Bill Gibson had never heard of Buchenwald. "I never even knew what a concentration camp was."

"We were all taken down to what they called the 'little camp.' There was no place for us to sleep other than the rocks, no place to live, even," Gibson says. "We were all issued...a pair of britches and I remember an old army shirt and a little cloth hat... When a German walked by you removed your hat and stood at attention or suffered the consequences."

They soon found out that there were between 35,000 and 45,000 prisoners at Buchenwald. "The Jews had to wear the yellow star. Homosexuals had to wear a certain colour. Murderers had to wear a certain coloured star. Those were the semi-permanent occupants," Gibson explains.

When Carter-Edwards arrived at Buchenwald he remembers "SS guards milling around, with guns and dogs, beating people, herding them into the direction of the camp. It was an absolute terror. The bestiality! We [the airmen] remained together [and] were treated the same as the rest. As we entered the camp we saw the electrified barbed wire fences, the towers, guns, guards. We couldn't believe our eyes. We saw these walking skeletons, men with bulging or sunken eyes, the walking dead..."

He still remembers the food: "Occasional crusts of coarse, terrible black bread and a watery vegetable soup with fleas, lice, and maggots floating in it."

There is no question that the Germans knew that the Allied airmen were who they said they were. When Carter-Edwards was first arrested, he identified himself as a Canadian airman.

"Prove it," challenged his captor.

Carter-Edwards opened his shirt and revealed his ID tags.

The German grabbed the tags, twisted them, threw them away, and said, "Now, prove who you are."

Because there were German munitions plants very close to Buchenwald, making parts for V1 or V2 rocket bombs, American Flying Fortresses repeatedly bombed the area.

"They (the Americans) knew we were there," says Gibson, "because they dropped leaflets...to the effect that this is how we treat prisoners of war in the United States. They had pictures of [their] prison camps. I'm sure that they knew we were there or otherwise they wouldn't have dropped the leaflets. But we weren't allowed to touch them on threat of death."

Ed Carter-Edwards was seriously ill with pneumonia and pleurisy at two different times in Buchenwald. He was sent to an "infirmary" but given no medical treatment at all. What saved his life was a French doctor, also a prisoner, who "got hold of a big syringe and drained the fluid out of my lungs."

"I prayed a lot. Maybe my prayers were answered. Maybe it gave me the inner resistance to fight all this, but it helped me."

Bill Gibson remembers being injected "in the left breast with...a greenish-looking stuff, slime green. We were all injected with the same needle, they just refilled the syringe." He has no idea what the contents were or what the purpose was, "but I know some of the fellows today have trouble with their left breast swelling."

Carter-Edwards confirms this. "Oh, yes... I also had that. I got the needle in the left breast. Mine swelled, I still have [occasional] swelling to this day."

He also remembers another form of mistreatment: "When a guard came up to you, you had to stand to attention with your hands palm up. If you made anything resembling a fist you got either a rifle butt in the face or a bullet in the stomach."

Another Canadian airman at Buchenwald was J. Ewart Prudham, who later said what he saw in the camp was "unbelievable." He remembers hearing about the brutal execution of captured Allied agents in September 1944. They were hung on meat hooks in the cellar of the crematorium and slowly strangled.

"There were thirty-three British agents in Buchenwald at the time we were there," says Bill Gibson. One of them was Frank Pickersgill, brother of former Liberal cabinet minister Jack Pickersgill, according to Gibson. There were also several European aristocrats among the prisoners, "but they were not shot. Their way of execution was death by strangulation with a piano wire."

(A report of Frank Pickersgill's death appeared in Canadian papers on May 12, 1945. The Canadian Press story said Pickersgill had been on a secret mission for the British War Office and was "executed in a German prison camp three weeks after his arrest by the Germans in August, 1944.")

Of the roughly 165 Allied airmen imprisoned at Buchenwald between August and November, 1944, twenty-seven were Canadians. Besides those already mentioned, they included Art Kinnis of Victoria, Stan Heatherington of Windsor, Ontario, and Les Head from Manitoba.

Some of the Canadians who spent time at Buchenwald formed the K.L.B. Club. The initials stand for Koncentration Lager Buchenwald. Active in the organization is Ed Carter-Edwards, who told a *Toronto Star* writer in 1987 he was hoping to get the Canadian government to acknowledge the airmen's role in what he termed "one of the darkest pages of our history."

Carter-Edwards concedes it is a difficult story to accept. "Most people, when you tell them your story, they believe but they don't believe. The first thing they say is, 'Are you Jewish?' You say, 'No.' Then they say, 'Where's your tattoo?' You never got tattooed in Buchenwald, you got tattooed in Dachau or Belsen. So they do not believe you. [Eventually] you kept it all to yourself. It's only in the last fifteen years or so that it's come to light again."

Arguably, Bill Gibson's ordeal has been the hardest. By the time he was liberated, he had a broken collar bone ("it was never fixed") and, when he got to England, he learned his pilot had laid a charge of insubordination against him. (The pilot had escaped from the train bound for Buchenwald.) The interrogating officer told him the charge was going to be "ignored" but Gibson was told "not to tell anybody what you have seen or where you have been for a period of thirty years."

After Gibson got home to Halifax a doctor at Camp Hill (Veterans) Hospital examined his shoulder and told him he was entitled to a pension, so Bill went to see a "pensions advocate."

"And this doctor, when I went into his office, his first words to me were, 'The trouble with you guys that were overseas is that you come back here and think the country owes you a living.' So I said, 'Doctor, don't say another word or I'm going to punch you right in the face."

Gibson was granted a disability pension of $3.75 a month. He candidly acknowledges that he had "mental problems," that he "went on a drunk for the first year," but then he quit drinking. He was put on pain-killing drugs, which he took for fifteen years, until, with the help of his family doctor, he got off the pills. But he kept going before pension boards and kept being rejected.

"And the reason I was rejected was 'pre-enlistment ailment not aggravated by wartime service.' [It was] psychological, they said. And I said, if I'd had that before I went to the recruiting unit, would you take me into the air force, would you let me be a tail gunner and protect your life?" Over the years, he went before "at least twenty-five boards." He kept appealing their negative decisions.

One day, several years later, he got a phone call from a lawyer who was the son of the offensive camp doctor at Camp Hill Hospital. This lawyer gave him new hope. Gibson was sent to a psychiatrist who came up with a new diagnosis for his problem: "post-traumatic stress syndrome." After much backing and filling, over many years, he got a lump-sum "compensation" payment of $26,000.

Bill Gibson, who will be seventy in September 1995, looks gaunt and troubled. Ed Carter-Edwards is troubled, too, as he talks about the battle that began after Buchenwald. "We don't know what the government's justification is. I have personally been fighting our government for close to fifty years... I have written to everybody. The communication goes to a certain level and then it just stops. It ceases to exist. You don't even get a response."

In a 1987 article about Carter-Edwards in *The Toronto Star*, a researcher at the Department of National Defence was quoted as saying that "historians know Canadians died in other German concentration camps." But he also said he "could find no documentation in his archives that described the experience of Canadian airmen in Buchenwald."

In 1990, both Bill Gibson and Ed Carter-Edwards testified before a Senate sub-committee on veterans affairs, and the committee recommended "that the rates of compensation provided for under the Prisoner of War Compensation Act be reviewed."

Nothing came of the recommendation.

In summer 1993, Ed was one of several Allied airmen (another was British, a third American) flown to Germany by the National Film Board to take part in a documentary film about the Buchenwald experience. He hoped this film would help "the cause," but was not very confident.

The closest ally they have had, he says, has been Senator Jack Marshall, who has been "supportive of our cause." Then he adds, somewhat wistfully, "He'll probably be retiring soon..."

Not even their captors acknowledged their experiences. When Bill Gibson was transferred to Stalag Luft III towards the end of the war, "a German Air Force colonel came out to us and says, 'Where did you people come from?' We said, 'Buchenwald concentration camp.' He said, 'Such places don't exist in Germany.'"

16

Land of Promise—and Promises

The blood was barely dry on the battle wounds before Canada was in the grip of a new pastime: advising veterans.

In *Maclean's* magazine, Blair Fraser wrote an article about "handling" returned veterans, in which he related that the Department of Veterans' Affairs in Ottawa was running a series of two-week courses in personnel counselling for counsellors in the three services and in the rehabilitation centres. "It's an education," Fraser wrote, "to sit in at these classes and listen to the cross-examination the instructor gets from the young returned men who are his pupils."

Colonel Richard S. Malone, head of public relations for the Canadian Army, doled out advice to returning soldiers in a magazine article in July 1945. Among other things, he suggested: "People's daily interests back here are miles apart from our daily concerns of the past. It is our way of living that has to be changed if we are to get back into step again quickly, not theirs."

Another magazine article started out bluntly: "The Canadian soldier is just about the biggest problem Canada has to face in the future." It went on to warn of the "dangers" of a new political party dominated by veterans, which would run the country "onto the rocks of financial ruin…"

Even *The Maple Leaf* wagged an editorial finger in an article headlined "Veterans Warned Against Creating New Depression," which told veterans not to expect too much from the postwar economy.

It seems to have come as a considerable shock to Canada that the postwar period was going to be difficult. Generally, Canadians wanted to get "back to normal." Many veterans, on the other hand, felt that "normal" wasn't good enough. Having fought valiantly for their country, they felt something more was owed them. Many employers welcomed "the boys" back with genuine feelings of gratitude and loyalty. Some did not.

Jim Smart spent five years with the electrical mechanical engineering branch of the army, the last one in a group of seventy-three Canadians on a hush-hush mission in Australia, instructing the military there on the developing technology of what came to be known as radar. When he finally got home in February of 1946, he was welcomed back to his job with General Electric in Toronto and stayed with that company until 1979.

Don McLennan from Galt, Ontario, spent four years overseas and was injured in an accident in England. Before the war, he had worked at the St. Catharines branch of the Bank of Toronto. After the war he went back to the bank and "was told I should take a step or two backwards to make up for all the time I'd been away... I didn't feel I should take a step or two backwards..."

Tom Watson had worked in the Canadian Bank of Commerce in Vernon, B.C., before joining the RCAF. By the end of the war, he had served five years, done three tours of operations, and been decorated. When he was being interviewed about his postwar plans, he said he wasn't sure, but he might go back to banking. "So they gave me a slip of paper saying I'd make a good clerk."

Jack Stoddard didn't get into the army until 1944, when he was eighteen. Much of his service was spent as a guard in various POW camps. He was still in uniform until late August 1946, partly because "you didn't get out unless you had a job to go to.

"I had to have a letter, which I got, from Imperial Oil that I was going to have a job there...and I was to present that letter, which I did, and that's how I was eventually discharged from the Canadian Army."

Don Carty, who served three years in the RCAF, went back to his native Saint John, "back to the old status quo." He found he was "just another black face on the street." Don remembers, too, that though his brother, Clyde, had served as a firefighter in the air force, he had similar difficulties in finding employment. "Though he went to various prominent people," Don recalls, "they didn't want to be identified as the person giving 'those people' an opportunity."

But going uphill was nothing new for Don Carty. He slogged through a succession of menial jobs before finding employment in the post office, where he stayed for much of his working life. The job allowed him to indulge his passion for writing.

Not all black Canadians had the same experience. Wendell Sharp, who served five years in the army, was twenty-two when he returned to civilian life and says he had "no problems" in making the adjustment. "I got a job with Smith Transport and I drove for them for quite a few years. And I went to night school."

Perhaps Sharp found postwar life comparatively easy after some of his wartime experiences of racism. Early in the war, he and 400 other paratroopers had been sent to Fort Benning, Georgia, for training with the U.S. Army. Although Sharp himself managed to put up with the hostility of southern racists, the Canadian officers objected to the practice of segregation that was standard procedure in the U.S. forces. After three or four weeks, the Canadian colonel in charge had his paratroopers transferred to Shilo, Manitoba, for training.

Wendell was one of four Sharp brothers who served in Canada's armed forces. Walter, his older brother, was in the Royal Canadian Army Service Corps in Brantford. He found some of the NCOs rough on black soldiers, and there were restaurants and bars in Brantford where "they didn't want us." Dorothy Gollinger, who married Walter just after the war, says that "some of them [black Canadians] were told it's not a black man's war. But when things started to get pretty rough over there, they began to accept anybody."

Aubrey was the only Sharp brother to go overseas, where he served in an armoured unit in Italy and Germany. After his return, he and a few other black Canadian servicemen established the Toronto Negro Veterans' Association, because, as his sister-in-law Dorothy Sharp says, "black veterans who had served overseas for Canada came home to find they were not recognized or welcomed by white veterans who they had stood shoulder-to-shoulder with in combat."

Billy O'Connor, who produced, wrote, and/or appeared in many army shows during the war, says the worst period was the several months after the war. The army was so "backed up" in processing discharges for its members that "the men were grumpy as hell." Instead of a show a week or so, Sergeant O'Connor had to come up with shows virtually every day to keep the boys happy.

"They were getting drunk all the time," says O'Connor, "and the worst part of it was they weren't sending any money home to their wives. They were spending it all on booze and stuff... It was nerves. They weren't drunks, they [just] wanted to get out and back to their jobs because a lot of them were afraid they would lose their jobs."

Arthur Wood found that "jobs were few and far between" in postwar Canada. Wood had spent three years as a radio technician with the RCAF during the war. While waiting for an opening at Trans-Canada Airlines, he worked as a spare driver on a horse-drawn milk wagon in downtown Winnipeg. "I was fortunate in having a loyal, loving wife. Many marriages did not survive those difficult years."

For Margaret Los, who spent the war as a Wren, the adjustment back to civilian life was difficult, too, because "I married a man that I'd known, but I found he wasn't willing to accept independence in me. We had a lot of very bad differences about that... He didn't see why I wanted to go to night school...or college... He wouldn't stop me, but he resented that a lot of the time that could have gone into better housekeeping was spent on something else."

William Moore, an ack-ack gunner in the war, acknowledges that his home town of Napanee, Ontario, "seemed strange" to him. "It was hard to settle down for the first couple of years," he says. "We were carefree, we partied half the time."

"It was real hard," agrees Fred Weegar. He had served with the Algonquin Regiment and become a POW. "My dad was a druggist down here on the Danforth [in Toronto]. So he wasn't pushing me at all. We used to go golfing every day. [I was] just too pooped. Dad wanted me to finish school and be a druggist. I didn't want to, but I did, and went back to my old school. It was no good. I couldn't concentrate. I could have done it a year later, but I just couldn't retain anything."

Coming home was equally difficult for Gordon Gross. An RCAF mid-upper gunner on Halifax bombers, Gross remembers that "everything was so different in Canada to what I had expected. Everyone seemed to be so far removed from the hostilities of the war, and no one seemed to understand or maybe didn't care about what had happened across the pond. The attitudes of many people were unrealistic and difficult to accept... Things had certainly changed in Canada... The booming wartime economy was now in transition and there didn't seem to be any space for the new work force emerging from active service..."

Phil Marchildon had travelled a long way from his Penetanguishene, Ontario, home. An outstanding major league baseball pitcher, he had been signed by the Philadelphia Athletics in 1940 and had won seventeen games the following year. In 1942 he returned to Canada, joined the RCAF, went overseas, and, on his twenty-sixth combat mission, was shot down over Denmark. He spent the rest of the war in the infamous Stalag Luft III. When he returned home, things seemed odd to him. "What seemed strangest of all," he recalled, "was that things looked exactly the way I remembered them...as if the war had never happened."

Another change to the Canadian landscape was the presence of war brides, mostly from Britain—close to 28,000 of them—and 13,000 children of wartime marriages.

Eileen Simpson was with the Canadian Red Cross, greeting war brides arriving in Hamilton, and she remembers the excitement of Canadian families waiting for the new brides. "They would be in little family clusters and in almost every case someone in each group would be holding a huge bouquet of flowers...

"The first time we met the train we wondered how the war bride and the family would recognize each other, but we had forgotten the magic of snapshots which had been exchanged both ways across the ocean... It was amazing how quickly they were recognized by the waiting families and the cries of welcome echoed throughout the station... It was an especially emotional moment for grandparents seeing their grandchild for the first time..."

At the end of the war, Grace Grant was a CWAC major, stationed in Halifax and greeting many of the war brides. "They were coming to a strange country and their husbands mostly were still in England. They were going to their in-laws and there was an awful lot of apprehension...

"There was one woman," she remembers, "who was a very la-de-da type of English... And I said, 'Are you all set, you know where you are going? You know who your husband's people are, are they meeting you?'

"Well, she said she was going to Kapuskasing to her husband's 'estate.' I thought, oh no... I often wonder what happened to that poor woman in Kapuskasing."

Grant says it was difficult to meet the war brides. "These gals were very anxious to get over to this side; they wanted to get out of England...with the rationing and everything. And I think they thought they were going to the promised land when they came over here. Which I suppose by comparison it was in those days."

For many of them, perhaps most, the promised land worked out reasonably well—after a while. Eva MacLeod came over in 1946, four years after her marriage to Gordon MacLeod in England. Arriving in Halifax, her first impression "was seeing Gordon in civvies, which I had never done before. He had a stupid hat on. I sat on it all the way from Halifax; couldn't stand it. I felt very lonesome, and I said if I could just see one face that I knew I'd be happy. But Gordon was very good..."

After all these years (the MacLeods celebrated their fiftieth anniversary in 1992) she still misses England, mostly at Christmas. "We were a very close family and everybody at Christmas always got together. And I found the Canadians not as family-oriented. Even then...they didn't seem as close as we were."

Eva MacLeod belongs to the Nova Scotia War Brides Association, which has about 200 members in the Westville/New Glasgow area. "When we get together, it's as though [we] all have something in common," she says.

Wallace Bambrough was married in England and brought his war bride over to Toronto, shortly after he got home. How did she feel about coming to Canada? "It didn't make any difference, she had plenty of guts," he says with admiration. "They had to, because where she lived they [the Germans] tried to get the airport every night."

William Moore also married an English girl. She came over in 1946, "and we're still together," he says, with satisfaction.

One war bride, quoted but not identified in a CP story, was awed, if not pleased, by the plains of Saskatchewan. "Heavens," she gushed, "do they never end?"

Madge Janes, originally of Bournemouth, England, met RCAF Spitfire pilot John Trull in England. Madge was serving in the Women's Royal Naval Service as a highly skilled code-breaker. They were married late in the war and he preceded her back to Canada. When he was told a definite date for her arrival, Trull and his parents drove to Toronto from St. Thomas, booked rooms at the Royal York Hotel, and went across the street to Union Station to await Madge's train.

"When the train arrived," he recalls, "there were about 500 war brides on it. And they had a big platform set up down on the concourse of Union Station and they were announcing the girls' names and bringing them out to a wild round of applause. They had a band and it was quite a show and quite a welcome."

Madge remembers her arrival, as well as the trip over from England to Halifax. "One of the girls I came with," she says, "was a lovely girl who ended up in New Brunswick. Her husband had been killed. However, she came out just to see his parents, which I thought was a lovely thing to do."

At John's suggestion, Madge had brought few clothes with her, the idea being they would go shopping in Toronto as soon as she arrived. They had a rousing celebration that night and got up the next morning to go and buy clothes for Madge.

"We got going up Yonge Street and, my gosh, all the stores were closing. Banners were coming out. Streamers were coming out of the windows and a dental office upstairs was throwing teeth out and they were clattering down the street," John remembers. "All the stores were closing up and everybody was announcing that it was VE Day, and of course it was a tremendous thrill to know it was finally over...[but it] was mixed with a bit of disappointment that they couldn't have waited half a day until Madge got some clothes."

Mona Trevartan of Leicester, England, served in an anti-aircraft battery from 1941 to 1945 (in England, some women were in second-line combat). She served first in England, then in Northern Ireland. During the war she met Bert Hawboldt, a Canadian serviceman, whom she married in 1944 in London.

When she came out to Canada in June 1946, and settled in Trenton, Nova Scotia, all Mona remembers was that it was "a big shock... So many trees, so vast, everything wide. Everything in England is close... But the people were friendly—well, most people were. Of course, you may get an odd one or two, but that's true no matter where you go. But, no, I found Canadians very receptive..."

Alan and Blanche Lund, who were married while they were in *Meet The Navy*, went on to a long, successful career, mostly on CBC television programs. Lund also staged many stage shows, including *Anne of Green Gables*.

Not all of the war brides succeeded in the promised land. Jean Kelly, originally of Greenock, Scotland, married John McAllister, a naval officer, and came to Canada in 1946. She and John lived in a cabin near Kirkfield, Ontario. On Labour Day weekend, 1948, Jean McAllister shot and killed her husband. Her trial in Lindsay that November became something of a media circus. But evidence at the trial established that McAllister had been abusing her, both physically and mentally, for some time. In the end, she was convicted of manslaughter, with a strong recommendation for mercy, and was sentenced to three years in prison.

For many who served in the war, the trip home was memorable. As a member of the Women's Division of the RCAF, Hilda Ashwell had served overseas. She recalls the marked difference between the trip over and the celebration coming home.

"I had gone overseas on a troopship, very over-crowded, with little food and narrow escapes from submarines," she remembers, "but I came back on the *Queen Elizabeth*." Although the ship was not fitted out as a luxury liner, "it was exciting luxury to us who had been on English rations, and in acute danger, for two years."

Joe Baker was on the westbound *Queen Elizabeth*, where "I got seasick, deathly sick. And they suggested that I go up and get some fresh air, as much as I possibly could. So I went up on the deck and I was just sitting there...

"Suddenly there were these four or five guys walking along and one was my brother. I hadn't seen him for about four years. So I waited until they got right to me and I just said, 'Hey, Ol, how you doing?'"

Alan Skaife, originally from Montreal, remembers his trip home on a hospital ship, *New Amsterdam*, bound for New York. "I must say, the American people were marvellous... There were nine or ten Canadians at that time aboard the ship, some badly wounded. I wasn't. But before we even disembarked, a pile of people came on, Bell Telephone people, and you couldn't see the side of the ship for lines. Every person on that American ship had the opportunity, no matter where, to phone home. That was smart."

When Captain Leonard Davies, a doctor in the Royal Canadian Army Medical Corps, was dispatched from Kingston to New York City to meet incoming Canadians aboard the *Queen Mary*, there was a similar rousing American welcome at the docks. "I was to meet and escort the Fort Garry Horse regiment home to Winnipeg. When the troops came off the ship, the American Red Cross had canteens on the pier, with men and women providing our boys with coffee, cigarettes, and chocolate bars...[even though] they had disembarked at midnight. Then we were taken by barge across the Hudson River to Hoboken, New Jersey, where the trains were waiting for us... At about two or three in the morning as we arrived in Hoboken, our troops were piped ashore by American veterans of the First World War...and again the Red Cross were there with sandwiches and candy bars...

"In contrast, when we arrived in Toronto, about eleven o'clock that morning, there was nobody there at the station. Nobody. No Red Cross. No officials. No coffee. No candy. No cigarettes. Nothing. It just seemed that the country couldn't have cared less. It was the most disgraceful thing I ever saw."

Many who returned were profoundly changed by their experience of war. Don McLennan has been a resident of Sunnybrook Health Science Centre (Canada's biggest veterans' hospital) since 1966. "I am a happy veteran," he says, dismissing his health problems. "I take problems philosophically, they don't worry me. I'm still alive and I thank God for that. And for my family and friends, the home, the country. We have so much."

Joe Baker, who ran into his brother on his trip home, lives now in a retirement home in Toronto. He readily acknowledges that the war changed him because "I was just an ordinary guy that couldn't care less about anything, in a sense. I don't know whether I'd found myself or not, I guess I hadn't. But when I got overseas and I lived in all the devastation and I looked at the whole thing, when I came home I had determined then that I was going to try to do something that would be of benefit to others. And I became a preacher. I was with the Youth for Christ International...and that did change my life."

Army nurses Kay Christie and May Waters—the only Canadian women to become prisoners of war (in Hong Kong)—continued their selfless nursing careers after returning home in 1943. May Waters died in 1987, at the age of eighty-four. Kay Christie died in 1994, aged eighty-two.

Most veterans look back on the war as a difficult experience, but one they would not have missed for the world. Says Don MacNeil, former RCAF pilot: "You made friendships at that time that you could never make in peacetime. The bond was so strong."

Asked if serving in the navy changed his life, Murray Westgate says: "Oh, yeah! I would have never left Regina. I would have been selling shoes in Eaton's." Instead, having matured in the service, he carved out a successful acting career for himself.

Another man who was "changed" by wartime experience was Victor Albota. He had joined the RCAF in Ottawa as a photographer, but his life was really altered the moment he boarded the *Queen Elizabeth* in Halifax, where "we all received as a gift from the government of Canada a carton of cigarettes and as I did not smoke I put them in my kit bag."

He was soon based near York, England, and noticed that "nearly all the English people smoked, so I started to carry those gift cigarettes when I was not on duty." Albota began offering cigarettes to people he met in pubs, but they tended to be suspicious, wondering what was wrong with the cigarettes and why he wasn't smoking them himself. "So I would light up. It was not long [before] I began to enjoy smoking... When on leave in London, I would go to the Canadian Red Cross, where we could obtain sweaters, socks, and a couple of cartons of cigarettes absolutely free; and from home in Canada my parents would send me cigarettes which only cost a dollar a carton. Pretty soon I was smoking two packs a day." He quit smoking in 1957 and never went back to it. However, "I will always remember that I would not have smoked those fifteen years if I had not received that carton from the government of Canada."

Bill Brydon was nine years old when Winston Churchill became prime minister of Britain, in 1940. Bill was evacuated to Canada, where he spent most of the war years. He returned to Canada in 1956 and later became a successful actor. In 1993, Brydon appeared in the CBC mini-series *Dieppe*. He played the role of Churchill.

Ronald Brent Bartlett Taylor's very name is a wartime story. His mother, Lynne Fisher, met his father, Ron Bartlett, while he was a pilot trainee in Medicine Hat, Alberta. Their son was born in Medicine Hat and "then whisked off to England, later in 1944." The family had an emotional reunion at the Thundersley railway station, when the RAF pilot was on leave after flying his Lancaster bomber on several missions.

Later the same year, Bartlett, Sr., was shot down on a bombing mission. His widow later married Colin Taylor, a pilot whom Ron Bartlett, Sr., had helped train. That's how Bartlett's son grew up with all those proud names.

Nordeau Goodman was with the 45th Canadian Army Transport Company in England and on the Continent. He is now a resident of Camp Hill (Veterans) Hospital in Halifax. "I did mature... I certainly had a feeling of adventure as a youth, you know. I was always active, I enjoyed activity, and how much was instilled in me and how much was there in the first place, I'm not really sure. I enjoyed my association with the men, I really did and still do. I've been to a number of reunions, and I enjoy it very much. It's intriguing, you know, I tell stories, and it's come home to me a number of times that each and every soldier, sailor, whatever, has his own war. My memories are unique to me."

Reunions: some veterans look forward to them; others avoid reunions completely.

The Royal Canadian Artillery Memory Association holds annual reunions, usually at the Canadian Legion Hall in Westville, Nova Scotia. Most of the members served with the 4th Light Anti-Aircraft. Thirty-five members came to the 1993 reunion, some from as far away as Alberta. Most of the afternoon was spent gabbing, tossing back a few beers, catching up on the news, and reminiscing about wartime experiences. At the evening session there were informal speeches, starting with good-natured joking and ending with emotional tributes to fallen comrades. Fred ("Jeep") Jones, the regimental sergeant major, spoke glowingly of his "boys," evoking memories of their trials and sacrifices in the war. The next morning there was a quiet memorial service at which the men again thought and talked about their brothers-in-arms who were no longer present.

Roy Harbin never bothered with reunions until 1994, when the Royal Canadian Navy was commissioning a new frigate, HMCS *Montreal*, namesake of the ship on which he had served. He went to Montreal for the occasion, as did some forty of his shipmates, including the old *Montreal*'s skipper, Captain C. L. Campbell, "now ninety-five years old and walking with a cane."

The veterans sat and talked "with everybody sneaking looks at each other's name tags, trying to remember who they were."

At one point, Harbin met a shipmate named Hank Trout, from "somewhere in Alberta," who told him that soon after he had gone home, at the end of the war, he had received a twenty-dollar bill in the mail—from Harbin.

"He couldn't remember what it was for," says Harbin. "And I couldn't even remember sending it."

Legion halls from one end of the country to the other are the natural gathering places for veterans. They meet, drink, throw a few darts, pass the time, joke about each other's wartime shortcomings, and talk about the war.

But most of the talk is about the lighter moments—the time Joe got busted for returning late from a leave, or when Gord and Harry inadvertently set fire to the captain's tent, or the way Jim looked when the sergeant bawled him out for not cleaning his rifle, or the party where everybody got so bombed nobody could drive back to camp.

Doug MacFarlane tells about the two war veterans trading yarns and reminiscing about the war.

"It was a helluva war," says one.

"Yeah," grins the other, "but it was better than no war at all."

They talk about the "good" times, the silly incidents, the clowning and capering. Rarely do they trade stories about the bad times. The scars are still there, and it's better not to scratch at them.

Sergeant Louis M. Androlia served overseas with the Royal Canadian Artillery. His son Mark says his father "never talked of the horrors of war, only the fun times...and the friends he made and lost." Soon after Sergeant Androlia died in 1975, Mark and his brother received a letter from Vancouver, from a man named Ralph Sketch. Sketch had been Louis Androlia's captain during the war and he described an action in March 1945, when the Canadians were crossing the Rhine, one of the last great battles of the war. The artillery unit was ordered to provide a huge preliminary barrage to cover the crossing of the river. One Bofors gun was needed to continue firing after the barrage "so that the glow of its tracer shells...would mark the left margin of the crossing... A Bofors gun produces 120 gun flashes a minute. I was virtually condemning the gun crew to destruction."

Captain Sketch sent for Androlia. He described the terrible mission and then said, "I know you've just got married, Sergeant. Do you think you should take this on?"

Androlia promptly replied: "This job's for me, Cap'n."

At the height of the action, Androlia's gun misfired. According to Sketch, "Androlia...pushed aside his loading gunner, opened the top cover plate and wrenched out the shell... It blew up in his face... We got (him) to a field hospital, hoping rather to spare him pain than to save his life. He lived, became the father of four fine sons...but he has not been able to see since the night of March 24, 1945."

It was not until Mark Androlia received that letter—thirty years after the war—that he learned how his father had lost his sight that night on the Rhine.

Some veterans have missed out on the recognition of their efforts. George Hutton, an RCAF gunner who became a POW, relates that many years after the war, an old buddy asked him why he wasn't wearing the Defence of Britain medal. Hutton had never received one, but decided to look into it. He found out that the length of his service in Britain was not enough to qualify him for the medal. It was a few days shy of the minimum requirement. And no, his four months as a prisoner of war did not count.

Not all veterans are needy, of course. Alan Erson, who served in the merchant navy, called the Department of Veterans Affairs a couple of years ago to see if he could find out what, if any, veterans benefits he was entitled to. The woman he talked to asked what his family income was. When he told her, she snapped that he didn't need help.

"I said, 'No, I don't need help, I was just wanting to know," he says. After they ran down a list of health and income supplements that he wasn't entitled to, the woman got a bit huffy and asked what it was he wanted.

"I said, 'Well, when I was a kid I had two buddies, one in the air force and one in the army. And when they got out they got three acres of land under the Veterans Land Act. So,' I said, 'I'd like my three acres now, and if it's all right with you, I'd like mine at King and Bay Streets.'

"She said, 'Oh, I'll get to work on it right away.'

"I said, 'When you got it, call me.'

"She hasn't called yet."

Veterans' benefits helped nurse Peggy Tucker and RCAF pilot Arnold Lonsdale, who got married in October 1945. ("He was still in uniform," she says. "Actually, it was very handy, because then he didn't have to worry about a tux.") Her husband had to stay in Ottawa, so she returned to her work at the Hospital for Sick Children in Toronto. "Then I got pregnant and we got a little house in Ottawa. The only reason we got that was because he was a veteran."

Lloyd McCallum, of Halifax, likes to play down his wartime service (five years in the army) because it was not especially glamorous or life-threatening. A few years ago, he read that there was a move afoot to have the names of all veterans put on a war memorial, alongside those who were killed. He sent a letter to the River John branch of the Royal Canadian Legion, in which he described how unheroic his own service had been. He listed some occasions that constituted how close he came to becoming a casualty. They included, "When I was shivering in my nudity under the slow drip of semi-warm water in the outside showers at Aldershot in sub-zero weather," and, "When I was trying to locate (at night) the least unclean outside latrine in the old Leopold Barracks in Ghent when I (and all other personnel) had diarrhea and only one book of matches."

The Canadian Merchant Navy Association still lobbies for greater benefits for its members. In 1991, it presented a brief titled "It's

Almost Too Late" to a Senate subcommittee on veterans affairs. The Hong Kong Veterans Association continues to fight for greater recognition of their grievances. And after much lobbying from veterans groups, in 1994 the federal government announced that it would strike a medal specifically for veterans of the Dieppe raid. The Koncentration Lager Buchenwald Club still pushes for recognition of the sufferings of its members. But for many it is too late, and for those who are left, it is nearly so.

Bill Gibson has never stopped fighting. Almost four decades after his ordeal, he appeared on the television program *Front Page Challenge*. During the interview, Pierre Berton asked him what he thought of people like Ernst Zundl and Jim Keegstra, who say that the holocaust never happened. "I said," he recalled, "that it's great they live in a country where they can say that, and that I'm sorry that they do, but they should be punished for saying such things."

In different ways, born of different experiences of camaraderie or pain, the veterans remember. Each year on Remembrance Day, they gather by the thousands at cenotaphs in cities and towns across Canada. They wear their fifty-year-old medals, stand stiffly, and listen solemnly to the speeches of the politicians and dignitaries, and they think about that time in those distant places and those men who did not come back.

Joe Oggy, who went in on D-Day after being told he and his buddies had "fifteen minutes to live," has gone to Remembrance Day ceremonies in recent years, stood by the cenotaph, and recorded on tape what he remembers of that dreadful day. Much of it is painful, even now, but Joe still goes, still talks his way through the difficult memories. It is his way of making sure he won't forget—not that there's much danger of that.

"D-Day is the most vivid," says Joe. "After that, battle after battle is cloudy compared to that first impression. You always remember that first part."

But it took a long time to get over the war. "I used to wake up screaming," Joe says, "because you could see the tall, tall grass, the way the wind blows it when the bullets are going through it... The fellows (at the Y in Montreal, where I lived after the war) used to pound on the door. I'd say, 'What's wrong?' They'd say, 'You're screaming.' It took a long time."

Some veterans do their remembering publicly. In May each year, RCN veterans in Toronto gather aboard the destroyer HMCS *Haida*, Canada's most famous warship, to commemorate the Battle of the Atlantic. Serving mostly in the English Channel, *Haida* dispatched two destroyers, a U-boat and fifteen other ships. HMCS *Haida* is now one of only two surviving Canadian warships from the Second World War. (The other is HMCS *Sackville*, a corvette.)

Some veterans go to church services. Others gather at Legion Halls for reunions. Some do it privately.

Roy Harbin, who was twenty when the war ended, is a big, heavy-set RCN veteran who looks as if he had been a football player in his youth—which he was. He attended Northern Vocational High School in Toronto and in 1942 the team on which he played won the city senior football championship.

He has a picture ("somewhere," he grins) of that football team—twenty-eight strong, young athletes, many of them too young to go into the service until the following spring. Of the twenty-eight boys in that picture, either seven or eight were killed in the war. (Harbin wears #49 in the team photograph.)

"Every Armistice Day, ever since the end of the war," Harbin says, "I sit down and I write down the names of all the guys I knew that were killed... When young people now think of the guys that went to war, they think [of] old guys like you and I, you know. But if you went to a school and said to them, 'Take your football team from this year and think of one quarter of them being missing, killed in the next two years,' they couldn't imagine it."

And so, at eleven o'clock on the morning of each Remembrance Day, Roy performs his little ritual, his own private way of paying homage to his high-school teammates of half a century ago.

"Well," he says, without any accompanying smile, "lest we forget." Then he smiles. "I'm not quite sure whether my list has gotten shorter over the years. I don't know how many I had the year before, you know? I don't remember them all this year..."

Bibliography

Allen, Ralph. *Ordeal by Fire.* Doubleday, Toronto, 1961

Broadfoot, Barry. *Years of Sorrow, Years of Shame.* Doubleday Canada Limited, 1977.

Bruce, Jean. *Back the Attack.* Macmillan of Canada, 1985

Burns, Max & Ken Messenger. *The Winged Wheel Patch.* Vanwell Publishing Ltd., St. Catharines, Ont., 1993

Cambron, Kenneth. *Guest of Hirohito.* PW Press, Vancouver, B.C., 1990.

Cameron, James M. *Pictonians in Arms - A Military History of Pictou County, N.S.* University of New Brunswick, 1969.

Canadian Bank of Commerce. *War Service Record 1939-1945.* Canadian Bank of Commerce, 1947

Carter, David J. *Behind Canadian Barbed Wire.* Nesbitt Publishing Co., Brooks, Alta., 1980s.

Colombo, John Robert. *New Canadian Quotations.* Hurtig Publishers, Edmonton, Alta., 1987.

Coughlin, Bing & MacFarlane, J. Douglas. *Herbie.* Thomas Nelson & Sons (Canada) Limited, 1946.

Dancocks, Daniel G. *In Enemy Hands (Canadian Prisoners of War, 1939-45).* Hurtig Publishers, Edmonton, Alta., 1983.

Durand, Arthur A. *Stalag Luft III, The Secret Story.* Patrick Stephens Limited, 1988.

Easton, Alan. *50 North.* Ryerson Press, Toronto, 1963.

Essex, James W. *Victory in the St. Lawrence: Canada's Unknown War.* The Boston Mills Press, Erin, Ontario, 1984.

Feldman, Seth (Editor) *Take Two - A Tribute to Film in Canada.* Irwin Publishing, Toronto, 1984.

Ferguson, Ted. *Desperate Siege: The Battle of Hong Kong.* Doubleday Canada Limited, 1980.

Giesler, Patricia. *Valour Remembered.* Veterans Affairs Canada, 1981.

Goodspeed, Lt. Col. D.J. (Editor) *The Armed Forces of Canada 1867-1967.* Directorate of History, Canadian Forces Headquarters, 1967.

Hadley, Michael L. *U-Boats Against Canada*. McGill-Queen's University Press, 1983.

Ito, Roy. *We Went to War*. Canada's Wings, Stittsville, Ont., 1984.

Kenney, Mart. *Mart Kenney and His Western Gentlemen*. Western Producer Prairie Books, Saskatoon, 1981.

Klippenstein, Lawrence (Editor) *That There Be Peace, Mennonites in Canada and World War II*. Manitoba CO Reunion Committee, Winnipeg, 1979

Koch, Eric. *Deemed Suspect - A Wartime Blunder*. Goodread Biographies, 1980

Kreisel, Henry. *Another Country*. NeWest Publishers Limited, Edmonton, Alta., 1985.

LaViolette, Forrest E. *The Canadian Japanese and World War II*. University of Toronto Press, 1948.

Lennon, Mary Jane & Charendoff, Syd. *On the Home Front*. The Boston Mills Press, Erin, Ontario, 1981.

Macpherson, K. R. *Canada's Fighting Ships*. Samuel Stevens, Hakkert & Co., 1975.

Marchildon, Phil & Kendall, Brian. *Ace*. Penguin Books, Toronto, 1993.

McNeil, Bill. *Voices of a War Remembered*. Doubleday Canada Limited, 1991.

— & Wolfe, Morris. *Signing On (The Birth of Radio in Canada)*. Doubleday Canada Limited, 1982

Melady, John. *Escape from Canada*. Macmillan of Canada, 1981.

Milberry, Larry & Halliday, Hugh A. *The Royal Canadian Air Force At War 1939-1945*. Canav Books, Toronto, 1990.

Munro, Ross. *Gauntlet to Overlord*. Macmillan Co. of Canada Ltd. 1946.

National Press Club Anthology. *A Century of Reporting*. Clarke, Irwin & Company Limited, 1967.

Omatsu, Maryka. *Bittersweet Passage*. Between The Lines, Toronto, 1992.

Phillips, Carol. "The Heroes Among Us," *Canadian Biker Magazine*. Victoria, B.C., 1992.

Phillips, Ruth. *Meet The Navy, The History of the Royal Canadian Navy's World War II Show*.

Powley, A. E. *Broadcast from the Front*. A.M. Hakkert Ltd., 1975

How, Douglas (Editor) *The Canadians At War (1939/45)*. The Readers Digest Association (Canada) Ltd., 1968

Redman, Stanley R. *Open Gangway (An Account of the Halifax Riots, 1945)*. Lancelot Press, Hantsport, N.S., 1981.

Robertson, Terrence. *The Shame and The Glory—Dieppe*. McClelland & Stewart Limited, 1962.

Rowland, Barry D. & MacFarlane, J. Douglas. *The Maple Leaf Forever*. Natural Heritage/Natural History Inc. 1987.

Schull, Joseph. *The Far Distant Ships: An Official Account of Canadian Naval Operations in the Second World War*. Queen's Printer, Ottawa, 1961.

Shapiro, Lionel. *They Left The Back Door Open*. Ryerson Press, Toronto, 1944.

Simonds, Peter. *Maple Leaf Up—Maple Leaf Down*. Island Press, New York, 1946.

Stacey, C. P. & Wilson Barbara M. *The Half Million (The Canadians in Britain, 1939-1946).* University of Toronto Press, 1987.

Stephens, W. Ray. *The Canadian Entertainers of World War II.* Mosaic Press, Oakville, Ont., 1993

Takata, Toyo. *Nikkei Legacy.* NC Press Limited, Toronto, 1983.

Toews, J. A. *Alternative Service in Canada During World War II.* Mennonite Brethren Church, Manitoba.

Villa, Brian Loring. *Unauthorized Action—Mountbatten and the Dieppe Raid.* Oxford University Press, 1994.

Periodicals

Atlantic Advocate
Canadian Business
Canadian Medical Association Journal
Cottage Life
Liberty
Life
Maclean's
Mayfair

Royal Canadian Legion
Saturday Night
The Star Weekly (Tor.)
Time
Variety
Weekend
Wings (RCAF Magazine)

Newspapers & News Agencies

British United Press
The Calgary Herald
The Canadian Press
The Edmonton Journal
The Globe and Mail (Toronto)
The Halifax Chronicle-Herald
The Halifax Herald
The Hamilton Spectator
The Kingston Whig-Standard
The Lethbridge Herald
The London Daily Express Journal
The London Daily Mail
The London Daily Telegraph
The Maple Leaf (Canadian Army)
The Meaford Express
The Gazette (Montreal)
The Montreal Standard
The Montreal Daily Star
The New York Times
The Niagara Falls Evening Review

The North Bay Nugget
The News Chronicle (London)
The Owen Sound Daily Sun Times
The Ottawa Citizen
The Regina Leader-Post
Reuter's News Agency
The Saint John Telegram-Journal
The St. Thomas Times
The Saskatoon Star-Phoenix
The Sudbury Daily Star
The Times of London
The Toronto Star
The Toronto Telegram
The United Press
The Vancouver Province
The Vancouver Sun
The Windsor Star
The Winnipeg Free Press
The Winnipeg Tribune

Other Sources

Black River Productions
Canadian Association of Retired Persons
Canadian Broadcasting Corporation
Canadian Forces Photographic Unit
Department of National Defense
Fran Dowie
Ex-Air Gunners Association of Canada (N. Alta. Branch)
Japanese Canadian Cultural Centre, Toronto
Harry Rasky
National Congress of Italian Canadians
National Film Board of Canada
Public Archives of Canada
Real Radio
Sunnybrook Health Science Centre, North York, Ontario
Veterans Affairs Department, Ottawa
Who's Who In Canada

Interviews

Bennie Amirault
Dick Arai
David Armour
Eve (Arnoldi) Armour
William E. Austin
Joe Baker
Wallace Bambrough
Everett Baudoux
Henry Beaudry
Stephen A. Bell
Dave Broadfoot
William Brydon
Elaine (Leiterman) Campbell
Norman Campbell
John Carling
Ed Carter-Edwards
Donald Carty
Gordon E. Clarke
Arthur L. & Elva Cole
Grace Collyer
Kristine Culp
Leonard Davies

Fred Davis
Dick Dee
Marie (Philp) Dee
Harold Doig
Gordon M. Drodge
Ronnie Egan
Alan Erson
Victor Feldbrill
Larry Foley
Livingston ("Cap") Foster
Bob Garvin
Hector Gaudet
Bill Gibson
Clyde Gilmour
Murray Ginsberg
Robert Goodier
Nordeau Goodman
Henry Gordon
Joyce Gordon
Freddy Grant
Thelma (Ransom) Grant
Norman Griesdorf

Paul Grosney
Tom Guy
Margaret (Los) Haliburton
Roy Harbin
Mona Hawboldt
Jim Hazlewood
Ren Henderson
Dave High
Peter Hobley
Brock Hunghberger
George Hutton
Bob Jarvis
Nadia (Boshuck) Jarvis
Catherine Jolly
Fred Jones
Eric Koch
Bill Kuinka
Sam Levine
Peggy (Tucker) Lonsdale
Blanche Lund
Jack MacCormack
David MacDonald
George E. MacDonald
J. Douglas MacFarlane
Alan MacLeod
Eva MacLeod
Gordon MacLeod
Don MacNeil
Lloyd McCallum
Donald J. McLennan
Lloyd Malenfant
Terry Manuel
William Moore
Ervine Morris
Frank Moritsugu
Beth Munro

Billy O'Connor
Joe Oggy
Frank Pellerin
Cliff Perry
Kay (Cochrane) Poulton
Ron Poulton
Jack Rae
John S. Reddekopp
Lewis & Josephine Robinson
Walter & Dorothy Sharp
Wendell Sharp
Tsitomu Shimizu
Vic Shoji
Frank Shuster
Alan Skaife
Jim Smart
Ken Smith
Maggie (Morris) Smolensky
Jack Stoddard
Toyo Takata
Hubert Thistle
Jerry Thornton
John & Madge Trull
Archie Van Hee
Andrew van Rassel
Frank Vines
Don Warner
Thomas Watson
Fred Weegar
Murray Westgate
Herbert Whittaker
Lorne Wickie
Jennifer Wilder
Harvey Willis
James Wilson
Scott Young

Correspondents

Mrs. Dorothy Adamic
Mrs. Isabel Adamson
Margaret Adcock
Frances J. Ailes
Victor Albota

George Aley
S. M. Anderson
Mark Androlia
Ted Arnold
Hilda E. Ashwell

Thomas Avill
A. E. Baker
Arthur Barnard
Mrs. Patricia Barnett
E. H. Bay
William E. Beales
Miss M. A. Bennett
D. A. Benson
Mrs. Winnifred Binnie
Gordon A. Black
Harry Bowes
Marcel Braitstein
T. Brooks
E. A. Brown
Charles Carter
Lois Christie
Mary C. Clark
John Cleave
A.S.R. Cole
Roy Leonard Cornwell
Frank J. Corring
Mr. & Mrs. William Coutts
Anne M. Crawley
Russell A. Cushman
Mrs. Monica Czanyo
Mrs. N. A. Davidson
Kenneth F. Davies
Mrs. Lillian A. Delaney
George Devonshire
John Dortmans
Albert Drager
Liam Dwyer
John N. Dyment
Mrs. Emma Edwards
Carman Eldridge
Doug Elwood
Ivy Emery-Miller
G. M. Farrow
Mrs. Norma Frew
Mr. & Mrs. Cliff Florence
David W. Francis
Beatrice M. Geary
A. Gilbert
Veronica Gizuk

Frank & Margaret Grehan
Gordon A. Gross
Hannah Grossman
Ed Hall
Joyce M. Harper
R. J. Hanlon
Mr. E. A. Healy
Dave High
Pat Hobbs
Peter Hobley
E. F. Horton
John D. Howley
Mrs. M. Ignatieff
Ms. Marie Jackman
Al Jared
Shirley Jarvis
Anthony Johansen
Mrs. Catherine Jolly
Brian H. Jones
Rev. Richard Jones
Rachel Kanner
Terry Kennedy
Lawrence Killoran
Jim Kirk
Pauline Laidlaw
Lou Lanser
Mrs. Lois Laycock
Pauline LeBlanc
Peter S. Lennie
Ernie Long
Mrs. Eileen MacLennan
Mr. & Mrs. Don M. Macfie
John Macfie
John S. Mair
H. Berenice McKague
R. C. McKenzie
M. McKillop
Mrs. Betty McLean
John Maycock
Bert W. Merrill
M. Mills
W. R. Moore
Mrs. Bette Mulvihill
Jay D. Murphy

Mrs. Isobel Murray
Mike Olson
Mrs. Ruth V. Patrick
Bruce C. Pendlebury
Harry Pope
W. K. Rankin
Arthur & Elspeth Read
Hartley Rogers
Jack Russell
Margaret Ruttan
Eileen C. Sally
Claire Sandford
Sam Shantz
Ellen M. Simpson
Mrs. Grace Smith
D. Crawford Smyth
E. R. Souris
Marion Spanton
W. Ray Stephens
Yvonne Stevenson
Bruce & Margaret Sturrock
Otto H. Sulek
W. J. Swanson
Mrs. Diana Taschereau

John E. D. Tayler
Brent B. Taylor
Alan Towsley
Donald A. Tracy
Eunice Tristram
John Turnbull
Mrs. C. Vandenbosch
Lt. Col. David Veitch
Mrs. Margaret Vorvis
R. & Mrs. Gordon W. Ward
M. Waring
Ms. Jill Warlow
Bill Warshick
Mrs. Helene Weaver
Mrs. Muriel O'Brien Whomsley
Helen & Art Wood
J. Ralph Wood
Mrs. Wynne Wooley
W. N. Wright
Leslie Wyle
Oliver & Velma Wylie
J. Ross Young
Mrs. Estella Yule

Index

294 DAYS OF VICTORY

Jared, Al, 210
Jarvis, Bob, 6, 215
Johnson, Air Marshal, 231
Johnstone, Sgt. Ross, 83
Jones, Brian H., 192, 244
Jones, Fred ("Jeep"), 277
Jones, Moreland, 83
Joyce, Sqdn. Ldr. Bob, 138

Kallman, Helmut, 105
Kane, Jack, 141
Kapinsky, Howard, 164
Kaufman, Hans, 105
Kazakoff, Sub. Lt. Mike, 180
Keegstra, Jim, 280
Kellock, Justice R. L., 223
Kelso, Cpl. Henry, 18
Kelso, Cpl. John H., 18
Kenney, Cpl. Harold, 175
Kenney, Mart, 241
Kettison, Boyd, 6
Kidd, George, 134, 253
King George VI, 20, 150, 186, 197
King, George, 56
King, Prime Minister Mackenzie, 47, 51, 72, 74, 81, 225, 228, 238
Kinnis, Art, 263
Knight, L/S Herbert, 180
Koch, Eric, 74, 103, 104, 105
Krahn, Kornelius, 74
Kreisel, Henry, 103, 105
Kuinka, Bill, 158
Kyser, Kay, 71

Lafitte, Francois, 103
Lambert, Freddie, 165
Lauder, Murray, 161

Lawson, Sister Elizabeth, 51
Lawson, Col. (later Brig.) J. K., 17, 19
Leadbetter, Elmer, 164
Leider, Jack, 50
Leiterman (Campbell), Elaine, 67, 166, 190, 191
Levine, Sam, 159, 160, 161, 162
Lillie, Bea, 141
Lion, Edgar, 104
Liri Valley, 121, 135
Livingston, Neal, 103
Lockhart, Andy, 37
Loevinsohn, Walter, 104
Long, Ernie, 202, 203
Lonsdale, Arnold, 69, 213, 279
Lord Haw Haw, 44, 45
Los (Haliburton), Margaret, 66, 67, 184, 185, 269
Lund, Alan, 141, 148, 273
Lund (Harris), Blanche, 141, 148, 149, 153, 273
Lynch, Charles, 122
Lynn, Vera, 70, 141, 189

MacCormack, John, 8, 58, 59
Macfie, John, 225
MacDonald, David, 222
MacDonald, L/S Duncan, 181
MacDonald, George ("Pinky"), 51, 52
MacDonald, Hazel, 162
MacDonald, Joyce, 211
MacFarlane, J. Douglas, 1, 2, 133-140 passim, 233, 246-256 passim, 277
MacKenzie, Lt. Col. Donald Alexander, 175